CAMBRIDGE STUDIES IN LINGUISTICS

The Syntax of Welsh

In this series

1 DAVID CRYSTAL: *Prosodic systems and intonation in English*
2 PIETER A. M. SEUREN: *Operators and nucleus*
3 RODNEY D. HUDDLESTON: *The sentence in written English*
4 JOHN M. ANDERSON: *The grammar of case*
5 M. L. SAMUELS: *Linguistic evolution*
6 P. H. MATTHEWS: *Inflectional morphology*
7 GILLIAN BROWN: *Phonological rules and dialect variation*
8 BRIAN NEWTON: *The generative interpretation of dialect*
9 R. M. W. DIXON: *The Dyirbal language of North Queensland*
10 BRUCE L. DERWING: *Transformational grammar as a theory of language acquisition**
11 MELISSA BOWERMAN: *Early syntactic development**
12 W. SIDNEY ALLEN: *Accent and rhythm*
13 PETER TRUDGILL: *The social differentiation of English in Norwich*
14 ROGER LASS and JOHN M. ANDERSON: *Old English phonology*
15 RUTH M. KEMPSON: *Presupposition and the delimitation of semantics*
16 JAMES R. HURFORD: *The linguistic theory of numerals*
17 ROGER LASS: *English phonology and phonological theory*

**Issued in hard covers and paperback*

THE SYNTAX OF WELSH

A TRANSFORMATIONAL STUDY OF THE PASSIVE

G. M. AWBERY

Assistant Keeper, Department of Oral Traditions and Dialects
Welsh Folk Museum, St Fagans

Is-Geidwad, Adran Traddodiadau Llafar a Thafodieithoedd
Amgueddfa Werin Cymru, Sain Ffagan

CAMBRIDGE UNIVERSITY PRESS

CAMBRIDGE

LONDON · NEW YORK · MELBOURNE

Published by the Syndics of the Cambridge University Press
The Pitt Building, Trumpington Street, Cambridge CB2 1RP
Bentley House, 200 Euston Road, London NW1 2DB
32 East 57th Street, New York, NY 10022, USA
296 Beaconsfield Parade, Middle Park, Melbourne 3206, Australia

First published 1976

Printed in Great Britain at the
University Printing House, Cambridge
(Harry Myers, University Printer)

Library of Congress Cataloguing in Publication Data

Awbery, G M 1947–
The Syntax of Welsh.

(Cambridge studies in linguistics; 18)
Revision of the author's thesis, Cambridge University, 1973.
Bibliography: p.
Includes index.
1. Welsh language – Voice. 2. Welsh language – Grammar, Generative. I. Title. II. Series. PB2171.A9 1976 491.6'6'82421 76-11489
ISBN 0 521 21341 X

Contents

Preface

This book is a revised version of my dissertation 'The passive in Welsh', which was submitted in September 1973 for the degree of Ph.D. of Cambridge University. The work was begun while I was a postgraduate student in Cambridge in 1968–9, but the bulk of the research was carried out while I was a lecturer in the Department of Phonetics at Leeds University. I am grateful to Leeds University for providing a grant towards the cost of publication.

I should like to thank my two supervisors for their help during this time; Dr P. A. M. Seuren originally suggested the topic for research and supervised the early stages, and Dr T. Moore supervised the later stages of the work. I have also benefited from the comments of my two examiners, Dr E. Fudge and Dr R. Hudson, from discussions with other linguists, in particular P. Meara, and from the intuitions of my Welsh-speaking friends and relations. I should also here like to thank Mr J. L. M. Trim, who first taught me linguistics and has always been a great source of encouragement and stimulation.

The Welsh language is not deficient of any of the properties which are considered essential to a good language...

It is not a mere sorry dialect as they are apt to imagine, incapable of being reduced to the rules of general grammar.

J. Hughes, *An Essay on the Ancient and Present State of the Welsh Language*, 1822

Introduction

Till now work on Welsh within the framework of transformational grammar has been limited both in scale and in scope. It has been confined to a small number of articles and these have concentrated mainly on questions of phonology.[1] This book is an attempt to rectify this situation, providing a full length study of Welsh within the transformational framework and concentrating on syntax. Owing to the dearth of previous work in this area this is bound to be an exploratory study, raising many questions for which no definite answers can be given. However, interesting explanations can be offered for much otherwise puzzling data which has caused difficulties within traditional and structuralist approaches, and it is felt that raising problems which have till now gone unnoticed is itself useful.[2]

It is hoped that this book will be of interest to those who are working in the field of Welsh and the Celtic languages generally, as providing a new perspective on the language, offering new answers to some old questions and raising new questions instead. It is also hoped that the book will be of interest to those who are working in the field of transformational grammar, as providing an example of the approach being applied to a new family of languages. Any substantive work on linguistic universals must be based on such detailed studies as this for an increasing number of new languages. It should perhaps be pointed out that this is primarily a contribution to the study of Welsh rather than to the theoretical base of transformational grammar, but theoretical issues are discussed where they arise in the course of the analysis.

The basic theoretical framework adopted is that developed by N. A. Chomsky in *Aspects of the Theory of Syntax* (1965). This may appear a rather odd choice at first sight since there have been considerable developments in syntactic theory since that date. It does however have an important advantage in the context of this study. It is a fairly clear and well understood theory which is easily accessible in published work. Much of the later work is relatively fragmentary and a great deal of it is in an unpublished form. When one is dealing with a new language it is useful to have a clear theoretical position so that issues of theory and actual analysis are not both being raised at the same time. Besides this pragmatic justification there is in fact support for this type of framework from the analysis itself. At several points it is clear that there is a considerable split in the Welsh data between syntactic relationships and semantic ones. This is more consistent with the *Aspects* approach than that put forward in the generative semantic approach where a close link between semantics and syntax is assumed. The assumptions of the model are presented briefly in an Appendix, as is the notation adopted for expressing transformations.

This study is not corpus-based but is based on my own judgements of grammaticality and those of my informants. Nor is it a study of any one dialect but rather of standard literary Welsh. If any dialect bias has crept in it will be from the usage of South East Wales, but this seems unlikely. It is also a purely synchronic account with no discussion of previous states of the language.

The topic selected for detailed discussion is the syntax of passive sentences of the type shown in (1).

(1) Cafodd y lleidr ei ddal gan yr heddlu.
Got the thief his catching by the police.
i.e. The thief was caught by the police.[3]

This is the passive equivalent of (2).

(2) Daliodd yr heddlu y lleidr.
Caught the police the thief.
i.e. The police caught the thief.

In order to justify the analysis proposed for this construction it proves necessary to discuss a wide range of other constructions which resemble this passive in various ways. These include simple and complex active sentences, 'impersonal' passives, certain adjectival and nominal forms, and a range of constructions where the verb *cael* appears. The syntactic issues raised therefore touch on many aspects of Welsh syntax, some of which have not previously been considered relevant to each other.

The discussion of active sentences in Chapter 1 forms the basis for the rest of the study. It is argued that certain active forms which are normally considered to be simple sentences should in fact be analysed as complex sentences, with a sentence containing a tenseless verb embedded below a tensed auxiliary verb. The rules required are formulated.

In Chapters 2 to 4 the analysis is extended to passive forms and it is argued that they too should be analysed as complex sentences with a tenseless active sentence embedded below a tensed auxiliary verb, in this case *cael*. The rules formulated in Chapter 1 to account for the active forms also figure in the derivation of passives, with the addition of a rule postposing the subject of the embedding into a prepositional phrase. It is further argued that many of the rules formulated so far must be postcyclic or last-cyclic rather than cyclic. And an attempt is made to explain restrictions on what forms may passivise.

Chapters 5 and 6 contain a further discussion of the extra subject-postposing transformation which was required in order to account for the passive. In Chapter 5 this rule is compared with similar rules in other constructions in an attempt to provide independent motivation for it. This attempt is not wholly successful and in Chapter 6 a different approach is adopted. There it is suggested that comparison of the passive and another set of constructions supports the view that the prepositional phrase is already present in deep structure. The movement transformation is replaced by a deletion transformation. Even here however there remain problems and it is not possible to provide a definite solution.

Finally, in Chapter 7, the main conclusions of the study are presented and some of the implications of the analysis pointed out.

1 *Active sentences*

In this chapter an analysis of the structure of active sentences is presented, which will provide a basis for the discussion of passive forms in later chapters. In section 1.1 simple active sentences are considered, and in sections 1.2 to 1.5 sentences containing periphrastic forms of the verb are discussed. It is suggested that they should be analysed as complex sentences containing a tenseless embedding.

1.1 Simple active sentences

1.1.1 Phrase structure The simple active sentence in Welsh consists of a sentence-initial verb, which is followed by the subject, object and any prepositional phrases in this order. Examples are given below.

(1) Diflannodd y ci.
Disappeared the dog.

(2) Gwelodd y dyn y ci.
Saw the man the dog.

(3) Soniodd y dyn am y ci.
Spoke the man about the dog.

(4) Rhoddodd y dyn y ffon i'r ci.
Gave the man the stick to the dog.

In traditional grammars of Welsh it is assumed that the sentence consists of two units, subject and predicate (Richards 1938 p. 5). This view is retained in more recent, structurally orientated, treatments such as Watkins (1961). The motivation for this division into subject and predicate seems to be a universalist semantic one rather than syntactic. For instance Watkins claims that 'it is difficult to imagine any kind of language which would not include something to talk about (subject) and something to say about it (predicate)'[1] (Watkins 1961 p. 183). In the course of their accounts of Welsh syntax however these writers do not make use of this predicate unit consisting of the verb, object and any prepositional phrases. They refer only to the individual items such as verb or object.

In the course of this analysis no clear evidence emerges to support an underlying division of the sentence into subject and predicate. At no point does it seem necessary to consider the verb, object and prepositional phrases as one unit. It is therefore assumed that the verb, subject, object, and prepositional phrases are separate constituents in deep structure as well as surface structure. The tree (5) will represent on this analysis an approximation to the deep structure of (2).

(5)

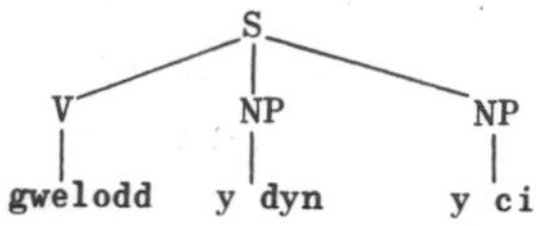

However the analysis presented in this study is not crucially dependent on the lack of a predicate constituent in deep structure, and could be very simply adapted should it become necessary in the light of future work to assume that such a constituent is in fact present. An additional rule would be needed to front the verb. Problems relevant to the issue will be discussed as they arise in the course of the book.

1.1.2 Verbal inflection The verb is inflected for tense and aspect. Compare the form of the verb *gweld* (see) in (2) with the forms it takes in (6) and (7).

(6) Gwêl y dyn y ci.
Sees the man the dog.

(7) Gwelai y dyn y ci.
Was seeing the man the dog.

The details of which tense and aspect are realised by each inflection are not relevant here. It will be assumed that each verb is marked in the deep structure with syntactic features [$+\alpha$ tense] and [$+\beta$ aspect], which will be realised as an inflection of the verb by a morphological rule. The deep structure of (2) will then be more accurately represented as (8) with the uninflected form of the verb *gweld* (see). In this case the morphological rule will give the inflected form *gwelodd*.

(8)

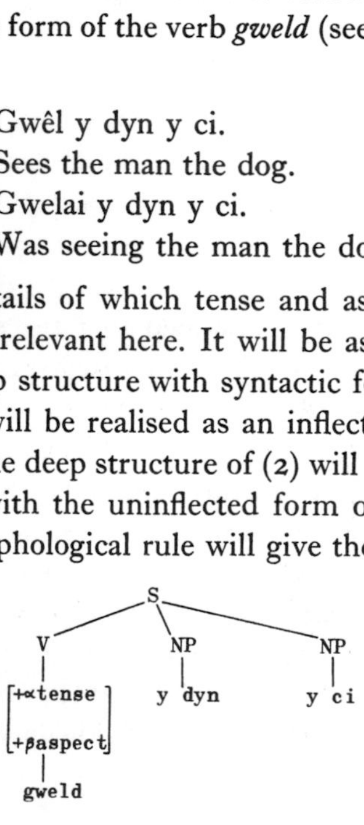

The inflections of the verb vary not only for tense and aspect but also for person and number. The person and number of the verb depend on the subject of the sentence, but the effect on the verb depends on whether the subject is a pronoun or a noun.

If the subject of the sentence is a personal pronoun, the the verb agrees with it in person and number, having a different inflection for each person and number combination.

(9) Gwelais i y ci.
Saw I the dog.
(10) Gwelodd ef y ci.
Saw he the dog.
(11) Gwelsant hwy y ci.
Saw they the dog.

Here (9) differs from (10) in person and (10) differs from (11) in number. In both cases the inflection changes.

If the subject is a noun then the verb agrees with it in person but not in number. The 3sg inflection is used with both singular and plural nouns.

(12) Gwelodd y dynion y ci.
Saw the men the dog.
(13) *Gwelsant y dynion y ci.
Saw the men the dog.

The singular noun subject in (2) and the plural noun subject in (12) take the same inflection of the verb as the singular pronoun subject in (10). The inflection which appears with the plural pronoun subject in (11) is not possible with the plural noun subject in (13).

If it is assumed that the subject is marked with features specifying person, number and whether the subject is a pronoun or not, then two agreement rules can be formulated to account for these forms. One rule copies the person and number features of a pronoun subject onto the verb. This is formulated as (14).

(14) <u>T. Subject-Verb Agreement (Pronoun) (obligatory)</u>

```
SD. (S V    NP       X )
             |
          [+pro ]
          [αno  ]
          [βpers]
     1 2     3       4
```

SC. Copy the features [αno] and [βpers] onto 2.

The other rule marks all verbs with noun subjects with the features [sg no] and [3pers]. This rule is formulated as (15).

(15) T. Subject-Verb Agreement (Noun) (obligatory)

```
SD. (S V    NP      X )
            |
          [-pro]

     1  2    3      4

SC. Add the features [sg no] and [3pers] onto 2.
```

These two agreement rules must precede the morphological rules which realise the inflection of the verb, since the morphological rules must be able to refer to the features of tense, aspect, person and number all together.

1.1.3 Mutation of direct object In Welsh, words do not always retain the initial sound of their isolation form. In certain lexical and syntactic environments the initial sound is changed systematically to give one of the three different mutation forms. For instance, an initial *c-* may be changed to initial *g-*, the soft mutation form, to initial *ch-*, the aspirate mutation form, or to initial *ngh-*, the nasal mutation form. The lexical item *ci* (dog) may appear in any of the three forms *gi*, *chi*, or *nghi* besides its isolation form *ci*.[2]

The direct object of the inflected verb must appear in its soft mutation form. The initial sound of the leftmost lexical item in the direct object consituent must be changed into the corresponding soft mutation initial. The sounds affected and the corresponding soft mutation initials are shown in (16).

(16) *Basic sounds* p, t, c, b, d, g, m, ll, rh
Soft mutation b, d, g, f, dd, zero, f, l, r

In the examples discussed so far the leftmost item in the direct object constituent is the definite article *y* (the). The initial sound is not subject to the soft mutation since it does not appear in the list given in (16), and so the direct object of these forms has not been affected. In (17), however, where the direct object is indefinite there is no overt determiner. The noun *ci* is now the leftmost item in the direct object constituent and therefore appears in its soft mutation form as *gi*.

(17) Gwelodd y dyn gi.
Saw the man (a) dog.

The problems which arise in giving a generative account of mutation forms have been discussed in Awbery (1973a) where it is suggested that words should be marked with the feature [+α mutation] late in the syntactic derivation. In the phonological component this feature will trigger the correct phonological changes. A rule may therefore be formulated as in (18) to mark the direct object with the feature [+soft mutation].

```
(18)  T. Soft Mutation of Direct Object (obligatory)

      SD. (S V  NP  NP  X )
          1  2  3   4   5

      SC. Add the feature [+soft mut] onto 4.
```

1.1.4 Subject deletion A personal pronoun subject may optionally delete. It may be present, as in (9), or absent, as in (19).

(19) Gwelais y ci.
Saw (I) the dog.

The verbal inflection indicates which pronoun has been deleted. Ambiguity arises if one of the 3sg pronouns is deleted since the verbal inflection does not indicate the gender of the subject pronoun. The deleted subject of (20) could be either *ef* (he) or *hi* (she).

(20) Gwelodd y ci.
Saw he/she the dog.

The deletion rule may be formulated as in (21).

```
(21)  T. Pronoun Subject Deletion (optional)

      SD. (S V     NP      X )
                   |
                 [+pro]

          1  2     3       4

      SC. Delete 3.
```

Some writers have suggested that in these forms the subject of the sentence is somehow contained in the verbal inflection, and the pronoun merely helps to clarify the inflection. A noun on the other hand is seen as the true subject of the sentence (e.g.Richards 1938 p. 29). The motivation for this distinction seems to be that a noun adds new information while a pronoun adds nothing new to the information already contained in the verbal inflection, except in the case of 3sg pronouns. Richards contrasts the Welsh data with the situation in English where the pronoun *I* is said to be the true subject because the verb has no personal inflection. No syntactic evidence has emerged in the course of this analysis to support such a big difference between sentences with noun and pronoun subject, and so it is assumed throughout that both types of subject are to be considered full constituents of the sentence.

1.1.5 Rule ordering Some of the transformations discussed above must apply to the sentence in a particular order. T. Subject-Verb Agreement (Pronoun) must precede T. Pronoun Subject Deletion. If the pronoun subject were deleted before the verb is made to agree with it then there will be no subject for the verb to agree with. T. Soft Mutation of Direct Object must also precede T. Pronoun Subject Deletion. If the reverse ordering were adopted, then after T. Pronoun Subject Deletion applied the object would immediately follow the verb, as in (22).

(22) Gwelais gi.
Saw (I) (a) dog.

It does not seem possible to formulate T. Soft Mutation of Direct Object in a way which can distinguish the object in (22) from the subject in forms which have not undergone T. Pronoun Subject Deletion. In both cases the noun phrase concerned immediately follows the verb. But this distinction must be made, since soft mutation of the subject is ungrammatical, as in (23).

(23) *Diflannodd gi.
Disappeared (a) dog.

T. Soft Mutation of Direct Object must therefore apply first so that the object can be unambiguously specified. It is worth pointing out however that this problem would not arise if there were an underlying predicate constituent as the object would be unambiguously specified within this constituent even after subject deletion.

It was pointed out in section 1.1.2 that the morphological rules realising verbal inflections must follow the two agreement rules. Similarly, the phonological rules which carry out the sound changes required by the soft mutation must follow T. Soft Mutation of Direct Object.

The ordering of rules is therefore that shown in (24). The rules are shown in order of application. Any two rules which must be ordered relative to each other are linked by an arrow. If a pair of rules is not linked in this way then there is no ordering relation between them.

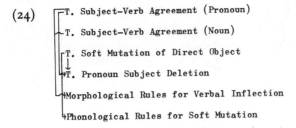

(24)
T. Subject-Verb Agreement (Pronoun)
T. Subject-Verb Agreement (Noun)
T. Soft Mutation of Direct Object
T. Pronoun Subject Deletion
Morphological Rules for Verbal Inflection
Phonological Rules for Soft Mutation

The nature of the ordering constraint varies. The morphological and phonological rules are not applicable until the preceding transformations have marked the verb and object respectively with the features that trigger these rules. On the other hand, the transformational rules could apply in a different order though this would lead to incorrect outputs.

A sample derivation is given below. This is the derivation of (22), repeated here.

(22) Gwelais gi.
Saw (I) (a) dog.

The deep structure is shown in (25). Note that the features of number, person and pronominality have been inserted on the subject.

(25)

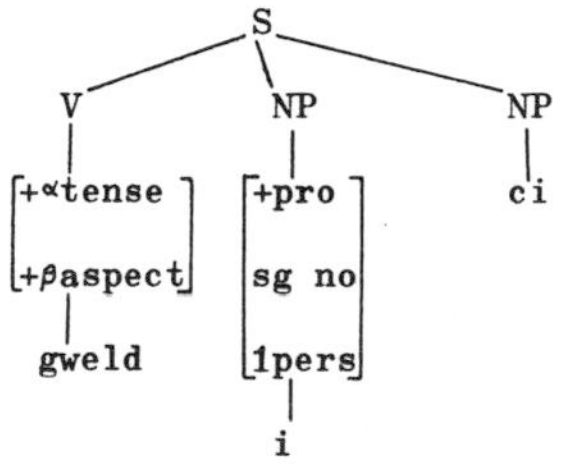

T. Subject-Verb Agreement (Pronoun) gives the structure (26).

(26)

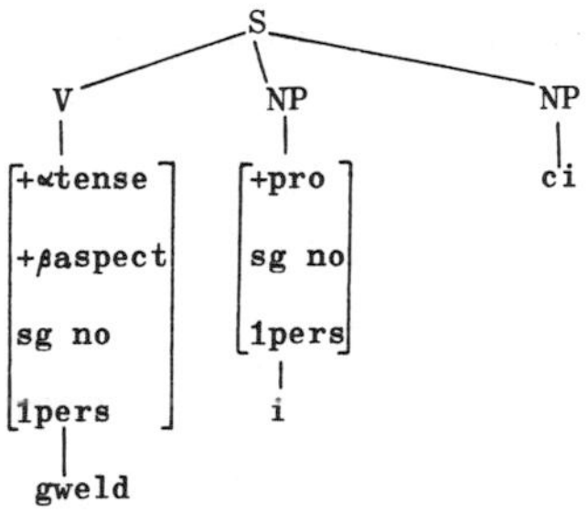

T. Soft Mutation of Direct Object applies, giving (27).

(27)

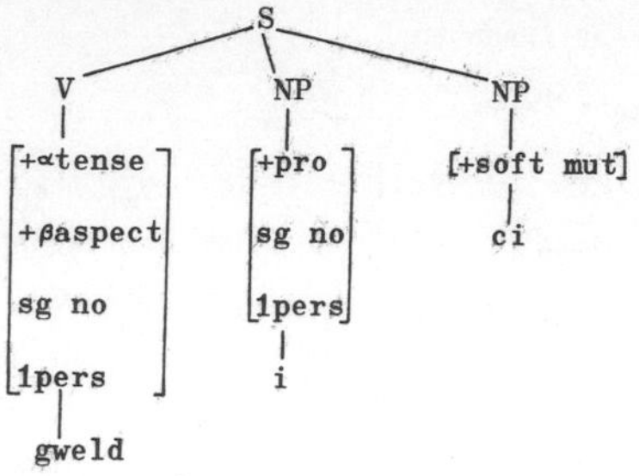

T. Pronoun Subject Deletion gives (28).

(28)

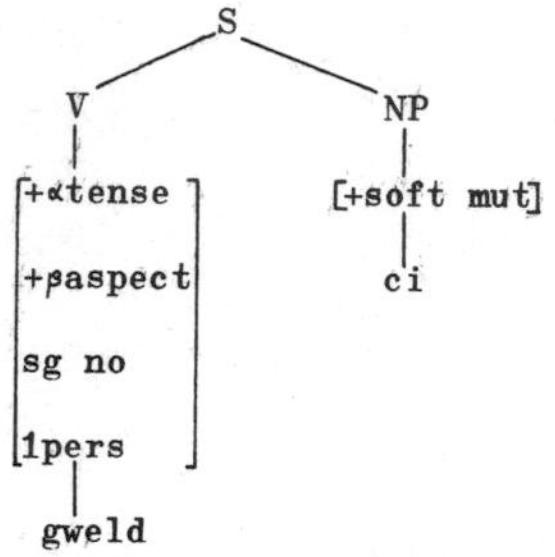

Morphological rules realise the verbal inflection, giving (29).

(29)

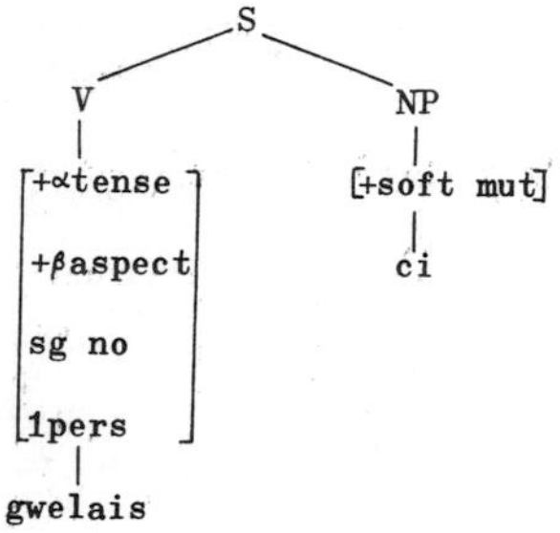

Finally phonological rules give the correct mutation form of the direct object, giving the form (30).

(30)

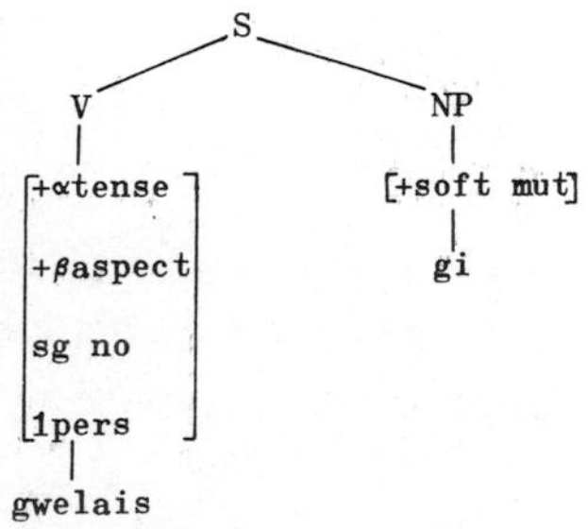

1.2 Periphrastic forms

1.2.1 Periphrastic forms The inflected verb of the simple sentence discussed above in section 1.1 cannot express all tense and aspect combinations. Those tense and aspect combinations which cannot be expressed by an inflected verb are expressed by what are traditionally called the periphrastic forms of the verb.[3] Examples are given below.

(31) Mae'r dyn yn gweld y ci.
Is the man in seeing the dog,
i.e. The man sees the dog.
(32) Mae'r dyn wedi gweld y ci.
Is the man after seeing the dog.
i.e. The man has seen the dog.
(33) Bydd y dyn yn gweld y ci.
Will be the man in seeing the dog.
i.e. The man will see the dog.

It is generally agreed that *yn* indicates continuous aspect and *wedi* indicates perfective aspect. The inflected forms of *bod* (be) realise the remaining tense and aspect features.

Although these forms differ semantically from the simple sentences in section 1.1 only in the tense and aspect which they express, the syntactic differences between them are considerable. In the simple sentence the inflected verb is followed by a subject noun phrase and then optionally by an object noun phrase. In the periphrastic forms an inflected form of the verb *bod* (be) is followed by the subject, an aspect marker, then an uninflected form of the lexical verb, and finally by the object noun phrase. If a prepositional phrase is present it follows the object, as in (34).

(34) Mae'r dyn wedi rhoi ffon i'r ci.
Is the man after giving (a) stick to the dog.

How should these forms be analysed in surface structure?

1.2.2 The verb and subject The inflected form of *bod* (be) resembles the verb of the simple sentence syntactically. It appears in sentence-initial position, followed immediately by the subject. It is inflected for tense, as can be seen from (31) to (33) above. It is also inflected for number and person, agreeing with a pronoun subject in both features, as in (35) to (37).

(35) Yr wyf i wedi gweld y ci.
Am I after seeing the dog.
(36) Mae ef wedi gweld y ci.
Is he after seeing the dog.
(37) Maent hwy wedi gweld y ci.
Are they after seeing the dog.

(35) and (36) differ in person and (36) and (37) differ in number. In both cases the inflection changes. With a noun phrase subject we again find the 3sg form of the verb for both singular and plural subjects. The same form of the verb appears in (31) with a singular subject and (38) with a plural subject.

(38) Mae'r dynion yn gweld y ci.
Is the men in seeing the dog.

The plural inflection found in (37) with a plural pronoun subject is ungrammatical in (39) with a plural noun subject.

(39) *Maent y dynion yn gweld y ci.
Are the men in seeing the dog.

If the subject is a personal pronoun it may optionally delete. Both (37) with a pronoun and (40) without one are grammatical.

(40) Maent wedi gweld y ci.
Are (they) after seeing the dog.

The two verbal agreement rules, T. Pronoun Subject Deletion, and the morphological rules realising verbal inflections must apply to the form of *bod* (be) and the subject noun phrase here just as they apply to the lexical verb and the subject in a simple sentence. This suggests that the two forms have structure in common, with *bod* corresponding to the lexical verb and the subject being identical in each case. Any other analysis will lead to a great deal of duplication and obscure the parallelisms between the two forms. The structure of the periphrastic type may then be given in part as shown in (41).

(41)

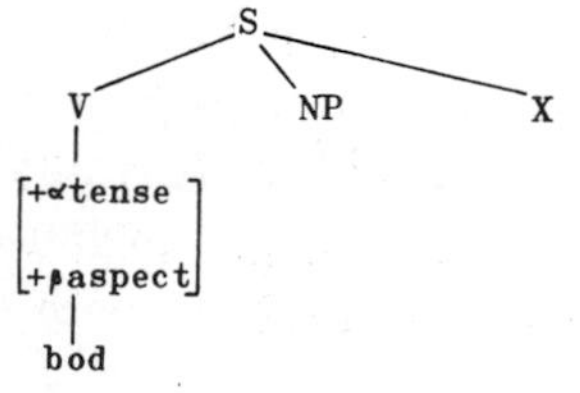

1.2.3 The uninflected verb If the inflected form of *bod* (be) corresponds to the inflected lexical verb of the simple sentence, there remains the problem of the uninflected verb in the periphrastic form. This is the item which corresponds lexically to the inflected verb in the simple sentence, but it differs in its syntax from this inflected verb. The lack of inflection is the obvious difference, but this is accompanied by other differences.

Whereas the direct object of the inflected verb in a simple sentence appears in its soft mutation form, the direct object of the uninflected verb does not. It retains its isolation form. Compare the mutation form *gi* of the object in the simple sentence (42) with the isolation form *ci* in the periphrastic sentence (43).

(42) Gwelodd y dyn gi.
Saw the man (a) dog.
(43) Mae'r dyn wedi gweld ci.
Is the man after seeing (a) dog.

A second difference is found in the treatment of personal pronoun objects. In a simple sentence a noun object and a pronoun object appear in the same position in the sentence, following the subject. Compare the noun object in (42) with the pronoun object in (44).

(44) Gwelodd y dyn ef.
Saw the man him.

In a periphrastic sentence however the noun object and pronoun object are treated differently. While the noun object follows the uninflected verb, as in (43), the pronoun object does not.

(45) *Mae'r dyn wedi gweld ef.
Is the man after seeing him.

Instead the pronoun object has two possibilities. It may either precede the uninflected verb, as in (46), or both precede and follow it, as in (47).

(46) Mae'r dyn wedi ei weld.
Is the man after his seeing.
(47) Mae'r dyn wedi ei weld ef.
Is the man after his seeing him.

The syntax of the uninflected verb and the direct object shows interesting parallelisms with the syntax of noun phrases consisting of a head noun and a possessive noun. In such forms the head noun precedes the possessive noun, and the possessive noun retains its isolation form, as in (48).

(48) ci plentyn
(a) dog (of a) child

If the possessive is a pronoun it may not follow the head noun in this way.

(49) *ci ef
(the) dog (of) him

Instead it may either precede the head noun, as in (50), or both precede and follow it, as in (51).

(50) ei gi
his dog

(51) ei gi ef
his dog him

The uninflected verb appears to correspond to the head noun and the direct object to the possessive.

Furthermore the pronoun forms in each case are identical. Compare the periphrastic forms in (46) and (47) with the possessive forms in (50) and (51). And in both cases the pronoun preceding the verb/head noun causes the same mutation. In the case of 3sg masc pronouns as here this is the soft mutation. In the case of 1sg pronouns as in (52) and (53) the nasal mutation is triggered, converting *gweld* (see) to *ngweld* and *ci* (dog) to *nghi*.

(52) Mae'r dyn yn fy ngweld i.
The man is in my seeing me.

(53) fy nghi i
my dog me

This similarity in the syntax of the two constructions can be most easily expressed if they have a similar structure. One way of accounting for the similarity is to assume that the uninflected verb and direct object form a noun phrase of the same sort as the noun phrase containing a head and possessive noun.

It may be objected that the presence of a preposed pronoun object is not necessarily to be seen as evidence for a noun phrase analysis of the uninflected verb and direct object, since inflected verbs in simple sentences may also take a preposed pronoun object. If the inflected verb is preceded by an assertion marker *fe*, then a pronoun object may appear between the assertion marker and the verb, as in (54). It may also follow it as in (55).

(54) Fe'i gwelais.
Assertion: him saw (I).

(55) Fe'i gwelais ef.
Assertion: him saw (I) him.

Clearly this is a very similar pattern to the one described above for the uninflected verb and possessives. There are however differences too. The pronouns preceding the inflected verb do not trigger the same mutations as in the uninflected verb or the possessive. For instance in (54) the 3sg masc pronoun leaves the following inflected verb in its isolation form, though it triggered the soft mutation form in the other cases. More significant perhaps is thc fact that a pronoun object may follow the inflected verb alone, while this is not possible for the two other forms. Compare (44) with (45) and (49). These differences suggest that the inflected verb is not the same type of structure as the uninflected verb and the possessive, and does not undermine the noun phrase analysis of the uninflected verb.

1.2.4 The aspect marker The aspect markers which appear in the periphrastic sentences are traditionally analysed as prepositions.[4] This analysis seems to be justified. The forms *yn*, *wedi*, and *ar* which appear as aspect markers in the periphrastic forms are identical to prepositions which appear elsewhere with a noun phrase object, as in (56) to (58).

(56) Mae Wyn yn nhŷ Ifor.
Is Wyn in (the) house (of) Ifor.

(57) Aeth hi adref wedi diwrnod hir o waith.
Went she home after (a) long day of work.

(58) Rhoddodd ef y llestri ar fwrdd y gegin.
Put he the dishes on (the) table (of) the kitchen.

Wedi does not require a mutation form of either a following noun or a following uninflected verb. *Ar* requires a soft mutation form of both. In (58) *fwrdd* is the soft mutation form of *bwrdd* (table), and in (59) *weld* is the soft mutation form of *gweld* (see).

(59) Mae ef ar weld y ddrama.
Is he on seeing the play.
i.e. He is about to see the play.

It will be assumed that *wedi* and *ar* are the same lexical item in both the periphrastic forms and the ordinary prepositional phrases.

A problem arises over the form *yn*. When it is used as an aspect marker it does not require the nasal mutation form of the uninflected verb. But when it is used with a noun phrase object it does require the nasal mutation form of the following noun. *Nhŷ* in (56) is the nasal mutation form of *tŷ* (house). The parallelism found between the two uses of *wedi* and *ar* breaks down here. It will be assumed here that in spite of this discrepancy, both uses of *yn* are instances of the same lexical item. It will be constrained to require mutation of a following noun only. This analysis preserves the parallelism of the structures of the various periphrastic forms. Those containing *yn* do not differ from the others in any major way.[5]

If the aspect markers are to be analysed as prepositions then this is further evidence that the uninflected verb and the direct object should be analysed as a noun phrase. They appear in a position normally occupied by a noun phrase, as object of a preposition, and are subject to the same mutation requirements, at least in the case of *wedi* and *ar*.

1.2.5 Surface phrase structure The surface structure analysis of the periphrastic forms seems to be that shown in (60), which represents (61).

(60)

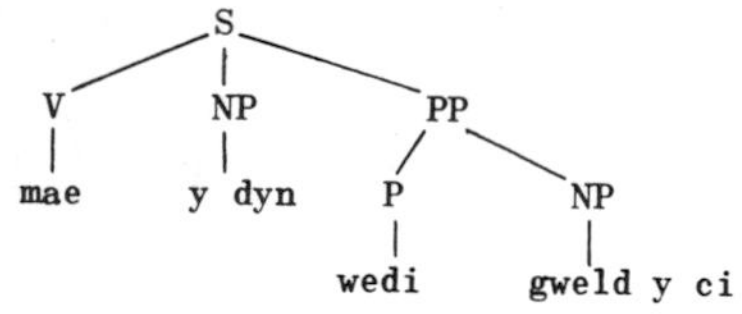

(61) Mae'r dyn wedi gweld y ci.
Is the man after seeing the dog.

The sentence initial inflected verb *bod* (be) is followed by the subject noun phrase. This is followed by a prepositional phrase whose preposition is the aspect marker and whose object is a noun phrase consisting of the uninflected verb and the direct object. The internal structure of this noun phrase will be discussed later.

This analysis is supported by parallelisms between the periphrastic forms and simple sentences of this general structure, such as (56). In both instances the prepositional phrase can appear as the focus of a cleft sentence. The prepositional phrase appears in sentence-initial position and the rest of the sentence takes the form of a relative clause whose antecedent is this prepositional phrase. The cleft form of (56) is (62), and the cleft form of (61) is (63).

(62) Yn nhŷ Ifor y mae Wyn.
In (the) house (of) Ifor that is Wyn
i.e. It is in Ifor's house that Wyn is.
(63) Wedi gweld y ci y mae'r dyn.
After seing the dog that is the man.

Here again there are problems with *yn*. If a periphrastic form with *yn* is clefted, as in (64), the *yn* must be deleted. (65) where the *yn* is retained is ungrammatical.

(64) Gweld y ci y mae'r dyn.
Seeing the dog that is the man.
(65) *Yn gweld y ci y mae'r dyn.
In seeing the dog that is the man.

It will be assumed here that this too is merely an idiosyncratic fact about the lexical item *yn* and not an indication that the structure of periphrastics with *yn* is different to that of the other forms.

1.3 The derivation of these forms

1.3.1 A complex sentence Although the uninflected verb displays certain characteristics of noun phrases, as was pointed out in sections 1.2.3 and 1.2.4, it also retains certain other characteristics in common with the inflected verb of a simple sentence.

The selection restrictions on the subject and object of the sentence are the same for the inflected and uninflected forms of the verb. Compare the forms in (66) to (69). The object noun phrase *llyfr* (book) is grammatical with both forms, while the object noun phrase *esgid* (shoe) is ungrammatical with both. Similarly, the subject noun phrase *merch* (girl) is grammatical while the subject noun phrase *ci* (dog) is not.

(66) Darllenodd y ferch y llyfr.
Read the girl the book.

(67) Mae'r ferch wedi darllen y llyfr.
Is the girl after reading the book.

(68) *Darllenodd y ci yr esgid.
Read the dog the shoe.

(69) *Mae'r ci wedi darllen yr esgid.
Is the dog after reading the shoe.

The subcategorisation of both forms of the verb is also the same. *Darllen* (read) is transitive in both its inflected and uninflected forms, while *rhedeg* (run) is intransitive in both.

(70) Rhedodd y dyn ymaith.
Ran the man away.

(71) Mae'r dyn wedi rhedeg ymaith.
Is the man after running away.

Other constraints are identical in the case of both the inflected and the uninflected verb. For instance, either both may take a manner adverb or neither may. *Darllen* (read) does allow a manner adverb, as in (72) and (73). *Gwybod* (know) does not, as in (74) and (75).

(72) Darllenodd y ferch y llyfr yn ofalus.
Read the girl the book carefully.

(73) Mae'r ferch wedi darllen y llyfr yn ofalus.
Is the girl after reading the book carefully.

(74) *Gŵyr y ferch yr ateb yn ofalus.
Knows the girl the answer carefully.

(75) *Mae'r ferch yn gwybod yr ateb yn ofalus.
Is the girl in knowing the answer carefully.

Not only do the inflected and uninflected forms of the verb share these syntactic features, but they also have the same lexical meaning. As was pointed out above in section 1.2.1 the only difference in meaning between a simple and a periphrastic sentence is in the tense and aspect expressed. The lexical meaning of the verb remains the same.

Unless the uninflected verb is analysed as a verb, a great deal of duplication of both syntactic and semantic information will be needed. It is therefore necessary to reconcile the need to analyse the uninflected verb as a verb and the need to analyse the unit formed by the uninflected verb and the direct object as a noun phrase.

These two requirements can be met if the periphrastic sentence is analysed as a complex sentence. The matrix sentence consists of the verb *bod* (be), the subject and a prepositional phrase whose preposition is the aspect marker. A second sentence is embedded below the object noun phrase of the preposition, containing the uninflected verb, the subject again and the object. On this analysis (76) will be the deep structure of (61), repeated here for convenience.

(61) Mae'r dyn wedi gweld y ci.
Is the man after seeing the dog.

(76)

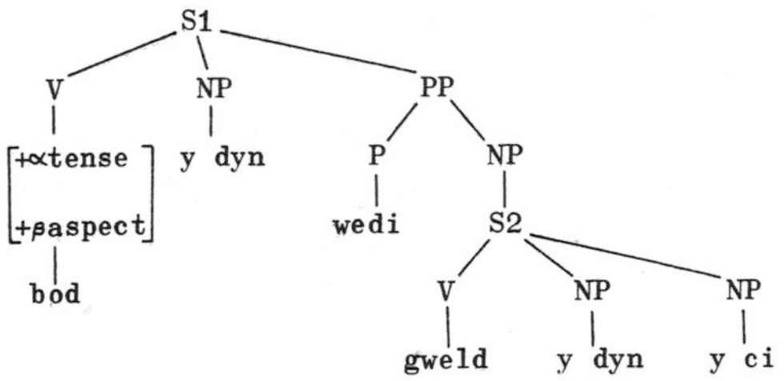

The uninflected verb is the verb of the embedded sentence, and its similarity to the verb of the simple sentence follows. The entire embedded sentence is embedded below a noun phrase node, so that it is possible to explain its noun phrase characteristics.[6]

1.3.2 Equi-subject deletion In the deep structure representation (76) the subject noun phrase appears twice, once as subject of the matrix sentence and once as subject of the embedded sentence. In the surface structure representation (60) however it appears only once, in the same position as the subject of the matrix in (76). It is therefore necessary to delete the subject of the embedded sentence on identity with the subject of the matrix sentence. This restriction is needed, since if any other subject noun phrase were deleted there would be no way of recovering it.

The rule deleting the subject of the embedding is formulated in (77).

(77)
```
T. Equi-Subject Deletion (obligatory)
SD. (S V NPx P (NP (S V NPx X ) ) )
       1 2  3  4   5  6  7  8  9
SC. Delete 8.
```

This rule will convert the deep structure (76) into the tree (78).[7]

(78)

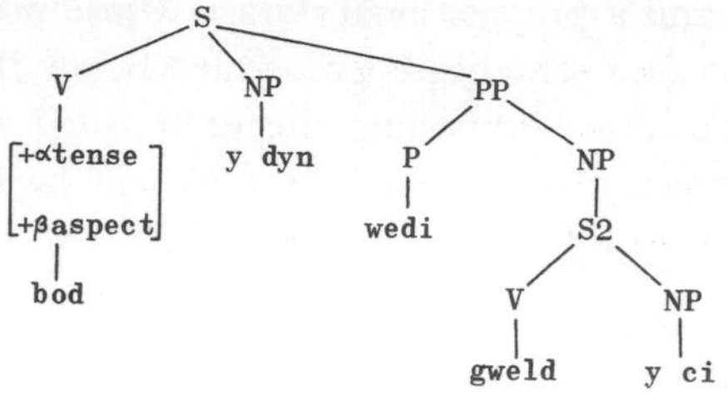

The direct object of the embedded sentence must not be marked for the soft mutation. It appears that the verb in the embedding must be tenseless, as will be shown in section 1.5 below, so mutation can be prevented by limiting T. Soft Mutation of Direct Object to tensed verbs. The revised version of this rule is given in (79).

(79) T. Soft Mutation of Direct Object (obligatory)[2]

SD. ($_S$ V [+tense] NP NP X)

1 2 3 4 5

SC. Add the feature [+soft mut] onto 4.

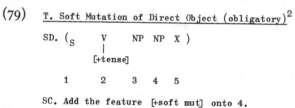

1.3.3 Possessive pronoun preposing The similarity between the syntax of the uninflected verb and its direct object and the syntax of a head and possessive noun phrase was pointed out above in section 1.2.3. In both the pronoun direct object or the pronoun possessive must appear to the left of the verb or noun, with an optional pronoun also following. A generalisation will therefore be caught if both can be accounted for by the same rule.

The structure of (80) seems to be that shown in (81).

(80) llyfr y dyn
(the) book (of) the man

(81)

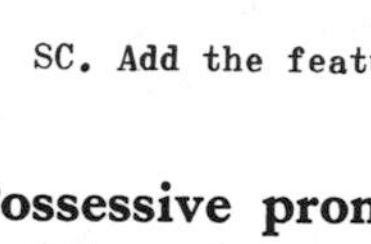

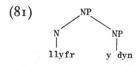

It is not clear how this structure is to be generated, and the problem will not be explored as it is not relevant to the topic of this study. It is assumed that at some stage in the derivation the structure of (82) is as shown in (83), identical except that the possessive is a pronoun rather than a noun.

(82) ei lyfr ef
his book him

(83)

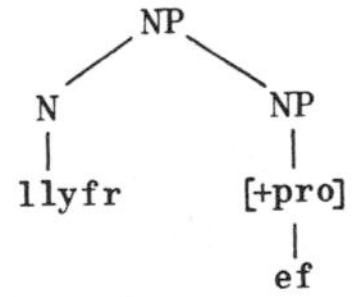

A rule is needed to copy the pronoun to the left of the head noun.

The preposed possessive pronoun seems to be a determiner in surface structure. It appears in the same position as a determiner relative to other items in the noun phrase, as in (84) and (85).

(84) y tri hen lyfr
the three old books

(85) ei dri hen lyfr ef
his three old books him

And the preposed pronoun cannot co-occur with a determiner, suggesting that the two forms are instances of the same category.

(86) *yr ei lyfr ef
the his book him

(87) *ei y llyfr ef
his the book him

The pronoun possessive must then be copied in the determiner position. The rule formulated in (88) is only an approximation as it is not clear if the pronoun should be copied onto an existing determiner node or if it creates a new determiner node.

(88) T. Possessive Pronoun Preposing (obligatory)

SD. ($_{NP}$ N NP [+pro])

1 2 3

SC. Adjoin a copy of 3 as left daughter of 1, dominated by the node Determiner.

This will give (89) as output if it is applied to (83).

(89)

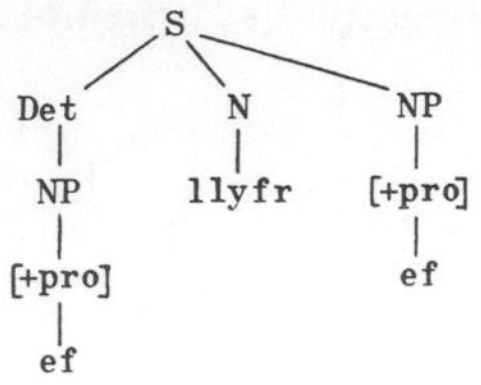

If T. Possessive Pronoun Preposing is to apply to the pronoun object of the uninflected verb as well as to possessives, then it must be modified. The structure of the noun phrase containing the uninflected verb and the direct object has been shown in section 1.3.2 to be (90).

(90)

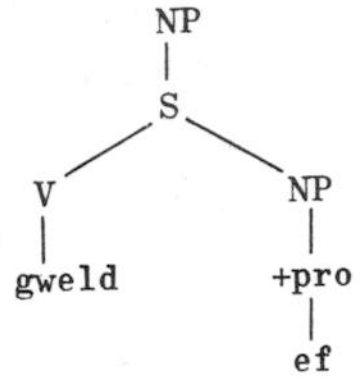

This differs from the possessive form in two ways, the additional sentence node and the presence of a verb rather than a noun. All that the two trees have in common is a noun phrase embedded in another noun phrase.

It is not possible to tell if the preposed pronoun object is a determiner in surface structure, since determiners of any other kind are ungrammatical with the uninflected verb, and so the tests used with the possessive cannot be used here.

(91) *Mae'r dyn yn y gweld y ci.
Is the man in the seeing the dog.

The parallelism of the form of the pronoun in both cases and the identical mutations triggered suggest that the pronoun is in both cases a constituent of the same type, and is dominated here too by the node determiner.

An attempt to extend T. Possessive Pronoun Preposing to account for both constructions is given in (92).

(92) T. Possessive Pronoun Preposing (obligatory)[2]

SD. $(_{NP} \left\{ \begin{matrix} \langle (_{S}\ V \rangle \\ N \end{matrix} \right\} \quad \begin{matrix} NP \\ | \\ [+pro] \end{matrix} \quad \langle) \rangle\ )$

$\quad 1 \qquad 2 \qquad\qquad 3$

SC. Adjoin a copy of 3 as left daughter of 1, dominated by the node Determiner.

This will give (93) as output if it is applied to (90).

(93)

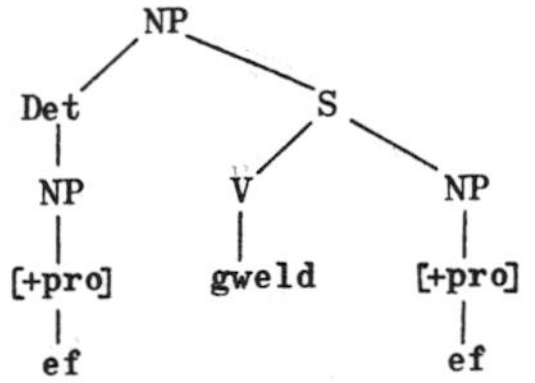

This is a complicated formulation and it would be more satisfying to find a simpler form for the rule. Unfortunately it is not possible to take advantage of what common structure there is and formulate a rule referring only to a noun phrase embedded within another noun phrase as this would be too wide. It would allow the rule to apply for instance to a form such as (94) to give (95).

(94) llyfr amdano ef
(a) book about him

(95) *ei lyfr amdano ef
his book about him

The structure of (94) is that shown in (96) where the pronoun is again a noun phrase embedded within a noun phrase. The preposing rule must however be prevented from applying here.

(96)

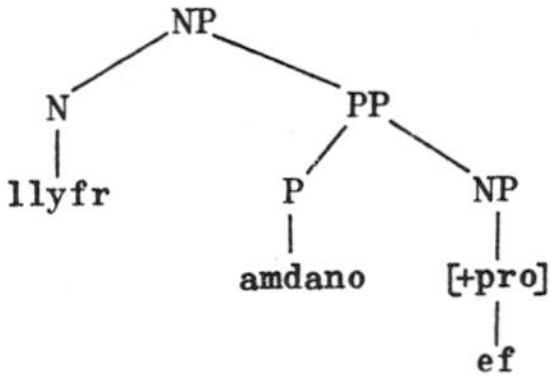

It is necessary therefore to retain the complex formulation of the preposing rule.

It is assumed that T. Equi-Subject Deletion must precede T. Possessive Pronoun Preposing. The basis for this assumption is the greater similarity which exists between the possessive noun phrase and the noun phrase containing the uninflected verb after this rule has applied. After the subject of the embedded sentence has been deleted, the pronoun object immediately follows the verb, just as the possessive immediately follows the head noun. If T. Possessive Pronoun Preposing applied before the subject of the embedding was deleted, then the problems of accounting for the two constructions with the same rule would be multiplied.

At a later stage in the derivation, a set of morphological rules must apply, giving the correct form of the preposed pronoun. These rules will convert (89) into (97) and (93) into (98).

(97)

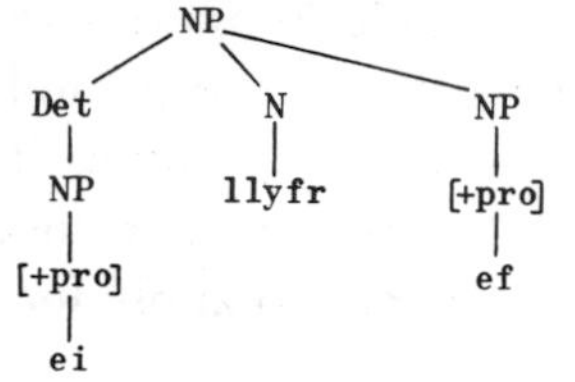

(98)

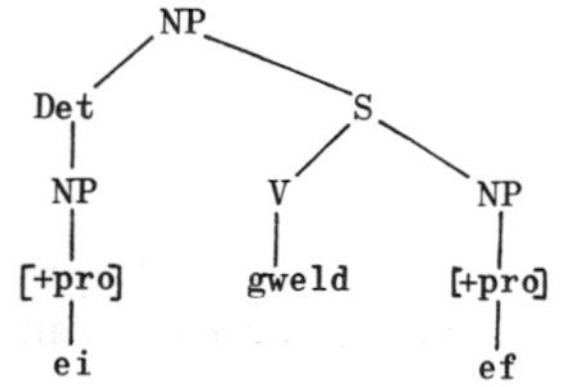

1.3.4 Mutation rules The preposed possessive pronouns require specific mutation forms of the following noun or uninflected verb. The rules marking them for the appropriate mutation forms must follow T. Possessive Pronoun Preposing. For instance the 3sg masc pronoun

(99)

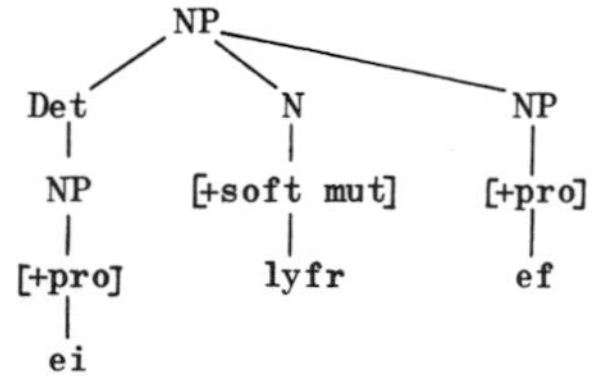

ei (his) requires the soft mutation form, so the output of the relevant mutation marking rules and the later phonological rules carrying out the phonological changes will be (99) and (100).

(100)

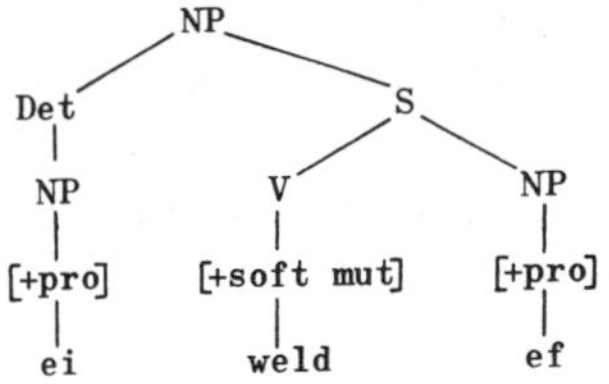

The general format of these mutation marking rules is given in (101), but the details of which mutation is involved will vary according to which pronoun is present.

(101) T. Preposed Pronoun Mutation (obligatory)

SD. ($_{NP}$ ($_{Det}$ NP [+pro, +αmut]) { <($_S$ V> / N } X <()>)

1 2 3 4 5

SC. Add the feature [+αmut] onto 4.

It seems likely that T. Preposed Pronoun Mutation must follow the morphological rules which give the correct form of the preposed pronoun. The shape of the preposed pronoun varies according to the preceding environment. For instance the 3sg masc pronoun takes the form *ei* in (102) but the form *w* in (103).

(102) Gwelais ei frawd ef.
Saw (I) his brother him.

(103) Rhoddais y llyfr i'w frawd ef.
Gave (I) the book to his brother him.

In this case the *ei* and *w* both trigger the same mutation, the soft mutation, so that it would not matter in which order the rules applied. This is not always the case however. In the case of 1sg pronouns the form corresponding to *ei* is *fy*, as in (104), and the form corresponding to *w* is *m*, as in (105).

(104) Gwelais fy mrawd i.
Saw (I) my brother me.

(105) Rhoddais y llyfr i'm brawd i.
Gave (I) the book to my brother me.

Here *fy* requires a following nasal mutation, and *m* retains the isolation form of the following item. Unless the rules specifying the form of the pronoun apply first here it will not be possible to specify correctly which mutation form is required, if any.

It is not only following nouns which are affected in this way. While in a normal periphrastic sentence the form of the preposed 1sg pronoun is *fy* as in (106), in a conjoined form the pronoun will take the form *m* when it follows the conjunction *a* (and), as in (107).

(106) Mae Ifor wedi fy ngweld i.
Is Ifor after my seeing me.
(107) Mae Ifor wedi fy ngweld i a'm galw i.
Is Ifor after my seeing me and my calling me.

As with a following noun, *fy* requires nasal mutation of the verb and *m* retains the isolation form.

1.3.5 More mutation rules Another set of mutation rules will be needed to mark the uninflected form of the verb if there is a noun object and so the verb immediately follows the aspect marker preposition. The only aspect marker preposition which actually requires mutation is *ar* which requires soft mutation, but the rule will be given below only in a very general format as many prepositions require mutation of the following item, with the actual mutation required depending on the particular preposition involved.

(108) T. Prepositional Object Mutation (obligatory)

SD. ($_{PP}$ P NP)
P: [+αmut]

1 2 3

SC. Add the feature [+αmut] onto 3.

This rule will give the correct form of the uninflected verb in (59), following *ar*.

The preposition only requires mutation of the verb if there is no item between them. If a pronoun object has been preposed and so intervenes between the preposition and the verb, as in (109), the preposition has no effect on the verb.

(109) Mae'r dyn ar fy ngweld i.
Is the man on my seeing me.

In this case it is the preposed pronoun that causes mutation of the verb, as was shown in section 1.3.4. This suggests that T. Prepositional Object Mutation should apply after T. Possessive Pronoun Preposing, since only then is it clear if the verb will immediately follow the preposition. If there is no pronoun object to prepose, then the preposition will cause mutation of the verb. If a pronoun has been preposed then it will block this rule and itself cause mutation of the verb.

1.3.6 Possessive deletion It was pointed out above in section 1.2.3 that there need not be a pronoun following the uninflected verb or head noun of a possessive, though one may be present. In section 1.3.3 a rule was formulated to account for those cases where there is a pronoun both preceding and following the verb or noun. A further rule is now needed to optionally delete the second pronoun form. This is formulated in (110).

(110) <u>T. Possessive Pronoun Deletion (optional)</u>

```
SD. (NP (Det   NPx     ) {<(S V>}   NPx     <()> )
                |        {  N   }    |
              [+pro]               [+pro]

     1   2      3          4          5

SC. Delete 5.
```

If this applies to the trees (99) and (100) the output will be (111) and (112) respectively.

(111)

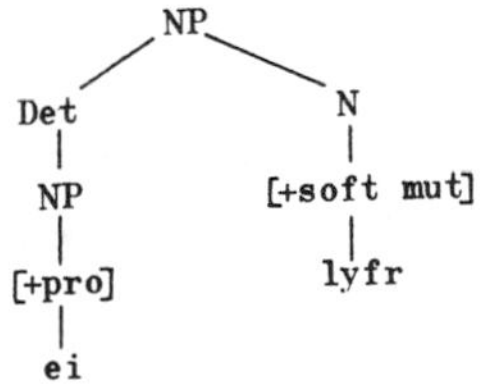

(112)

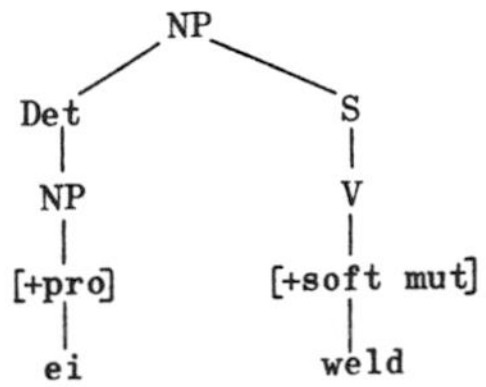

It does not seem to matter if this rule precedes or follows the rules giving the form of the preposed pronouns and the mutations of verb and noun, but it must follow T. Possessive Pronoun Preposing.

1.3.7 Rule ordering The following rules have been suggested in section 1.3 and should apply in the order shown below. Arrows link pairs of rules which are crucially ordered.

(113)
T. Equi-Subject Deletion
↓
T. Possessive Pronoun Preposing
↓
Morphological Rules for Preposed Pronouns
↓
T. Preposed Pronoun Mutation
T. Prepositional Object Mutation
T. Possessive Pronoun Deletion
Phonological Rules for Mutations

Of these rules, only T. Prepositional Object Mutation could apply in the wrong place in the ordering to give an incorrect output. It could precede instead of following T. Possessive Pronoun Preposing. The other rules cannot apply in any order other than that given here since each presupposes in its structural description the change carried out by the preceding rule. If the preceding rule has not yet applied then the rule following it in this table cannot apply because its structural description is not met.

In addition to these rules, some of those formulated in section 1.1 to account for simple active sentences must also apply in these periphrastic forms. These are the two versions of T. Subject-Verb Agreement, T. Pronoun Subject Deletion, and the morphological rules giving the correct inflection of the verb *bod* (be).

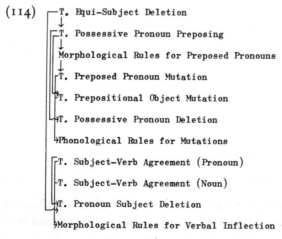

(114)
T. Equi-Subject Deletion
↓
T. Possessive Pronoun Preposing
↓
Morphological Rules for Preposed Pronouns
↓
T. Preposed Pronoun Mutation
T. Prepositional Object Mutation
T. Possessive Pronoun Deletion
Phonological Rules for Mutations
T. Subject-Verb Agreement (Pronoun)
T. Subject-Verb Agreement (Noun)
T. Pronoun Subject Deletion
Morphological Rules for Verbal Inflection

Of these, T. Pronoun Subject Deletion must follow T. Equi-Subject Deletion or the structural description of this latter rule will not be met. The other rules do not seem to be ordered relative to the rules in (113). The overall ordering so far then will be that shown in (114). None of these rules applies on the cycle of the embedded sentence. All apply on the cycle of the matrix sentence, either affecting only the matrix sentence or both sentences. The ordering shown in (114) appears then to be the ordering of these rules within the cycle.[8]

1.4 Parallelisms with other embeddings

1.4.1 Prepositional object embeddings All the rules formulated above to account for the periphrastic sentences are independently required to derive other instances of embedding where the matrix verb is not an auxiliary but a full lexical verb.

One such example is (115) which can be derived from the deep structure shown in (116).

(115) Blinodd Ifor ar ddarllen llyfrau.
Tired Ifor on reading books.
i.e. Ifor tired of reading books.

(116)

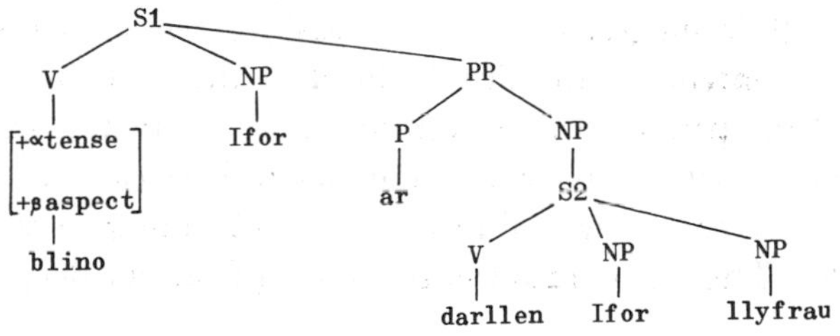

The subject of S2 is deleted by T. Equi-Subject Deletion, and the uninflected verb mutated by T. Prepositional Object Mutation. The object of S2 is left unmutated, as it follows an uninflected verb. Compare (115) with (43).

(117), which has a pronoun object, may be compared with (46).

(117) Blinodd Ifor ar ei ddarllen.
Tired Ifor on its reading.

This may be derived from the deep structure (118).

(118)

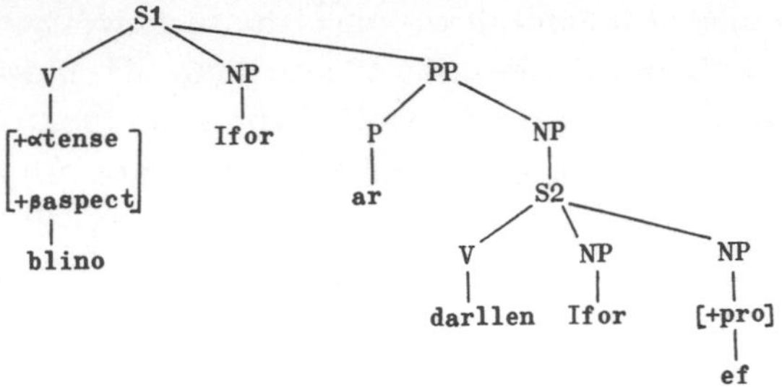

T. Equi-Subject Deletion deletes the subject of S2, and the pronoun object is copied to the left of the verb by T. Possessive Pronoun Preposing. Later the pronoun in the original position to the right of the verb is deleted by T. Possessive Pronoun Deletion, which is here optional as in the periphrastic forms. (119) where the pronoun is not deleted is also grammatical.

(119) Blinodd Ifor ar ei ddarllen ef.
Tired Ifor on its reading it.

The uninflected verb is mutated following the preposed pronoun.

1.4.2 Direct object embeddings In all the examples discussed so far, whether the embedding is below a lexical verb or an auxiliary verb, the embedded sentence has been the object of a preposition in the matrix sentence. The analysis suggested can be very easily extended to cases where the embedded sentence is the direct object of the verb in the matrix sentence, and the parallelism between forms with a matrix lexical verb and those with a matrix auxiliary verb holds in these cases too.

An auxiliary verb taking a direct object embedding in this way is *gallu* (be able). The form (120) can be derived from the deep structure (121).

(120) Gall Ifor ddarllen llyfrau.
Can Ifor reading books.
i.e. Ifor can read books.

(121)

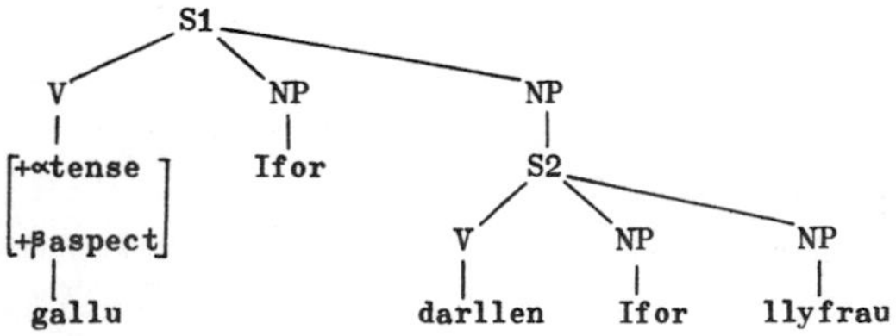

In order for T. Equi-Subject Deletion to apply to forms such as this it must be reformulated to omit direct reference to a preposition in the matrix sentence. A modified version of this rule is given in (122). The preposition is replaced by a variable which represents the presence or absence of the preposition. It is assumed that this variable is restricted to cover only items occurring within one sentence, an abbreviatory variable of the type discussed by Postal (1971 p. 115). This will prevent the rule from applying too far down the tree if there are intervening layers of embedding.

(122) T. Equi-Subject Deletion (obligatory)[2]

$$\text{SD. } (_{S}\ \text{V}\ \ \text{NPx}\ \ \text{X}\ \ (_{NP}\ (_{S}\ \text{V}\ \ \text{NPx}\ \ \text{Y}\ )\ )\ )$$

$$1\ \ 2\ \ 3\ \ \ 4\ \ 5\ \ \ 6\ \ 7\ \ 8\ \ \ 9$$

SC. Delete 8.

The uninflected verb is mutated as the direct object of the matrix verb, and the object of S2 is left unmutated.

(123) differs in having a pronoun object in S2.

(123) Gall Wyn ei ddarllen.
Can Wyn its reading

Here again T. Equi-Subject Deletion applies, and rules already discussed above copy the pronoun object, delete the original pronoun and mutate the verb.

Apparently identical are cases such as (124) and (125) where the embedding is the direct object of a lexical matrix verb rather than an auxiliary verb.

(124) Dymunai Ifor ddarllen llyfrau.
Wanted Ifor reading books.

(125) Dymunai Ifor ei ddarllen.
Wanted Ifor its reading.

The modified version of T. Equi-Subject Deletion can apply here too, and the other transformations are identical to those needed by the examples (120) and (123).

1.4.3 Subject raising in subject embeddings In those cases where the subject of the embedding is not identical to the subject of the matrix sentence T. Equi-Subject Deletion cannot apply. Instead the subject of the embedding appears in a prepositional phrase as the object of the preposition *i* (for). Again parallelisms appear between cases with an auxiliary matrix verb and cases with a lexical main verb.

An example of an auxiliary matrix verb taking an embedding of this type is *darfod* (happen) which expresses past punctual aspect. *Darfod* is an intransitive verb and the embedding is embedded below the subject of the matrix sentence, with (126) being derived from the deep structure (127).

(126) Darfu i rywun ddarllen llyfr.
Happened for someone reading (a) book.
i.e. It happened that someone read a book.

(127)

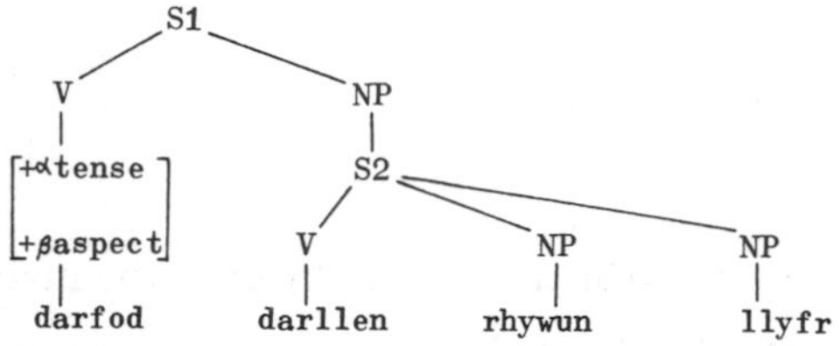

T. Equi-Subject Deletion cannot apply as there is no noun phrase in the matrix sentence identical to the subject of S2. Instead another rule moves the subject of the embedding to the left of the verb as the object of *i* (for).

The rules affecting the uninflected verb and the object of the embedding are the same here as in the cases where T. Equi-Subject Deletion has applied. In (126) the object noun is left unmutated. In (128), which has a pronoun object, the pronoun is copied to the left of the uninflected verb, the original pronoun is deleted, and the uninflected verb is mutated following the preposed pronoun.

(128) Darfu i rywun ei ddarllen.
Happened for someone its reading.

If T. Possessive Pronoun Preposing is to have the same formulation here as has been adequate till now, then the prepositional phrase containing the subject of S2 must be outside the noun phrase which dominates S2 at this point in the derivation. The rule which converts the deep structure (129) into the structure (130), which is the input to T. Possessive Pronoun Preposing, is shown in (131).

(129)

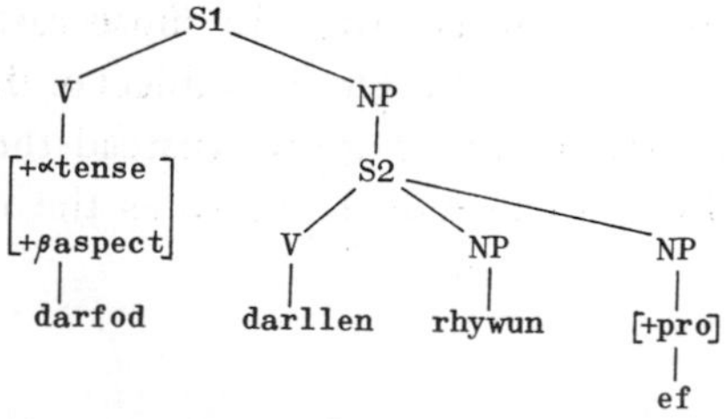

(130)

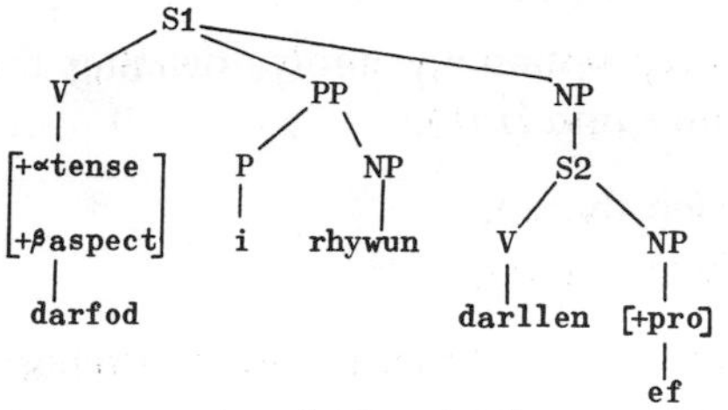

(131) T. Subject Raising (obligatory)

SD. $(_S\ V\ (_{NP}\ (_S\ V\ NP\ X\ )\ )\ )$

1 2 3 4 5 6 7

SC. Adjoin 6 as left sister to 3, in a prepositional phrase as object of the preposition i.

In (130) the pronoun object once again immediately follows the uninflected verb. T. Equi-Subject Deletion achieved this by deletion, and T. Subject Raising does so by movement.

Further rules apply to the prepositional phrase which is created by this rule. If the object of the preposition is a noun then it is marked for soft mutation by T. Prepositional Object Mutation. Here this converts *rhywun* (someone) to *rywun*. If the object of the preposition is a pronoun as in (132) then the preposition is inflected to agree with it in number and person, and in the case of 3sg pronouns in gender as well. Compare (133) and (134).

(132) Darfu iddynt hwy ddarllen llyfrau.
Happened for them reading books.

(133) Darfu iddo of ddarllen llyfrau.
Happened for him reading books.

(134) Darfu iddi hi ddarllen llyfrau.
Happened for her reading books.

The rule carrying out this agreement is formulated in (135). Morphological rules will give the correct inflections to the preposition.

(135) T. Preposition Agreement (obligatory)

SD. $(_{PP}\ P\ \ NP\ )$, where NP = [+pro, αno, βpers, γgend]

1 2 3

SC. Copy the features [αno], [βpers], [γgend] onto 2.

Later a further rule may optionally apply, deleting the pronoun, converting (134) for instance into (136).

(136) Darfu iddi ddarllen llyfrau.
Happened for (her) reading books.

This rule is formulated in (137). It must follow T. Preposition Agreement or there will be no pronoun for the preposition to agree with.[9]

(137) T. Pronoun Prepositional Object Deletion (optional)

SD. ($_{PP}$ P NP[+pro])

1 2 3

SC. Delete 3.

These two rules apply to prepositional phrases in general, not just to those that result from T. Subject Raising. In (138) only T. Preposition Agreement has applied, and in (139) both rules.

(138) Rhoddais y llyfrau arno ef.
Put (I) the books on it.

(139) Rhoddais y llyfrau arno.
Put (I) the books on (it).

A further mutation rule applies to give the soft mutation form of the uninflected verb following the prepositional phrase. The isolation form *darllen* (read) is converted to *ddarllen*. This rule will apply only in cases like (126) where the object of the uninflected verb is a noun. In cases like (128) where the object is a pronoun, this pronoun is copied between the prepositional phrase and the verb and it is this pronoun which triggers mutation of the verb. The rule giving a soft mutation form of the verb following a prepositional phrase is formulated in (140).

(140) T. Mutation of Embedded Verb (obligatory)

SD. ($_S$ X PP ($_{NP}$ ($_S$ V Y)))

1 2 3 4 5 6 7

SC. Add the feature [+soft mut] onto 6.

The ordering of rules required here is as follows. All those rules shown in (114) which affect the pronoun object of the embedding follow T. Subject Raising.

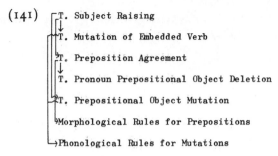

(141) T. Subject Raising
↓
T. Mutation of Embedded Verb
T. Preposition Agreement
↓
T. Pronoun Prepositional Object Deletion
T. Prepositional Object Mutation
Morphological Rules for Prepositions
Phonological Rules for Mutations

These same rules are required when the matrix sentence contains something other than an auxiliary verb. There are few lexical verbs which appear in this construction but lexical adjectives are quite common. Examples are shown in (142) and (143). In (142) there is a noun object and in (143) a pronoun object.

(142) Mae'n angenrheidiol i rywun ddarllen llyfrau.
Is necessary for someone reading books.
(143) Mae'n angenrheidiol i rywun ei ddarllen.
Is necessary for someone its reading.

In (142) the uninflected verb is mutated following the prepositional phrase and the object noun is left unmutated. In (143) the rules affecting a pronoun object have applied. In both the subject is raised into a prepositional phrase and mutated following *i*. In (144) the raised subject is a pronoun and the agreement rule has applied.

(144) Mae'n angenrheidiol iddi hi ei ddarllen.
Is necessary for her its reading.

1.4.4 Subject raising in object embeddings If the matrix sentence contains a lexical verb T. Subject Raising can apply not only where the embedding is the subject of the matrix sentence but also where it is the object of the sentence. For instance, in (145) the embedding is the direct object of the matrix.

(145) Dymunai Wyn i Ifor ddarllen llyfr.
Wanted Wyn for Ifor reading (a) book.

This can be derived from the deep structure (146) where the subject of the matrix is not identical to the subject of the embedding.

(146)

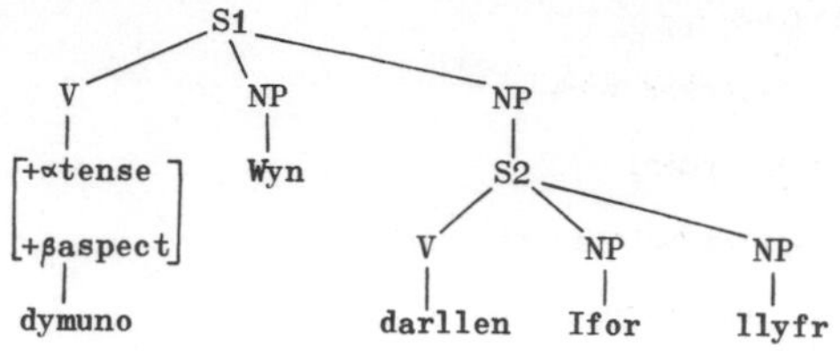

In order to account for such forms as this T. Subject Raising must be modified as shown in (147).

(147) <u>T. Subject Raising (obligatory)</u>[2]

SD. $(_{S}\ V\ X\ (_{NP}\ (_{S}\ V\ NP\ Y\ )\ )\ )$

1 2 3 4 5 6 7 8

Condition. X does not contain a noun phrase identical to 7.

SC. Adjoin 7 as left sister to 4, in a prepositional phrase as object of the preposition <u>i</u>.

This will now cover cases of both subject and object embedding. The variable in the rule is again an abbreviatory variable. There may or may not be a noun phrase subject in the matrix sentence. If there is one it may not be identical to the subject of the embedding. This rule converts the deep structure (146) into (148).

(148)

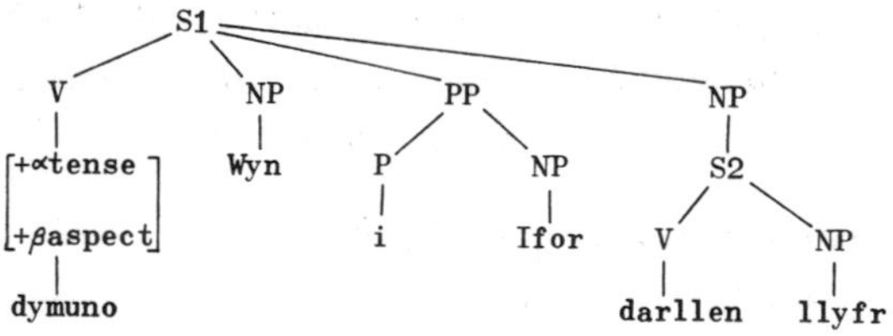

The later transformations will apply here as in the examples discussed already.

It appears that there are no instances of auxiliary verbs which take an object embedding of this type, undergoing T. Subject Raising. But it is predicted by this analysis that this is a syntactic accident, the result probably of semantic constraints. The syntactic patterning leads one to expect that the full range should be possible with auxiliary verbs and lexical verbs alike.

1.5 Uninflected verbs as tenseless verbs

1.5.1 Tenseless embeddings Till now the question of whether the verb of the embedded sentence is marked for tense or not has been ignored. It will now be suggested that it is not marked for tense or aspect at any stage in the derivation. The lack of inflection is due to this.

The tense and aspect of the uninflected verb are understood as being identical to that of the inflected verb in the matrix sentence. This is true of both the periphrastic forms and those with a lexical matrix verb. It might be thought that the verb in the embedding should be marked for tense and aspect in the deep structure and these features deleted on identity with the features of the verb in the matrix sentence. This analysis resembles the one used above in section 1.3.2 to justify T. Equi-Subject Deletion. In the case of examples such as (149) it appears to be a reasonable analysis.

(149) Dymunai Ifor ddarllen llyfr.
Wanted Ifor reading (a) book.

The features of tense and aspect on *dymunai* (wanted) might well be duplicated in the deep structure on *darllen* (read).

There are however problems in extending this analysis to the periphrastic forms. In the case of (150) the tense and aspect of the matrix sentence are expressed by a combination of the inflected form of *bod* (be) and the preposition *wedi.*

(150) Mae Ifor wedi darllen llyfr.
Is Ifor after reading (a) book.

If these features are not all attached to the verb in the matrix sentence, it is difficult to see how they can be duplicated in the embedding where the preposition is not available. The problems become even more acute in the case of a form like (151) where there are three sentences involved, according to the embedding analysis adopted here.

(151) Mae Ifor wedi bod yn darllen llyfr.
Is Ifor after being in reading (a) book.

The deep structure of (151) is (152). Here the tense and aspect of the entire form is expressed by the verb and preposition of S1 and the preposition of S2. The difficulties of duplicating all this in the embedded sentence S3 are multiplied.

(152)

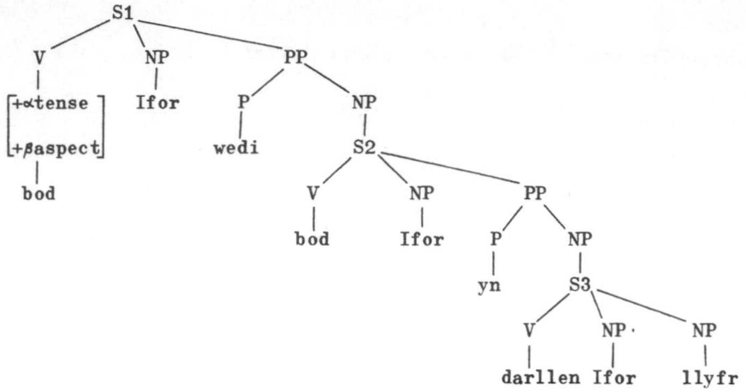

It is much easier to assume that the verb of the embedding is not marked for tense in deep structure. No deletion rules are now needed, and the tense and aspect of the embedded verb is a matter of semantic interpretation. Nor is this true only of the periphrastic forms. The same problems arise over deletion of tense and aspect in the case of embeddings below a lexical verb if that verb is itself embedded in a periphrastic form, as in (153).

(153) Mae Ifor yn dymuno darllen llyfr.
Is Ifor in wanting reading (a) book.

The tense and aspect of the uninflected verb *darllen* (read) here must be identical to those of *dymuno* (want) in the sentence above. And the tense and aspect of this must in turn be identical to those of the matrix sentence. But here these features are distributed over the verb and preposition, and the same problems arise as in the case of the ordinary periphrastic forms above. It appears then that in these cases too the embedded verb is better analysed as not marked for tense and aspect in deep structure.

The lack of tense and aspect in these uninflected verbs at all stages in the derivation and their noun-like syntax in surface structure suggest that it might be wrong to analyse them as verbs. Instead they should perhaps be analysed as nouns, lexically related to the corresponding verbs but still different lexical items.[10]

This approach however seems to be mistaken. There are other constructions in Welsh, discussed below in section 1.5.2, in which the verb is uninflected and has the same form as the uninflected verbs discussed here, but where it must be marked for tense and aspect in deep structure.

These features are deleted by a later rule. The superficially tenseless verb must be tensed and therefore a verb in deep structure, and the parallelism between these forms and the periphrastic sentences supports a verbal analysis of both.

1.5.2 Superficially tenseless verbs There is a set of embeddings which have an inflected verb in surface structure, as in (154) and (155). The embedding may be a simple sentence as in (154) or a periphrastic sentence as in (155).

(154) Dywedodd Emyr y deuai Ifor yno.
Said Emyr that would come Ifor there.
i.e. Emyr said that Ifor would come there.
(155) Dywedodd Emyr y byddai Ifor yn dod yno.
Said Emyr that would be Ifor in coming there.
i.e. Emyr said that Ifor would be coming there.

These embeddings differ from the ones so far discussed not only in having inflected verbs but also in other ways. For instance, the subject of the embedding is not necessarily deleted even if it is identical to the subject of the matrix sentence. Instead it is pronominalised, as in (156).

(516) Dywedodd Rhian y deuai hi yno.
Said Rhian that would come she there.

The pronoun subject may indeed be deleted as in (157).

(157) Dywedodd Rhian y deuai yno.
Said Rhian that would come (she) there.

But this deletion seems to be due to T. Pronoun Subject Deletion not to some version of T. Equi-Subject Deletion, since any pronoun subject may be deleted, as in (158), even if it is not identical to the subject of the matrix sentence.

(158) Dywedodd Rhian y deuech yno.
Said Rhian that would come (you) there.

These embeddings may take all tense and aspect combinations except for periphrastics where the verb *bod* (be) appears in its present or its imperfect form.[11] Sentences with embeddings of these two types are ungrammatical.

(159) *Dwêd Emyr y mae Ifor yn dod yno.
Says Emyr that is Ifor in coming there.

(160) *Dywedodd Emyr yr oedd Ifor yn dod yno.
Said Emyr that was Ifor in coming there.

This restriction holds only for positive statements. If the embedding is a question, as in (161), or a negative statement, as in (162), then these forms of the verb are grammatical.

(161) Gofynnodd Emyr a oedd Ifor yn dod yno.
Asked Emyr whether was Ifor in coming there.

(162) Dwêd Emyr nad yw Ifor yn dod yno.
Says Emyr that not is Ifor in coming there.

The gaps which this restriction causes are filled by embeddings containing the uninflected form of *bod* (be).

(163) Dwêd Emyr fod Ifor yn dod yno.
Says Emyr being Ifor in coming there.

(164) Dywedodd Emyr fod Ifor yn dod yno.
Said Emyr being Ifor in coming there.

(163) has the same interpretation as (159) would have, and (164) has the same interpretation as (160) would have. This is the same uninflected form of *bod* (be) as is found in a periphrastic sentence or embedded below a lexical verb, as in (165) and (166).

(165) Mae Wyn wedi bod yn darllen.
Is Wyn after being in reading.

(166) Dymunai Wyn fod yn enwog.
Wanted Wyn being famous.

The embeddings with uninflected forms of *bod* (be) which fit the semantic gaps left by the inflected verbs share certain syntactic characteristics with the inflected embeddings. For instance, if the subject of the embedding is identical to the subject of the matrix sentence, it is not deleted but rather appears in pronoun form, as in (167).

(167) Dywedodd Emyr ei fod ef yn dod yno.
Said Emyr his being him in coming there.

In order to show this parallelism these forms must somehow be grouped with the inflected embeddings.

These pseudo-inflected embeddings also share certain characteristics with tenseless embeddings, besides the form of the uninflected verb.

The pronoun object of the uninflected verb in the tenseless embedding appears either both preceding and following the verb or just preceding, as in (168) and (169).

(168) Mae Wyn wedi ei ddarllen ef.
Is Wyn after its reading it.
(169) Mae Wyn wedi ei ddarllen.
Is Wyn after its reading.

Similarly in the case of the pseudo-inflected embeddings the subject noun phrase appears in the same positions. In (167) it appears both preceding and following the verb, and in (170) it precedes the verb only.

(170) Dywedodd Emyr ei fod yn dod yno.
Said Emyr his being in coming there.

The two sets of parallelisms may be shown if the verb *bod* (be) is marked for tense and aspect in deep structure but these features are deleted at some stage in the derivation. It will then be unmarked for these features in the later stages of the derivation. This allows the full spread of tense and aspect possibilities in deep structure for these embeddings, so that apparently unmotivated gaps do not need to be explained. It also explains why the *bod* forms are interpreted as filling these gaps. And it allows for the similarities in syntax with the inflected forms over pronominalising rather than deleting the subject of the embedding. The later tenselessness of *bod* explains the similarities to the other tenseless forms.

A rule deleting the tense and aspect features in these cases does not meet the same problems as arose in the case of the rule discussed in section 1.5.1 since it is very limited in scope, affecting only the features of two inflections of *bod*. It resembles the rules which also apply to inflected embeddings to give the correct sequence of tenses. For instance, a rule must convert the present inflection of the verb in (171) to the imperfect form of (172).

(171) Dywedodd Emyr 'Nid yw Ifor yn dod'.
Said Emyr 'Not is Ifor in coming'.
(172) Dywedodd Emyr nad oedd Ifor yn dod.
Said Emyr that not was Ifor in coming.

Both types of rule apply on the cycle of the matrix sentence and affect the tense and aspect features of the embedded verb.[12]

1.5.3 A revised analysis The deep structure of the periphrastic sentences may now be formulated in more detail, with the embedded verb specified as unmarked for tense and aspect. The deep structure of (173) is (174).

(173) Mae Wyn wedi darllen y llyfr.
Is Wyn after reading the book.

(174)

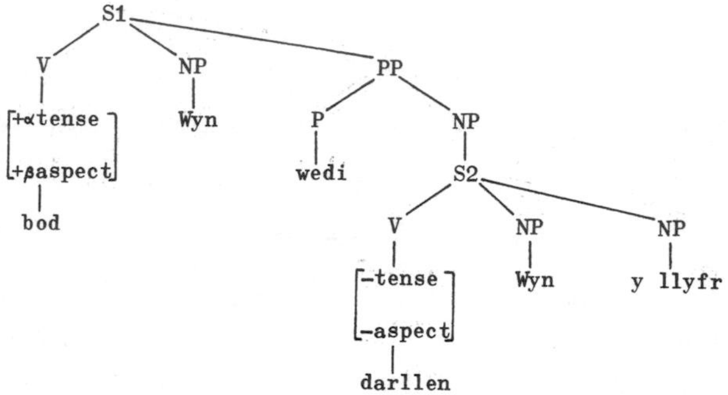

Similarly the verb of embeddings below lexical verbs is marked as [–tense] and [–aspect].

Certain transformations which are limited to these tenseless embeddings must now be reformulated to make this clear. It was pointed out in section 1.5.2 that T. Equi-Subject Deletion does not apply to embeddings which contain tensed verbs in deep structure. It must therefore be rewritten as (175).

(175) <u>T. Equi-Subject Deletion (obligatory)</u>[3]

SD. ($_S$ V NPx X ($_{NP}$ ($_S$ V [–tense, –aspect] NPx Y)))

1 2 3 4 5 6 7 8 9

SC. Delete 8.

Similarly T. Subject Raising only applies to forms with a deep structure tenseless verb. Neither in (154), where the verb of the embedding is inflected, nor in (163), where the verb was tensed in deep structure, is the subject of the embedding raised into a prepositional phrase. This rule must be rewritten as (176).

```
(176) T. Subject Raising (obligatory)[3]

      SD. (S V X (NP (S       V       NP  Y ) ) )
                              |
                          [-tense ]
                          [-aspect]

          1   2  3  4  5      6       7   8

      Condition. X does not contain a noun phrase identical to 7.

      SC. Adjoin 7 as left sister to 4, in a prepositional phrase
          as object of the preposition i.
```

T. Possessive Pronoun Preposing must also be restricted to tenseless forms.

```
(177) T. Possessive Pronoun Preposing (obligatory)[3]

      SD. (NP  { <(S       V        > }  NP     <)> )
               {           |          }  |
               {       [-tense ]      } [+pro]
               {       [-aspect]      }
               {  N                   }

          1      2                       3

      SC. Adjoin a copy of 3 as left daughter of 1, dominated by the
          node Determiner.
```

The morphological rules which follow on this rule will automatically be restricted to tenseless forms. T. Possessive Pronoun Deletion must also be rewritten as (178).

```
(178) T. Possessive Pronoun Deletion (optional)[2]

      SD. (NP (Det   NPx    )  { <(S       V       > }  NPx    <)> )
                     |         {           |         }  |
                   [+pro]      {       [-tense ]     } [+pro]
                               {       [-aspect]     }
                               {  N                  }

          1    2     3           4                      5

      SC. Delete 5.
```

Certain other transformations must be restricted to tensed verbs. These are T. Soft Mutation of Direct Object, which was reformulated in (79) above, the two verbal agreement rules, and T. Pronoun Subject Deletion. These are shown in (179) to (181).

(179) <u>T. Subject-Verb Agreement (Pronoun) (obligatory)</u>[2]

$$\begin{array}{lcccc} \text{SD.}\ ({}_S & \begin{array}{c} \text{V} \\ | \\ \begin{bmatrix} +\alpha\text{tense} \\ +\beta\text{aspect} \end{bmatrix} \end{array} & \begin{array}{c} \text{NP} \\ | \\ \begin{bmatrix} +\text{pro} \\ \alpha\text{no} \\ \beta\text{pers} \end{bmatrix} \end{array} & \text{X}\ ) \\ 1 & 2 & 3 & 4 \end{array}$$

SC. Copy the features [αno] and [βpers] onto 2.

(180) <u>T. Subject-Verb Agreement (Noun) (obligatory)</u>[2]

$$\begin{array}{lcccc} \text{SD.}\ ({}_S & \begin{array}{c} \text{V} \\ | \\ \begin{bmatrix} +\alpha\text{tense} \\ +\beta\text{aspect} \end{bmatrix} \end{array} & \begin{array}{c} \text{NP} \\ | \\ [-\text{pro}] \end{array} & \text{X}\ ) \\ 1 & 2 & 3 & 4 \end{array}$$

SC. Add the features [sg no] and [3pers] onto 2.

(181) <u>T. Pronoun Subject Deletion (optional)</u>[2]

$$\begin{array}{lcccc} \text{SD.}\ ({}_S & \begin{array}{c} \text{V} \\ | \\ \begin{bmatrix} +\alpha\text{tense} \\ +\beta\text{aspect} \end{bmatrix} \end{array} & \begin{array}{c} \text{NP} \\ | \\ [+\text{pro}] \end{array} & \text{X}\ ) \\ 1 & 2 & 3 & 4 \end{array}$$

SC. Delete 3.

1.6 Conclusions

One theme pervades the discussion in this chapter; the lack of a simple tie-up between semantics and syntax. The semantic differences between the simple active forms and the periphrastic forms are a matter of tense and aspect only, and no greater than the tense and aspect differences which hold between various simple actives. Yet syntactically they are very disparate, requiring different deep structure representations and different transformations in the derivation. Conversely, there are big semantic differences between the periphrastic forms and embeddings below lexical verbs, but from the point of view of syntax the two are very similar, requiring similar deep structure representations and the same transformations. The semantic difference between auxiliary and lexical verbs does not seem relevant syntactically. This theme will be further illustrated in the discussion of passive forms in the next chapter.

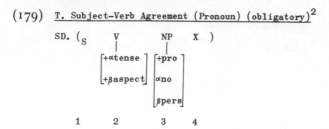

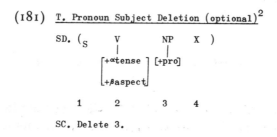

2 *Passive sentences*

In this chapter an analysis of passive sentences is presented, which builds on the analysis of actives already established. It is suggested that passives, like periphrastic forms, contain an embedded sentence with a tenseless verb. In sections 2.1. to 2.4 the derivation of straightforward passives is considered, and in section 2.5 some variations on this type. In section 2.6 a problem first raised in section 2.4.3 is followed up more fully.

2.1 Active and passive pairs

Examples of active and passive pairs are given in (1) to (6). Each pair of sentences appears to be synonymous.

(1) Rhybuddiodd y dyn y bachgen.
Warned the man the boy.
(2) Cafodd y bachgen ei rybuddio gan y dyn.
Got the boy his warning by the man.
i.e. The boy was warned by the man.

(3) Rhybuddiodd y plant y merched.
Warned the children the girls.
(4) Cafodd y merched eu rhybuddio gan y plant.
Got the girls their warning by the children.

(5) Rhybuddiai'r ferch y dyn.
Was warning the girl the man.
(6) Câi'r dyn ei rybuddio gan y ferch.
Was getting the man his warning by the girl.

In each case, the passive sentence has a sentence-initial inflected form of *cael* (get) of the same tense and aspect as the verb of the active. This is followed by a noun phrase identical to the object of the active. Then comes a pronoun of the same person, number and gender (if it is 3sg) as this noun phrase, and an uninflected form of the verb in the active. Finally there is a preposition *gan* (by) and a noun phrase identical to the subject of the active. These relationships are summarised in (7). Corresponding items are marked with the same subscript number.

(7)

Active	V_1	NP_2	NP_3			
	inflected					
Passive	cael	NP_3	$Pron_3$	V_1	gan	NP_2
	inflected			uninflected		

2.2 The surface structure analysis

2.2.1 Surface structure constituents The inflected form of *cael* (get) and the following noun phrase resemble the verb and subject of the simple active sentence in several syntactic characteristics. *Cael* is in sentence initial position and the noun phrase immediately follows it. *Cael* is inflected for tense and aspect, as can be seen by comparing (2) and (6). It also inflects for person and number, agreeing with the following noun phrase if this is a pronoun, as in (8) to (10).

(8) Cafodd ef ei rybuddio gan y ferch.
Got he his warning by the girl.

(9) Cawsant hwy eu rhybuddio gan y ferch.
Got they their warning by the girl.

(10) Cawsom ni ein rhybuddio gan y ferch.
Got we our warning by the girl.

(8) and (9) differ in number, and (9) and (10) differ in person. In both cases the verbal inflection changes. If the following noun phrase is a noun, then *cael* appears with the inflection which is found with 3sg pronouns. This is the case if the noun is singular as in (2) or plural as in (4). If the noun phrase is a pronoun it may optionally be omitted. Both (10) and (11) are grammatical.

(11) Cawsom ein rhybuddio gan y ferch.
Got (we) our warning by the girl.

The inflected form of *cael* and the following noun phrase therefore appear in the same place as the verb and subject of the simple active sentence. They display the same agreement patterns, and the noun phrase in both is optional if it is a pronoun. A generalisation is clearly lost if they are not given the same analysis. It is therefore assumed that *cael* and the following noun phrase are the verb and subject of the passive sentence.

The uninflected verb is preceded by a pronoun of the same form as the preposed pronouns discussed above in section 1.2.3. Compare the form *ei* (his) in the passive form (8) and in the possessive noun phrase (12).

(12) ei lyfr
his book

The parallelism extends to other pronoun forms. Compare the 3pl form in the passive (9) and the possessive (13).

(13) eu llyfr
their book

The pronoun causes the same mutation of the following item in both cases. *Ei* (his) requires the soft mutation form of the verb in (8) and of the noun in (12). *Eu* (their) retains the isolation form in both cases. This parallelism suggests that the pronoun and the uninflected verb should be analysed as a noun phrase of a similar structure to the noun phrases in (12) and (13). Otherwise a generalisation will be lost. The uninflected verb resembles the head noun and the pronoun resembles the possessive.

The noun phrase analysis is further supported by some evidence that this constituent is the direct object of the verb *cael* in surface structure. This claim is based on the fact that *cael* appears in other constructions where it does have a direct object, as in (14).

(14) Cafodd Emyr lyfr.
Got Emyr (a) book.

The noun phrase *lyfr* (book) appears in normal object position, immediately following the subject, and is in soft mutation form. Since the verb here is identical to that of the passive, and the pronoun and uninflected verb also immediately follow the subject in direct object position, it seems reasonable to assume that they too should be analysed as the object of *cael*. This analysis cannot be confirmed by soft mutation of the direct object, since the leftmost item is the pronoun which blocks mutation of the verb. There is however no evidence against this view.

It appears that the sequence of *gan* (by) and a following noun phrase is a prepositional phrase, as it shows the same patterns as were shown to be characteristic of prepositional phrases in section 1.4.3. If the noun phrase following *gan* is a pronoun, then *gan* is inflected to agree with it in person and number, as in (15) to (17).

(15) Cafodd y dyn ei rybuddio gennyt ti.
Got the man his warning by thee.
(16) Cafodd y dyn ei rybuddio gennych chwi.
Got the man his warning by you.
(17) Cafodd y dyn ei rybuddio gennym ni.
Got the man his warning by us.

If the pronoun is 3sg then *gan* agrees with it in gender too, as in (18) and (19).

(18) Cafodd y dyn ei rybuddio ganddo ef.
Got the man his warning by him.
(19) Cafodd y dyn ei rybuddio ganddi hi.
Got the man his warning by her.

The pronoun may optionally be omitted. Both (19) and (20) are grammatical.

(20) Cafodd y dyn ei rybuddio ganddi.
Got the man his warning by (her).

If the noun phrase following *gan* is a noun then *gan* triggers the soft mutation. In the examples discussed so far the definite article intervenes between *gan* and the noun, blocking the mutation, but in (21) where there is no intervening item the mutation is realised. *Ferch* is the soft mutation form of *merch* (girl).

(21) Cafodd y dyn ei rybuddio gan ferch.
Got the man his warning by (a) girl.

2.2.2 Surface phrase structure The surface structure of the passive sentence (21) is then that shown in (22).[1]

(22)

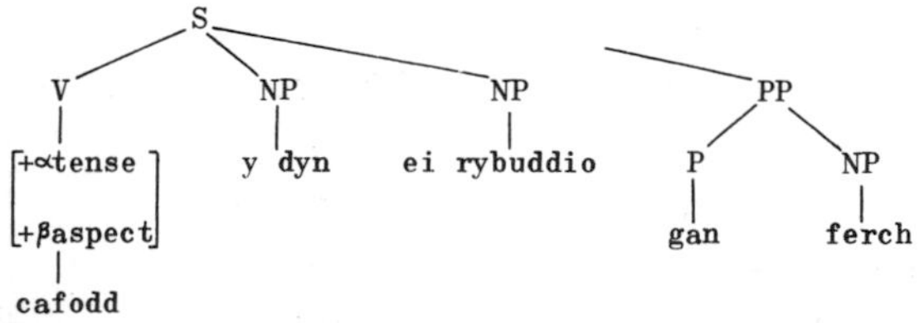

The main verb of the sentence is the inflected form of *cael* (get). The following noun phrase *y dyn* (the man) is the subject. The pronoun and uninflected verb form a noun phrase which is the object of *cael*. *Gan* (by) and the following noun phrase form a prepositional phrase. It is not yet clear however where the prepositional phrase should be attached in the tree.

There are two possibilities. Either the prepositional phrase is attached directly to the sentence node, as in (23), or it is attached to the same noun phrase node as the pronoun and uninflected verb, as in (24).

(23)

(24)

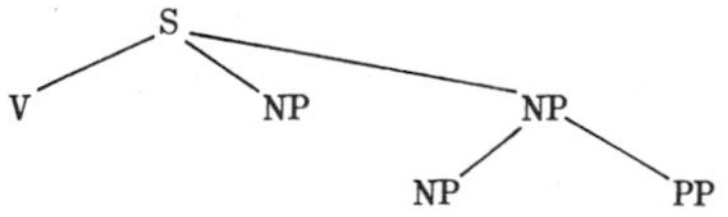

In (23) the noun phrase and the prepositional phrase are separate constituents. In (24) they form one constituent. The tree (23) is the same as the one suggested in section 1.1.1 for the active sentence (25).

(25) Rhoddodd y dyn y ffon i'r ci.
Gave the man the stick to the dog.

The tree (24) accounts for forms such as (26) where the prepositional phrase is part of the noun phrase it qualifies.

(26) Darllenodd y dyn lyfr am bysgod.
Read the man (a) book about fish.

The two forms have different possible cleft equivalents. The noun phrase and prepositional phrase of (25) may each appear separately as the focus of a cleft sentence, as in (27) and (28).

(27) Y ffon a roddodd y dyn i'r ci.
The stick that gave the man to the dog.

(28) I'r ci y rhoddodd y dyn y ffon.
To the dog that gave the man the stick.

They may not appear together as the focus of a cleft sentence.

(29) *Y ffon i'r ci a roddodd y dyn.
The stick to the dog that gave the man.

The reverse is true of (26). The noun phrase and prepositional phrase may appear together as the focus of a cleft sentence as in (30).

(30) Llyfr am bysgod a ddarllenodd y dyn.
(A) book about fish that read the man.

But neither the noun phrase nor the prepositional phrase may appear alone as the focus of a cleft sentence, as in (31) and (32).

(31) *Llyfr a ddarllenodd y dyn am bysgod.
(A) book that read the man about fish.
(32) *Am bysgod y darllenodd y dyn lyfr.
About fish that read the man (a) book.

The possible cleft forms of the passive may therefore show which of the two structures is correct. The prepositional phrase of the passive (21) may appear as the focus of a cleft sentence as in (33).

(33) Gan ferch y cafodd y dyn ei rybuddio.
By (a) girl that got the man his warning.

The noun phrase may not appear alone as the focus, as in (34), nor may both the noun phrase and prepositional phrase together, as in (35).

(34) *Ei rybuddio a gafodd y dyn gan ferch.
His warning that got the man by (a) girl.
(35) *Ei rybuddio gan ferch a gafodd y dyn.
His warning by (a) girl that got the man.

This pattern does not correspond entirely to either of the two forms (25) and (26).

The passive seems closer to the form (25), with the tree structure (23), since only with this form is it possible to have the prepositional phrase alone as focus. The ungrammaticality of (34) where the noun phrase is focus seems to be due to the operation of some other factor. Uninflected verbs which are the direct object in other constructions are also ungrammatical as the focus of a cleft sentence in many cases. For instance, it was shown in section 1.4.2 that the uninflected verb is the object of *gallu* (be able), and here too it cannot appear as the focus of a cleft sentence.

(36) Gall Ifor ganu.
Can Ifor singing.
(37) *Canu a all Ifor.
Singing that can Ifor.

This is not true of all such cases. For instance, the cleft form of (38) is (39), which is found grammatical by many speakers.

(38) Hoffai Ifor ganu.
Liked Ifor singing.

(39) Canu a hoffai Ifor.
Singing that liked Ifor.

The restriction holds of enough forms however for it to be a reasonable explanation of the failure of the passive to correspond entirely to the clefting pattern of (25).[2]

Had the structure of the passive been (24) one would expect all three cleft forms to be ungrammatical. (33) would be ungrammatical because the prepositional phrase cannot cleft alone in this type. (34) would be ungrammatical because of this and also because of the restrictions on uninflected verbs as focus. (35) would be ungrammatical because of the restriction on uninflected verbs. Since this pattern is not found, it seems best to adopt (23) as the surface structure of the passive.

The surface structure of (21) is (40) then on this analysis.

(40)

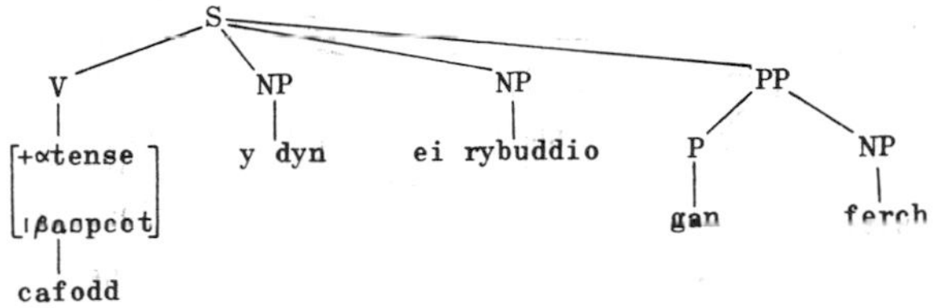

2.3 The deep structure analysis

2.3.1 The uninflected verb The uninflected verb may need to be analysed as a noun in surface structure, but it also retains certain verbal characteristics, which suggests that it must also be analysed as a verb if generalisations are not to be lost.

The same selection restrictions are found with the inflected verb in the active and the uninflected verb in the passive. If a pair of noun phrases is acceptable with the inflected verb in the active, then it is also acceptable with the uninflected verb in the passive, as in (41) and (42).

(41) Croesawodd y plant yr ymwelwyr.
Welcomed the children the visitors.

(42) Cafodd yr ymwelwyr eu croesawu gan y plant.
Got the visitors their welcoming by the children.

Conversely, if a pair of noun phrases is not acceptable with the inflected verb in the active then it is not acceptable either with the uninflected verb in the passive.

(43) *Croesawodd y bwrdd y gadair.
Welcomed the table the chair.

(44) *Cafodd y gadair ei chroesawu gan y bwrdd.
Got the chair its welcoming by the table.

The noun phrases do not appear in the same position in each case but the constraints are the same.

The noun phrases are also interpreted in the same way relative to the inflected and uninflected verbs. In both (41) and (42) it is the children who are doing the welcoming and the visitors who are being welcomed. The different positions of the two noun phrases in surface structure do not affect this. And the meanings of the inflected and uninflected forms of the verb are the same apart from tense and aspect specifications.

Further evidence of the verbal nature of the uninflected verb is the possibility of adverbs of manner co-occurring with it as in (45).

(45) Cafoldd y plant eu rhybuddio yn ofalus gan yr athro.
Got the children their warning carefully by the teacher.

Here again the parallelism with the inflected active appears since the same adverb may in each case appear with the inflected verb in the active.

(46) Rhybuddiodd yr athro y plant yn ofalus.
Warned the teacher the children carefully.

In both cases the adverb refers to the action of the same person, here the teacher. The adverb must be associated with the uninflected verb in the passive forms since *cael* alone in a construction where there is no uninflected verb cannot take such adverbs, as in (47).

(47) *Cafodd Wyn anrheg yn ofalus.
Got Wyn (a) present carefully.

2.3.2 A complex sentence If the passive is analysed in deep structure as a complex sentence, then the double nature of the inflected verb as both a verb and a noun can be accounted for, as well as certain other problems. The inflected form of *cael* and the following noun phrase are, on this analysis, the verb and subject of the matrix sentence. A second sentence is embedded below the object noun phrase node of the matrix sentence. The uninflected verb is the verb of the embedded sentence, and it takes the same subject and object as in the active. The deep structure of (21) which is repeated here is (48) on this view.

(21) Cafodd y dyn ei rybuddio gan ferch.
Got the man his warning by (a) girl.

(48)

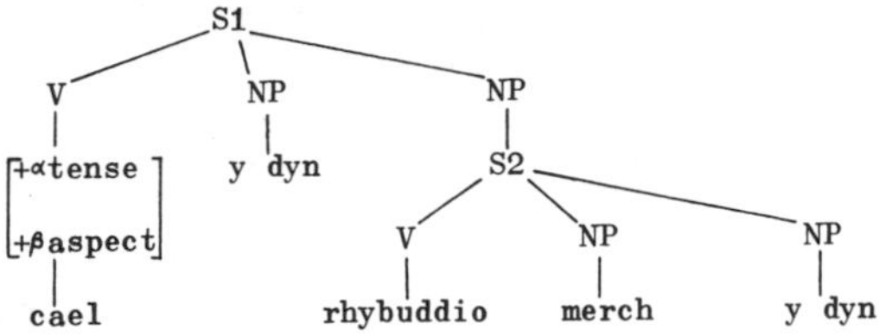

The uninflected verb is the verb of the embedded sentence, so that its verbal characteristics are accounted for. And it is embedded below a noun phrase node, so that its noun-like characteristics also follow.

Since the uninflected verb appears in a simple active embedding, no additional rules need be drawn up to account for the identical selection restrictions which it shows in the active and passive. The interpretation of the two noun phrases as subject and object of the uninflected verb follows automatically from this structure. Similarly the adverb of manner now refers to the actions of the subject of an active sentence, in the same way as it does in (46). From the point of view of surface structure the passive is exceptional since the adverb refers to the object of the preposition *gan*, not the subject. Here regularity is restored.

A further advantage of this deep structure analysis is that it provides a motivated source for the pronoun which precedes the uninflected verb in the passive. This pronoun is identical to the subject of the passive. In (48) there are two instances of this noun phrase, as subject of the matrix sentence and as object of the embedding. The subject of the matrix remains in this position. The object of the embedding is pronominalised and preposed.

2.3.3 A tenseless embedding The uninflected verb of the passive is not marked for tense and aspect and is interpreted as being identical to the inflected form of *cael* in the matrix sentence in those features. The same problems arise here as in the case of the tenseless embeddings discussed in Chapter 1. Should the uninflected verb be marked for tense and aspect in deep structure, with these features being deleted on identity with the tense and aspect features on the matrix verb? Or should it be unmarked for tense and aspect throughout the derivation?

The deletion account seems to be unworkable here, as in the case of the periphrastic forms. The problems do not show up in the case of forms like (21) where there is an inflected form of *cael* in the matrix sentence, as it is possible for the tense and aspect features to be duplicated in the embedding. It is in cases such as (49) that the difficulties are seen.

(49) Mae'r dyn wedi cael ei rybuddio gan y ferch.
Is the man after getting his warning by the girl.

Here the matrix verb *cael* is itself embedded in a periphrastic sentence. The tense and aspect features are spread over the inflected form of *bod* (be) and the preposition aspect marker. It is difficult to see how these features may be duplicated in the sentence containing *cael* and in turn in the sentence embedded below *cael.* The problems increase with more complicated forms such as (50).

(50) Mae'r dyn wedi bod yn cael ei rybuddio gan y ferch.
Is the man after being in getting his warning by the girl.

Here the tense and aspect features are spread over the inflected form of *bod* and two prepositions.

2.3.4 Relationship to other tenseless embeddings The analysis of passive forms resembles in many ways the analysis given in Chapter 1 of periphrastic forms. In both cases there is a close semantic relationship between the structure concerned and a simple active sentence, but this is not accompanied by a close syntactic similarity. The main verb of the passive or the periphrastic is different from the main verb of the corresponding simple active, with the main verb of the simple active appearing as an uninflected verb of the same form in each case. In both cases the uninflected verb seems best analysed as the verb of a sentence embedded below a noun phrase node, and it is not marked for tense and aspect in deep structure. The passive differs from the periphrastic in that the embedding is the direct object of the verb rather than the object of a preposition. In this it resembles other auxiliary forms such as *gallu* (be able).

There are also differences between the passive and the periphrastic forms over identity relations between the noun phrases in the matrix sentence and the embedding. In the periphrastic forms the subject of the matrix sentence and the subject of the embedding are identical in deep structure. The object of the embedding is not constrained at all. In the passive however it is the subject of the matrix sentence and the object of the embedding which must be identical. The subject of the embedding is not constrained. This pattern can be seen in (48) and is summarised in (51).

(51)

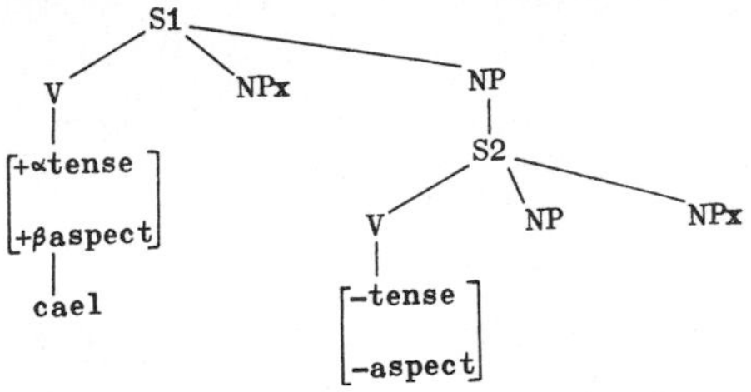

Nor is this pattern found elsewhere in the tenseless embeddings discussed in Chapter 1. Where the embedding is below a lexical or an auxiliary verb either the subject of the matrix sentence and the subject of the embedding are identical, as in sections 1.4.1 and 1.4.2, or there are no constraints at all requiring identity between noun phrases in the matrix sentence and the embedding, as in sections 1.4.3 and 1.4.4. The constraints on the passive seem to be unique to that construction.

This difference in identity constraints is reflected in the different treatment of the subject of the embedding. In the periphrastic forms and the other cases where the subject of the matrix is identical to the subject of the embedding, the subject of the embedding is deleted. In those cases where there are no identity constraints at all, the subject of the embedding is raised into a prepositional phrase to the left of the embedding as the object of *i* (for). In the passive however the subject of the embedding is raised into a prepositional phrase to the right of the embedding as object of the preposition *gan* (by).

2.4 The transformational derivation

2.4.1 Agent postposing A rule is needed to raise the subject of the embedding into the matrix sentence prepositional phrase, converting (48) into (52).

(52)

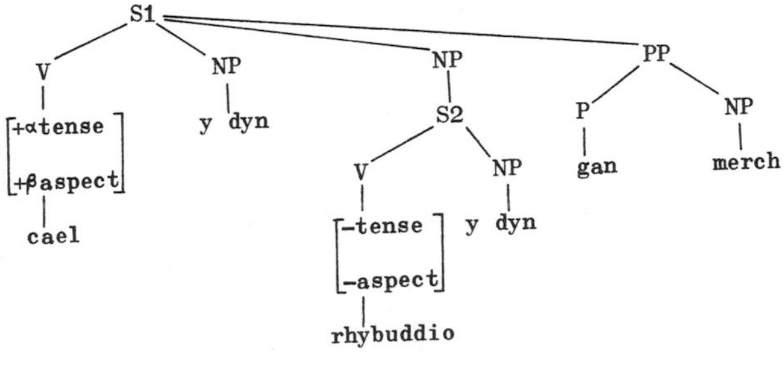

The rule can be formulated as shown in (53).

(53) <u>T. Agent Postposing (obligatory)</u>

```
SD. (S   V     NPx   (NP (S    V       NP  NPx  X  ) ) )
                               |
         cael              [-tense ]
                           [-aspect]

     1   2     3      4   5     6       7    8    9

SC. Adjoin 7 as right daughter of 1, in a prepositional phrase
    as object of the preposition gan.
```

The verb of the embedding is specified as [−tense] and [−aspect], so that the rule will not apply to forms where the verb of the embedding is inflected to give such ungrammatical forms as (54).

(54) *Cafodd y dyn ei rybuddiodd gan ferch.
Got the man his warned by (a) girl.

And it is necessary to leave these features unspecified for the *cael* (get) of the matrix sentence so that the rule may apply freely both to cases like (21) where *cael* is inflected and to cases like (49) where *cael* is itself an uninflected verb embedded in a periphrastic sentence. In both points T. Agent Postposing resembles the two other rules which affect the subject of tenseless embeddings. It was pointed out above in section 1.5.3 that both T. Equi-Subject Deletion and T. Subject Raising must have a tenseless verb in the embedding. It is also true that to account for such forms as (55) and (56), where the matrix verb *dymuno* (want) is itself an uninflected verb in a periphrastic sentence, the matrix verb in these transformations must be left unmarked for tense and aspect.

(55) Mae Ifor yn dymuno canu.
Is Ifor in wanting singing.

(56) Mae Ifor yn dymuno i Wyn ganu.
Is Ifor in wanting for Wyn singing.

T. Subject Raising must not apply to the deep structure (48) of the passive to give (57).

(57) *Cafodd y dyn i ferch ei rybuddio.
Got the man for (a) girl his warning.

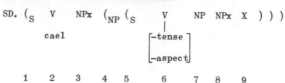

The formulation of T. Subject Raising given in section 1.5.3 would however allow this rule to apply to (48), as this is a complex sentence with a tenseless embedding where the subject of the matrix is not identical to the subject of the embedding. T. Subject Raising must therefore be prevented from applying by rule ordering. If T. Agent Postposing applies first to (48), the structural description of T. Subject Raising will no longer be available when that rule is reached.

Similarly, T. Equi-Subject Deletion must not apply to the passive, even if the subject of the matrix sentence is identical to the subject of the embedding, as in (58).

(58)

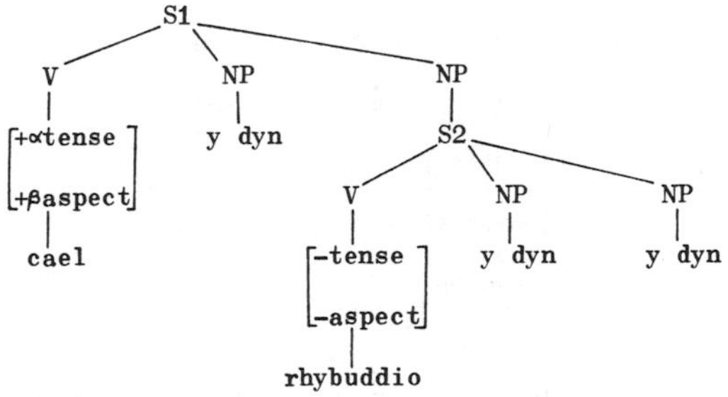

If T. Equi-Subject Deletion were applied to (58) the output would be (59).

(59) Cafodd y dyn ei rybuddio.
Got the man his warning.

This is a grammatical form, but it is not interpreted as the surface structure of (58). It is interpreted instead as the surface structure of a passive with an unspecified noun phrase as subject of the embedding, as will be discussed below in section 2.5.3. The surface structure of (58) is rather (60) where T. Agent Postposing has applied.

(60) *Cafodd y dyn ei rybuddio ganddo ef ei hun.
Got the man his warning by himself.

This form is ungrammatical, due to a general constraint which will be discussed in section 4.3. In order to prevent T. Equi-Subject Deletion from applying to the passive, this rule too must be ordered after T. Agent Postposing. The ordering established so far is therefore that shown in (61).

(61)

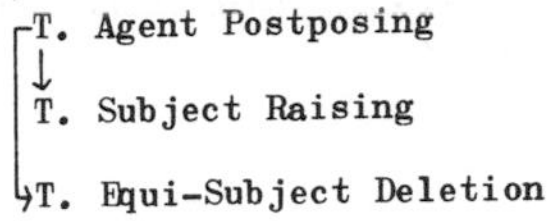

Even now however a problem remains, which cannot be accounted for by rule ordering alone. After T. Agent Postposing has applied, giving (52), there is nothing to stop T. Equi-Subject Deletion from applying to this tree, deleting the object noun phrase of the embedding, to give (62).

(62)

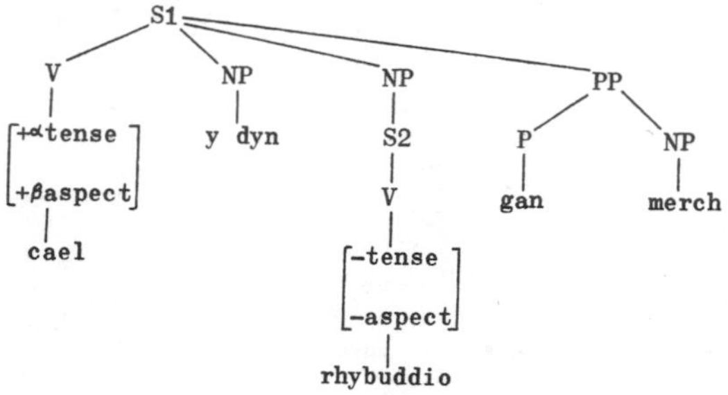

This is allowed by the ordering set up in (61), and by the VSO analysis adopted here for Welsh. On this analysis both subject and object are immediately dominated by the sentence node, and they are distinguished only by position in the string. The subject immediately follows the verb and the object follows the subject. If the subject is deleted however the object now immediately follows the verb and it is not possible to distinguish it from a deep structure subject.

A similar problem arises over the ordering of T. Equi-Subject Deletion and T. Subject Raising in the case of other embeddings containing a tenseless verb. The two rules may be ordered either as shown in (63) or as shown in (64).

(63) T. Equi-Subject Deletion
↓
T. Subject Raising

(64) T. Subject Raising
↓
T. Equi-Subject Deletion

If the ordering shown in (63) is adopted then a deep structure of the general type (65) is first converted by T. Equi-Subject Deletion into (66).

(65)
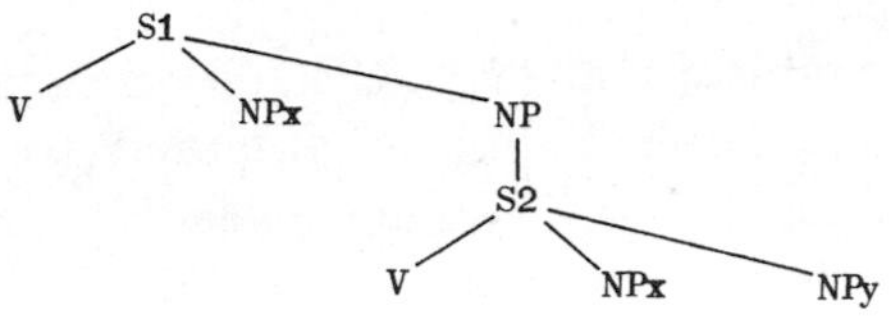

(66)
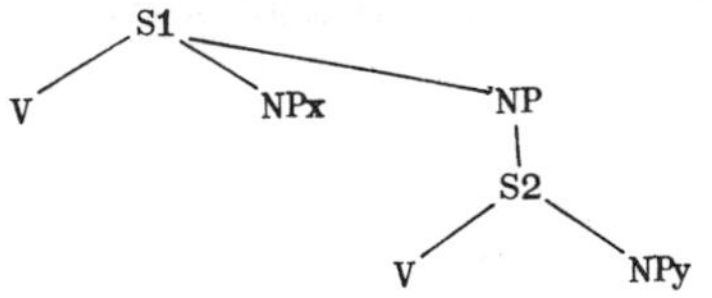

And then it can be converted into (67) by T. Subject Raising.

(67)
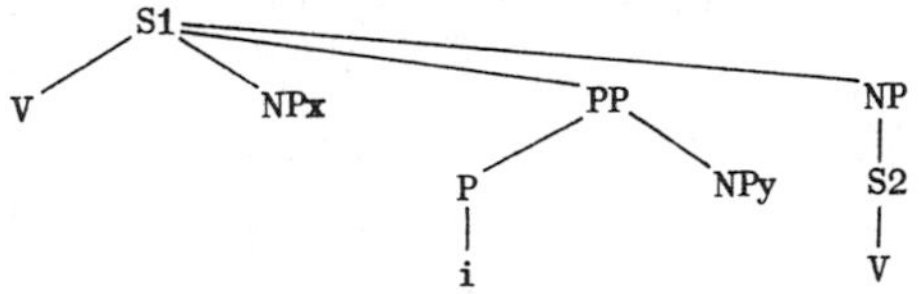

This will give ungrammatical outputs such as (68) instead of the correct (69).

(68) *Dymuna Wyn i lyfr brynu.
Wants Wyn for (a) book buying.

(69) Dymuna Wyn brynu llyfr.
Wants Wyn buying (a) book.

If on the other hand the ordering shown in (64) is adopted the reverse situation arises. A deep structure of the type shown in (70) is first converted into (71) by T. Subject Raising.

(70)
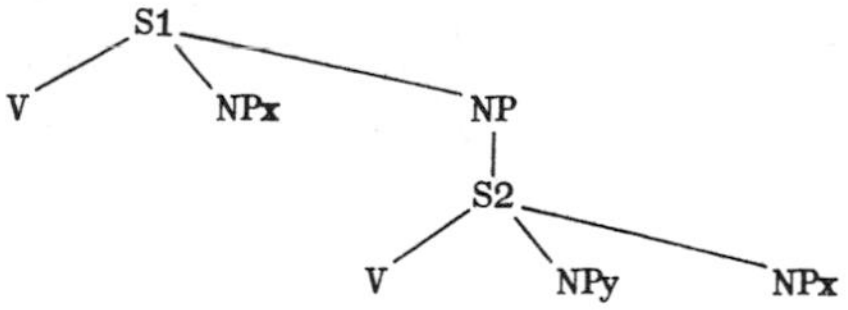

(71)
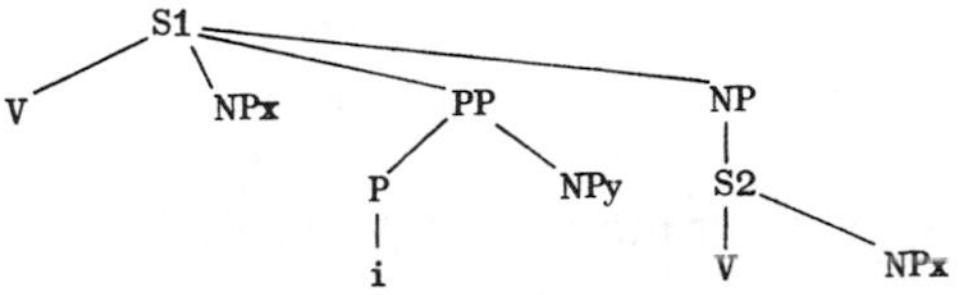

It is then converted into (72) by T. Equi-Subject Deletion.

(72)

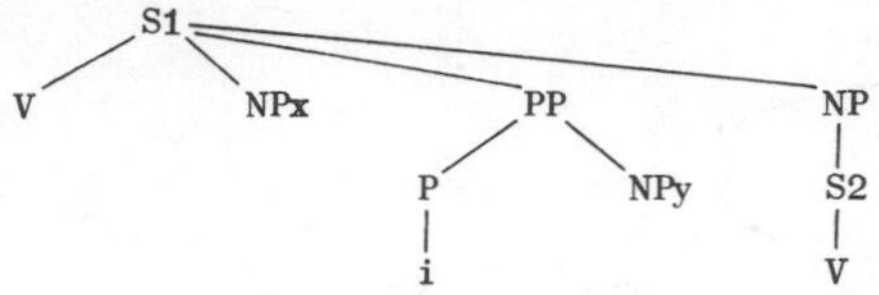

This will give the ungrammatical output (73) instead of the correct (74).

(73) *Dymuna Wyn i Ifor weld.
Wants Wyn for Ifor seeing.

(74) Dymuna Wyn i Ifor ei weld ef.
Wants Wyn for Ifor his seeing him.

Neither ordering of the two rules allows one to avoid this type of problem.

All three rules affecting the subject of the embedding are involved in this difficulty then, which is not limited to the passive. This may be an indication that the VSO analysis is mistaken and it would be better to adopt a subject and predicate split.[3] This would allow a distinct representation for the subject and object as in (75).

(75)

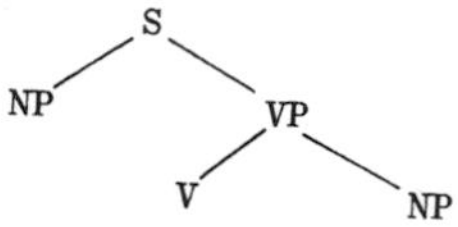

Even after the subject has been deleted it will still be possible to see that a particular noun phrase is the object as it is still dominated by the verb phrase node. An alternative approach is to have some sort of global derivational constraint which prevents more than one of the three rules applying to a single embedding. This latter solution is adopted here as it allows the otherwise satisfactory VSO analysis to be retained. Further information might of course force a reversal of this decision.

2.4.2 Agent phrase rules No new rules are required to account for the prepositional phrase with *gan* (by) which results from T. Agent Postposing. All the rules which affect it have been independently established in sections 1.3.5 and 1.4.3.

If the raised agent is a noun it must undergo T. Prepositional Object Mutation to give the soft mutation form. This will convert (52) into (76). If anything intervenes between the preposition and the noun, such as the definite article in (77), the mutation is blocked.[4]

(76)

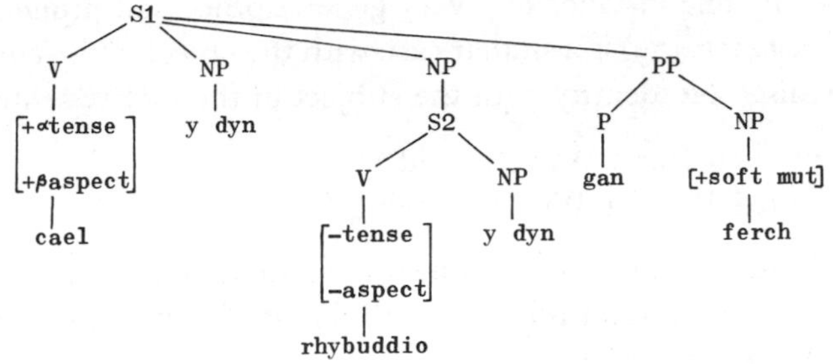

(77) Cafodd y dyn ei rybuddio gan y bachgen.
Got the man his warning by the boy.

If the raised agent is a pronoun, then the preposition must agree with it by T. Preposition Agreement to give such forms as (15) to (19). Morphological rules later give the correct inflection of the preposition. The pronoun may be deleted by T. Pronoun Prepositional Object Deletion to give (20). As was pointed out before this rule must follow T. Preposition Agreement or there will be no pronoun for the preposition to agree with.

2.4.3 Embedding rules The object of the embedding must be pronominalised on identity with the subject of the matrix sentence. This will give the tree (78).

(78)

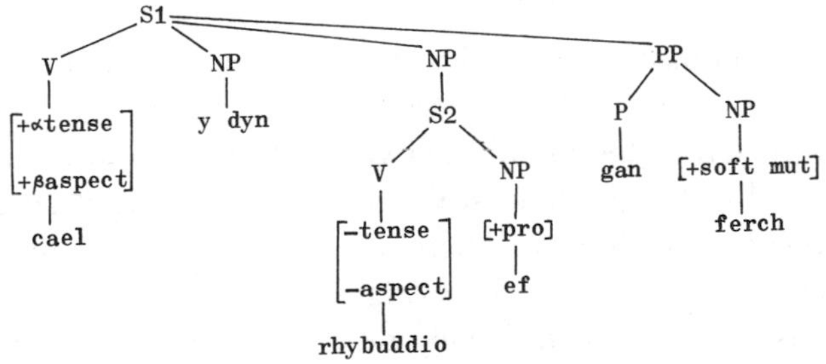

It is not clear if the pronominalisation rule should precede or follow T. Agent Postposing, since the main lines of the tree structure such as the presence of the S2 node remain the same after it has applied. It seems preferable that T. Agent Postposing should apply first, since it could be argued that once the object of the embedding has been pronominalised it is not identical to the subject of the matrix sentence and so T. Agent Postposing might be blocked.

This is only one instance of a very general process of pronominalisation. For instance, (79) is a similar case with the object of the embedding pronominalised on identity with the subject of the matrix sentence.

(79) Dymunai Ifor i Wyn ei weld ef.
Wanted Ifor for Wyn his seeing him.

An embedding is not necessary. The same pattern appears in (80) where the pronominalised noun phrase is still in the object of the matrix but this object is not an embedding.

(80) Darllenodd Rhian ei llyfr hi.
Read Rhian her book her.

The pronominalisation rule is formulated in (81).

(81) <u>T. Pronominalisation (obligatory)</u>

SD. $(_S$ V NPx $(_{NP}$ Y NPx Z))

1 2 3 4 5 6 7

SC. Add the feature [+pro] to 6.

If the subject of the matrix and the object of the embedding are pronouns then this rule applies vacuously, as in (82).

(82) Cawsom ni ein rhybuddio gan y bachgen.
Got we our warning by the boy.

The pronoun object of the embedding does not remain in its original position to the right of the uninflected verb. In surface structure it appears to the left of the uninflected verb, identical in form and mutations triggered to the pronoun which precedes the uninflected verb in other tenseless embeddings. There is one major difference. In the passive there is no pronoun following the uninflected verb, while in the other cases there may optionally be a pronoun in this position.

(83) *Cafodd y dyn ei rybuddio ef gan ferch.
Got the man his warning him by (a) girl.

(84) Mae merch wedi ei rybuddio ef.
Is (a) girl after his warning him.

There are two possible ways of deriving the preposed pronoun in the passive. A movement rule may move the pronoun from its position on the right of the uninflected verb to its surface structure position on the left of the verb. Or the derivation may involve two steps, first copying the pronoun on the left of the uninflected verb and then deleting the pronoun in the original position on the right of the uninflected verb. The first possibility amounts to a claim that the similarities between the passive and the other embeddings are accidental, and that a quite different process is involved in the two cases. The second possibility amounts to a claim that these constructions are very closely related and differ only in the application of one rule, if it is optional or obligatory. There seems no reason to assume that there is a major difference between the passive and the other embeddings on this point, so the second analysis is adopted here with the passive undergoing the same rules as the other embeddings. T. Possessive Pronoun Preposing, formulated in section 1.3.3, therefore applies to (78) to give (85).

(85)

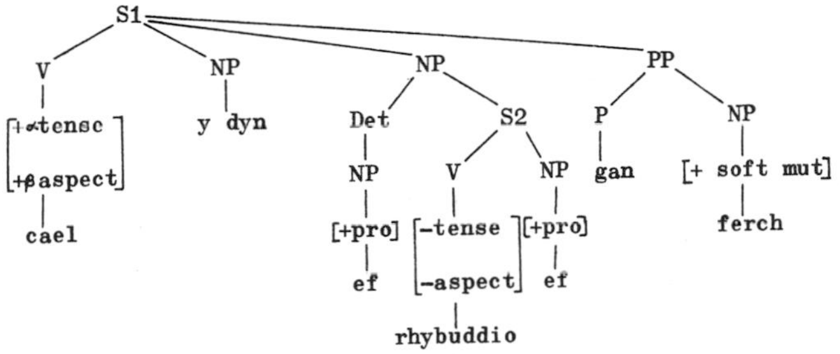

Morphological rules apply at a later stage in the derivation to give the correct form of the preposed pronoun, giving the tree (86).

(86)

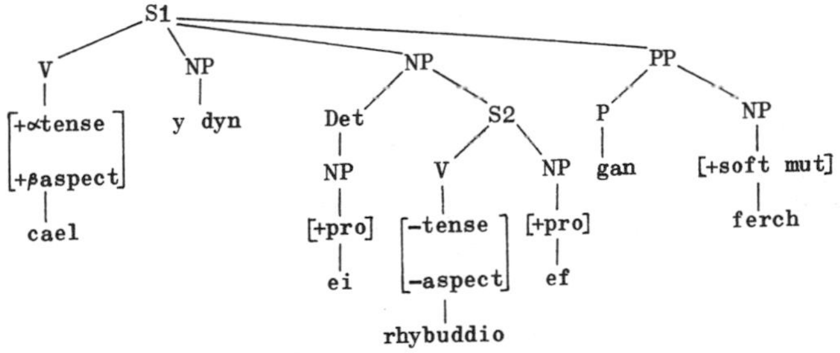

The form of the preposed pronoun varies according to context. For instance, it was pointed out in section 1.3.4 that the form of the 1sg pronoun is either *fy* or *m* depending on context. The same forms appear in the passive, as in (87) and (88).

(87) Cefais fy rhybuddio gan ferch.
Got (I) my warning by (a) girl.

(88) Cefais fy rhybuddio a'm dwrdio gan ferch.
Got (I) my warning and my scolding by (a) girl.

The preposed pronouns trigger different mutation forms of the uninflected verb by T. Preposed Pronoun Mutation, formulated in section 1.3.4, converting (86) into (89) where the uninflected verb appears in its soft mutation form.

(89)

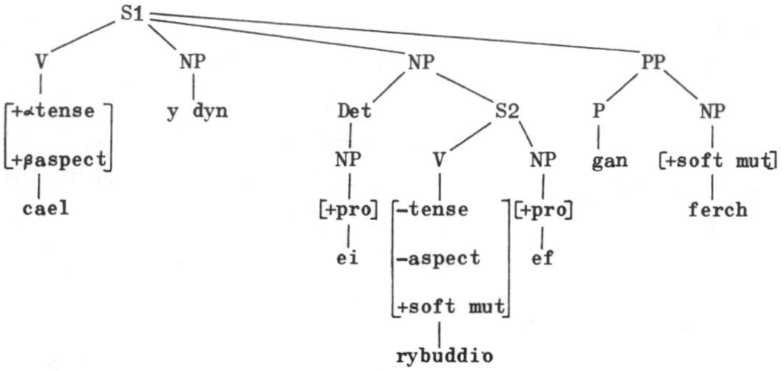

The different preposed pronoun forms required by different contexts require different mutation forms of the uninflected verb. For instance in (90) *fy* requires the nasal mutation form of the uninflected verb *gweld* (see) but *m* retains the isolation form of *galw* (call).

(90) Cefais fy ngweld gan y ferch.
Got (I) my seeing by the girl.
(91) Cefais fy ngweld a'm galw gan y ferch.
Got (I) my seeing and my calling by the girl.

Phonological rules later carry out the sound changes required by each mutation form.

The pronoun which follows the uninflected verb must be deleted by T. Possessive Pronoun Deletion, formulated in section 1.3.6. This rule must be obligatory here. It gives the output (92) when applied to (89).

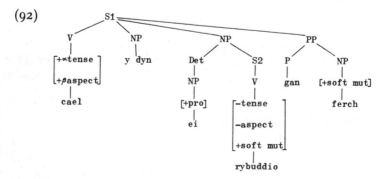

(92)

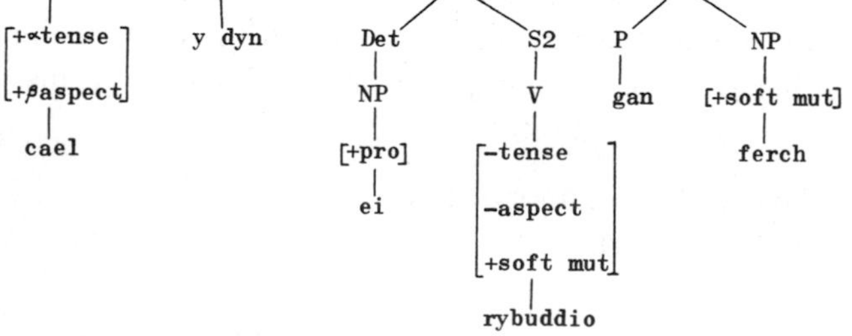

The question of why this rule should be obligatory in the passive will be further discussed in section 2.6.

2.4.4 Matrix sentence rules The verb and subject of the matrix sentence undergo the same rules as affect the verb and subject of a simple active sentence. The agreement rules apply, causing the verb to agree in person and number with a pronoun subject, or adding the features [3pers] and [sg no] to the verb if the subject is a noun. In the case of (92) T. Subject-Verb Agreement (Noun) applies, converting it into (93).

(93)

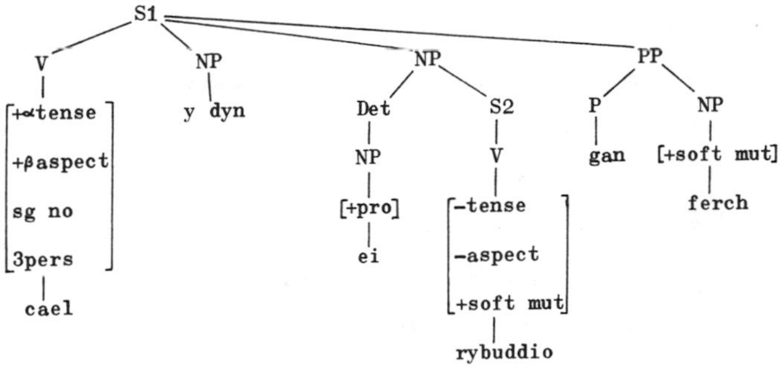

Morphological rules later give the correct inflection of the verb. In the case of a pronoun subject, such as (91), T. Subject-Verb Agreement (Pronoun) applies, and then optionally T. Pronoun Subject Deletion. T. Soft Mutation of Direct Object is blocked as the preposed pronoun which is the leftmost item in the direct object is not subject to soft mutation.

2.4.5 Rule ordering The ordering of the transformations referred to in this section is given in (94). All of these rules apply on the cycle of the matrix sentence, so this appears to be the ordering of rules within the cycle.[5] As usual, any rules crucially ordered are linked by arrows. Any rules not so linked are not crucially ordered.

Some of these rules must be applied in the order shown to prevent ungrammatical forms from being generated. It was shown in section 2.4.1 that T. Agent Postposing must precede T. Equi-Subject Deletion and T. Subject Raising to prevent ungrammatical forms. Similarly, T. Possessive Pronoun Preposing must precede T. Soft Mutation of Direct Object or the wrong mutation forms will be generated. In the cases just discussed the wrong ordering would allow the generation of in-

(94)

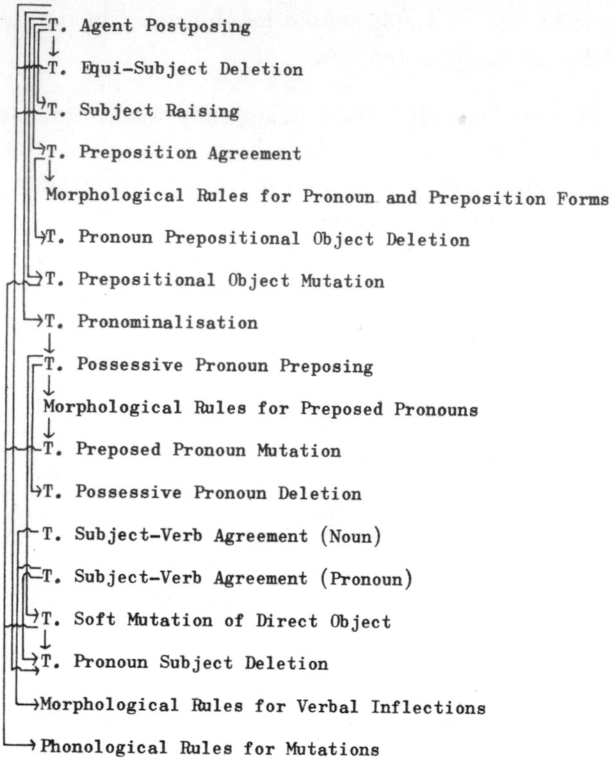

correct forms. In other cases the ordering shown is needed to allow all the rules to apply. Here the wrong ordering prevents the generation of correct forms. For instance, T. Pronominalisation must follow T. Agent Postposing; T. Possessive Pronoun Preposing must precede T. Possessive Pronoun Deletion; and T. Pronoun Subject Deletion must follow T. Agent Postposing. In these and other cases if the reverse ordering holds then the structural description of the rule which would apply second is destroyed before it is reached.

In the third type of case the ordering follows naturally from the formulation of the rule. Only after the first rule has applied is the structural description of the second met. For instance, none of the rules which affect prepositional phrases can apply till after T. Agent Postposing has produced the prepositional phrase. Similarly, only after T. Pronominalisation has applied can T. Possessive Pronoun Preposing and the subsequent rules apply.

2.5 Variations of the passive

2.5.1 Embedded passives It was pointed out above in section 2.3.3 that the matrix verb *cael* (get) of the passive is not always inflected. It may also be the uninflected verb of an embedding in a periphrastic sentence, as in (95), which has the deep structure (96).

(95) Mae Ifor wedi cael ei rybuddio gan y bachgen.
Is Ifor after getting his warning by the boy.

(96)

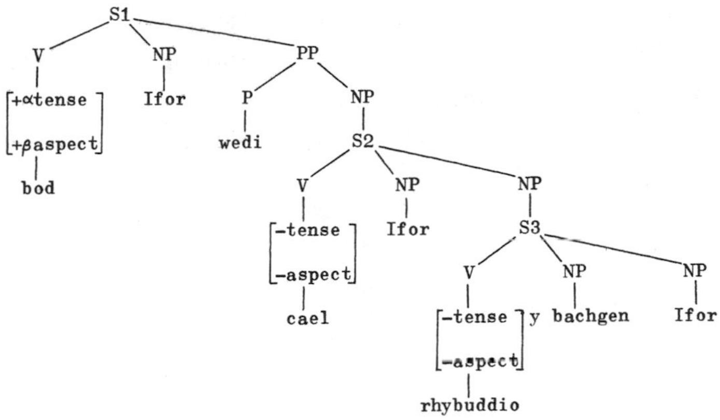

On the S2 cycle T. Agent Postposing applies here in the same way as it does in passives with an inflected form of *cael*. The rule was formulated in 2.4.1 without reference to the tense or aspect of *cael* so that it could be extended to cases like (95). The other rules which affect the prepositional phrase and the remains of the embedded active, here S3, also apply freely. On the S1 cycle the subject of *cael* is deleted by T. Equi-Subject Deletion. And the verbal agreement rule applies to give the inflected form of *bod* (be). The only difference between this type of passive and inflected passives is that the matrix sentence containing *cael* undergoes the rules which normally affect a tenseless embedding, and it is not till the higher sentence that verbal agreement comes into play.

In the same way, if the passive is embedded below a lexical verb as in (97), then on the S1 cycle T. Equi-Subject Deletion deletes the subject of *cael* and the verbal agreement rule applies to give the inflected form of the higher verb.

(97) Dymunaist gael dy rybuddio gan y bachgen.
Wanted (thou) getting thy warning by the boy.

In this case the subject of S1 is deleted by T. Pronoun Subject Deletion, and the uninflected form of *cael* appears in its soft mutation form as object of the inflected verb.

In the case of (98) the subject of *cael* is raised into the higher sentence by T. Subject Raising on the S1 cycle. The uninflected form of *cael* appears in soft mutation form as required when following this type of prepositional phrase.

(98) Dymunai Ifor i Wyn gael ei rybuddio gan y bachgen.
Wanted Ifor for Wyn getting his warning by the boy.

Again the rules for agreement apply to give an inflected form of the higher verb. In none of these forms is any extra rule needed. The specifically passive transformations apply on the *cael* cycle. *Cael* itself behaves as the verb of a tenseless embedding. The higher verb is inflected and undergoes the rules normal for a simple active sentence.

2.5.2 Cael deletion If the passive is embedded in a periphrastic sentence with the prepositional aspect marker *wedi* (after) as in (95), then the uninflected form of *cael* may be optionally omitted, giving (99).

(99) Mae Ifor wedi ei rybuddio gan y bachgen.
Is Ifor after his warning by the boy.

It seems justifiable to relate these two forms by a rule deleting the uninflected verb *cael*. The two forms are synonymous, and they are constrained in similar ways. For instance, it was pointed out above in section 2.4.3 that there may not be a pronoun following the uninflected verb in the passive, and that in this the passive differs from other embeddings. The form without *cael* is also restricted in this way, as in (100).

(100) *Mae Ifor wedi ei rybuddio ef gan y bachgen.
Is Ifor after his warning him by the boy.

The deletion rule is shown in (101).

(101) T. Cael Deletion (optional)

```
SD. (S bod NPx wedi (NP (S cael (NP (Det NPx ) V ) (PP gan NP ) ) ) )
                                           |
                                         [+pro]
       1   2    3    4   5   6     7  8    9    10    11  12  13 14
SC. Delete 7.
```

The rule must not apply before the cycle of the verb *bod* and the aspect marker *wedi*. Therefore the rules relevant to the passive, which all apply on the cycle of the verb *cael*, will all have applied. This is reflected in the structural description of the rule.

It must be restricted to embedded passives, since no other construction seems to allow deletion of the uninflected verb below *wedi*. If the uninflected lexical verb in (102) is deleted to give (103) the output is ungrammatical.

(102) Mae Ifor wedi darllen y llyfr.
Is Ifor after reading the book.
(103) *Mae Ifor wedi y llyfr.
Is Ifor after the book.

Similarly, if the deleted uninflected verb is another auxiliary verb as in (104) the result is ungrammatical.

(104) Mae Ifor wedi bod yn canu.
Is Ifor after being in singing.
(105) *Mae Ifor wedi yn canu.
Is Ifor after in singing.

Even embeddings of a very similar structure to the passive, with a further layer of embedding below the deleted uninflected verb and this lower verb preceded by a pronoun, are ungrammatical if the verb is deleted.

(106) Mae Ifor wedi bwriadu ei weld.
Is Ifor after intending his seeing.
(107) *Mae Ifor wedi ei weld.
Is Ifor after his seeing.

(107) is grammatical in a different meaning but not as an equivalent to (106).

Nor is this a rule which can delete any instance of *cael* below the aspect marker *wedi*. If *cael* has a noun phrase object rather than an embedding as in the passive, then the verb cannot be deleted.

(108) Mae Ifor wedi cael anrheg.
Is Ifor after getting (a) present.
(109) *Mae Ifor wedi anrheg.
Is Ifor after (a) present.

Only if *cael* is part of a passive can it delete below *wedi*. It is therefore necessary to show in the structural description that the rule applies only to passives.[6]

2.5.3 Unspecified embedded subjects So far all the passives considered have had a prepositional phrase consisting of the preposition *gan* and a noun phrase corresponding to the subject of the active. There are also passives with no such prepositional phrase, like (110).

(110) Cafodd y dyn ei rybuddio.
Got the man his warning.

In such forms no mention is made of the actor, and the subject of the embedded active in deep structure is an unspecified noun phrase. The deep structure representation of (110) is (111).[7]

(111)

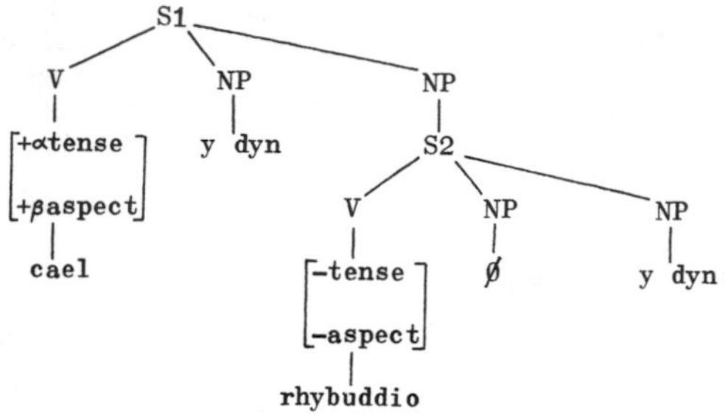

There are two ways of deriving (110) from (111). The first way is to allow T. Agent Postposing to apply as usual, giving the tree (112).

(112)

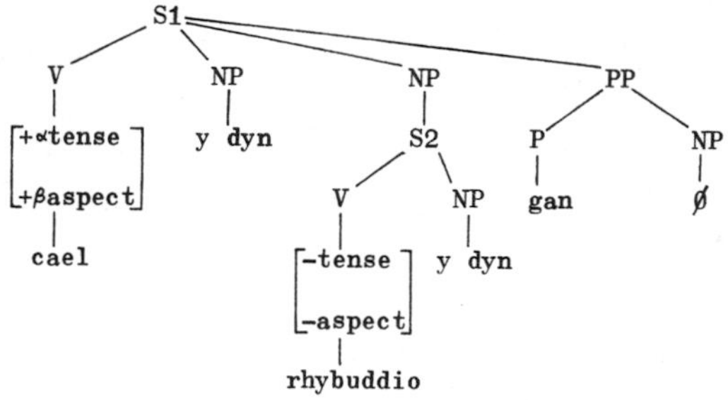

Later in the derivation the empty noun phrase in the prepositional phrase is deleted since it does not dominate any lexical items. The preposition *gan* is left without a noun phrase object and must be deleted since such isolated prepositions are ungrammatical in Welsh. Compare the ungrammatical passive (113) with the form (114) where the prepositional phrase originates in deep structure.

(113) *Cafodd y dyn ei rybuddio gan.
Got the man his warning by.

(114) *Gwelais y llyfr ar.
Saw (I) the book on.

(113) differs from the grammatical (115) in that the preposition *ganddi* in (115) has already been marked to show what the deleted pronoun object was.

(115) Cafodd y dyn ei rybuddio ganddi.
Got the man his warning by (her).

In the case of (113) where the object of *gan* was an unspecified noun phrase no such marking is possible.

The second way of deriving (110) is to delete the unspecified noun phrase subject of the embedding immediately, before T. Agent Postposing applies, giving the tree structure (116).

(116)

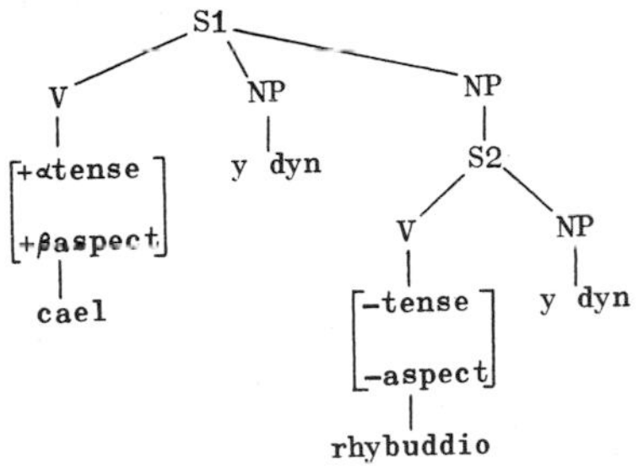

T. Agent Postposing does not apply and the rules affecting the prepositional phrase are irrelevant.

It appears that the first of these derivations may be preferable though there is no conclusive evidence. On the first derivation the agentless passives parallel more closely the full passives since T. Agent Postposing appears in the derivation of all passives. This analysis also allows an explanation of one way in which passives with an unspecified noun phrase subject in the embedding differ from other constructions with such a subject in an object embedding.

In the agentless passive the deep structure representation shows an embedding with an unspecified noun phrase subject and a matrix sentence with a full noun phrase subject. Other object embeddings resembling the passive in these aspects of its deep structure have no grammatical surface structure output. An example is the deep structure (117).

(117)

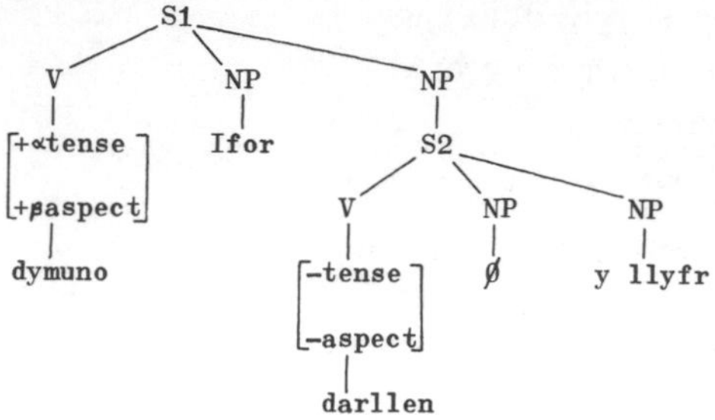

A general rule deleting the unspecified subject of an embedding below a matrix whose subject is a full noun phrase will give the output (118) in surface structure.

(118) Dymuna Ifor ddarllen y llyfr.
Wants Ifor reading the book.

But (118) does not have the same meaning as (117). It is interpreted as being derived from the deep structure (119) by T. Equi-Subject Deletion.

(119)

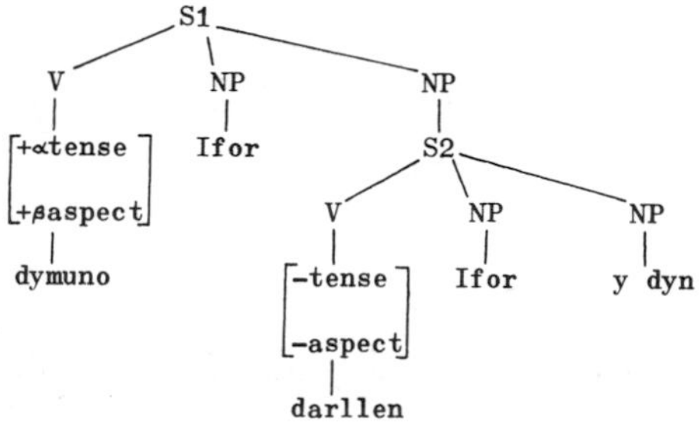

On the first analysis of the agentless passive suggested above this difference between the passive and other forms can be related to the fact that only in the passive does T. Agent Postposing apply, removing the unspecified noun phrase from the embedded sentence. In other constructions the unspecified noun phrase cannot be removed in this way and there is no general rule deleting such a subject noun phrase. It will still be present in surface structure, blocking the derivation. It is possible to distinguish between the passive and the other constructions on the second analysis too by limiting the rule deleting unspecified subjects to passives. But this requires an extra rule which is not independently motivated.

The rules which are needed to delete the unspecified object of *gan* and then *gan* itself are given in (120) and (121).

(120) <u>T. Unspecified Noun Phrase Deletion (obligatory)</u>

SD. ($_{PP}$ Prep NP)
NP → ∅

1 2 3

SC. Delete 3.

(121) <u>T. Preposition Deletion (obligatory)</u>

SD. ($_{PP}$ Prep)

1 2

Condition. 2 is not marked [+αpers], [+βno], [+γgend].

SC. Delete 2.

T. Unspecified Noun Phrase Deletion converts (112) into (122).

(122)

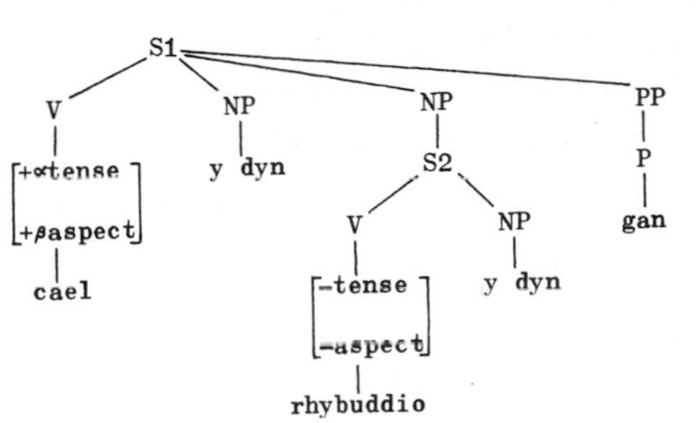

T. Preposition Deletion converts this into (123).

(123)

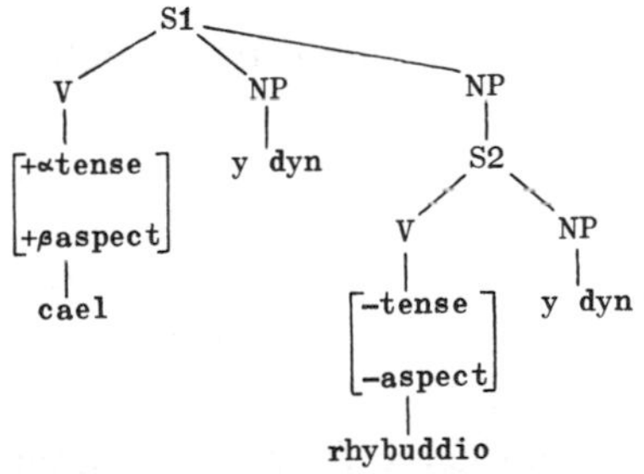

Both of these rules must follow T. Agent Postposing as this provides the prepositional phrase which is crucial to their structural description. T. Preposition Deletion must follow T. Preposition Agreement so that prepositions which have been marked for agreement with a pronoun object but later lose the pronoun object by T. Pronoun Prepositional Object Deletion are not also deleted. These rules are not ordered relative to the rules affecting the remains of the embedding or those affecting the matrix sentence. The ordering is summarised in (124).

(124) T. Agent Postposing
↓
T. Preposition Agreement
↓
T. Unspecified Noun Phrase Deletion
↓
T. Preposition Deletion

2.6 Possessive pronoun deletion

2.6.1 The problem It was pointed out in section 2.4.3 above that in the passive the uninflected verb may be preceded by a possessive pronoun but not followed by one too. (125) is grammatical but not (126).

(125) Cafodd Rhian ei galw gan y plentyn.
Got Rhian her calling by the child.
(126) *Cafodd Rhian ei galw hi gan y plentyn.
Got Rhian her calling her by the child.

In the case of other embeddings the pronoun following the uninflected verb is optional, as in (127) and (128).

(127) Bwriadai Rhian ei weld ef.
Intended Rhian his seeing him.
(128) Bwriadai Rhian ei weld.
Intended Rhian his seeing.

And the same is true of possessives with a head noun. Both (129) and (130) are grammatical.

(129) ei lyfr ef
his book him
(130) ei lyfr
his book

No explanations have so far been offered for this difference between the passive and the other forms. In this section the problem will be studied in more detail, and the passive will be compared with some other constructions which appear to be similarly restricted in an attempt to establish what they have in common.

2.6.2 'Easy' forms Adjectives such as *hawdd* (easy) take a tenseless subject embedding. In surface structure this appears to the right of the adjective, as in (131).

(131) Mae'n hawdd i Ifor weld Carys.
Is easy for Ifor seeing Carys.
i.e. It is easy for Ifor to see Carys.

An alternative form of this construction exists where the object of the embedding appears in surface structure as the subject of the matrix sentence. It also appears in the embedding, but in pronoun form, as in (132).

(132) Mae Carys yn hawdd i Ifor ei gweld.
Is Carys easy for Ifor her seeing.
i.e. Carys is easy for Ifor to see.

The pronoun form in the embedding is a preposed possessive pronoun, and just as in the passive there may not be a pronoun following the uninflected verb. (133) is ungrammatical.

(133) *Mae Carys yn hawdd i Ifor ei gweld hi.
Is Carys easy for Ifor her seeing her.

In the cases just given there is an overt subject in the embedding. There are also forms like (134) and (135) where there is an unspecified subject in the embedding.

(134) Mae'n hawdd gweld Carys.
Is easy seeing Carys.

(135) Mae Carys yn hawdd ei gweld.
Is Carys easy her seeing.

The same restriction appears here so that (136) is ungrammatical.

(136) *Mae Carys yn hawdd ei gweld hi.
Is Carys easy her seeing her.

The restriction crops up only where the object of the embedding has been copied in the subject of the matrix sentence. In (137), which is identical to (131) except in having a pronoun object in the embedding, there is no restriction.

(137) Mae'n hawdd i Ifor ei gweld hi.
Is easy for Ifor her seeing her.

Similarly with (138), which is identical to (134) except in the pronoun object, there is no problem either.

(138) Mae'n hawdd ei gweld hi.
Is easy her seeing her.

2.6.3 Purpose phrases A tenseless sentence may be embedded as the object of the preposition *i* (for) to express purpose, as in (139).

(139) Daeth y dyn i weld Emyr.
Came the man for seeing Emyr.
i.e. The man came to see Emyr.

If the subject of the embedding is an unspecified noun phrase, and the object of the embedding is identical to the subject of the matrix sentence, then the same restrictions appear here too.

(140) Ni ddaeth y dyn i'w anwybyddu.
Not came the man for his ignoring.
i.e. The man did not come to be ignored.

(140) with only a pronoun preceding the uninflected verb is grammatical but not (141) with a pronoun following it too.

(141) *Ni ddaeth y dyn i'w anwybyddu ef.
Not came the man for his ignoring him.

The form (141) is slightly old-fashioned and would probably be replaced by (142) with an embedded tenseless passive in normal usage, but the restriction seems clear.

(142) Ni ddaeth y dyn i gael ei anwybyddu.
Not came the man for getting his ignoring.

It is only in this particular type of purpose embedding that the restriction appears. In (143), which is identical to (139) except for the pronoun object, there is no restriction.

(143) Daeth y dyn i'w gweld hi.
Came the man for her seeing her.

Here the subject of the embedding is identical to the subject of the matrix. This is even true for cases where the object of the embedding is identical to the subject of the matrix. This gives a reflexive pronoun object, as in (144).

(144) Daeth y dyn i'w amddiffyn ei hun.
Came the man for his defending himself.

Similarly, if the subject of the embedding is different from the subject of the matrix, there is no restriction.

(145) Daeth y dyn i ni ei gweld hi.
Came the man for us her seeing her.
(146) Daeth y dyn i ni ei weld ef.
Came the man for us his seeing him.

It does not matter if the object of the embedding is identical to the subject of the matrix as in (146) or different from it as in (145).

2.6.4 Relatives, clefts and questions If the antecedent of a relative clause is identical to the object of an uninflected verb in the clause then the object is pronominalised and is restricted in this way. (147) with no pronoun following the uninflected verb is grammatical, but not (148) where there is a pronoun in this position.

(147) y dyn yr hoffwn i ei weld.
the man that should like I his seeing
i.e. the man that I should like to see
(148) *y dyn yr hoffwn i ei weld ef
the man that should like I his seeing him

If the antecedent is identical to a possessive pronoun in the relative clause with a lexical head noun rather than an uninflected verb then the restriction does not seem to hold. Both (149) and (150) are grammatical.

(149) y dyn y gwelais i ei fab
the man that saw I his son
i.e. the man whose son I saw
(150) y dyn y gwelais i ei fab ef
the man that saw I his son him

If the object of an uninflected verb in a sentence like (151) is clefted to give (152), then it is copied in sentence-initial position and the rest of the sentence takes the form of a relative clause with the clefted item as its antecedent.

(151) Hoffwn i weld Carys.
Should like I seeing Carys.
(152) Carys yr hoffwn i ei gweld.
Carys that should like I her seeing.
i.e. It's Carys that I should like to see.

The same restriction appears here, affecting the pronominalised form of the clefted object which is still in the embedding. (152) with only a pronoun preceding the uninflected verb is grammatical, but not (153) where a pronoun also follows it.

(153) *Carys yr hoffwn i ei gweld hi.
Carys that should like I her seeing her.

In the case of relatives resulting from clefting the restriction holds if there is a lexical head noun rather than an uninflected verb. In this they differ from normal relatives.

(154) Gwelais i lyfr Emyr.
Saw I (the) book (of) Emyr.
(155) Emyr y gwelais i ei lyfr.
Emyr that saw I his book.
(156) *Emyr y gwelais i ei lyfr ef.
Emyr that saw I his book him.

The same pattern emerges if the clefted constituent is negated, as in (157) and (158), or questioned, as in (159) and (160).

(157) *Nid Carys yr hoffwn i ei gweld hi.
Not Carys that should like I her seeing her.
(158) *Nid Emyr y gwelais i ei lyfr ef.
Not Emyr that saw I his book him.
(159) *Ai Carys yr hoffet ti ei gweld hi?
Question: Carys that wouldst like thou her seeing her?
(160) *Ai Emyr y gwelaist ti ei lyfr ef?
Question: Emyr that sawest thou his book him?

Wh. questions resemble cleft sentences in syntax. The questioned item appears in sentence-initial position, and the rest of the sentence takes the form of a relative clause with the questioned item as its antecedent. If the questioned item is the object of an uninflected verb as in (161) then it also appears in pronoun form in the relative clause.

(161) Beth yr hoffet ti ei weld?
What that wouldst like thou its seeing?
i.e. What would you like to see?

Here too the same restriction seems to hold. (162) with a pronoun following the uninflected verb is ungrammatical.

(162) *Beth yr hoffet ti ei weld ef?
What wouldst like thou its seeing it?

The restriction also holds if the possessive pronoun has a lexical head noun rather than an uninflected verb, as in the case of cleft sentences.

(163) Pwy y gwelaist ti ei lun?
Who that sawest thou his picture?
i.e. Whose picture did you see?

(164) *Pwy y gwelaist ti ei lun ef?
Who that sawest thou his picture him?

2.6.5 The structures of these forms The forms presented above which share the restriction on possessives with the passive have a variety of structures.

The 'easy' forms discussed in section 2.6.2 have the surface structure shown in (165), which represents the structure of (132).[8]

(165)

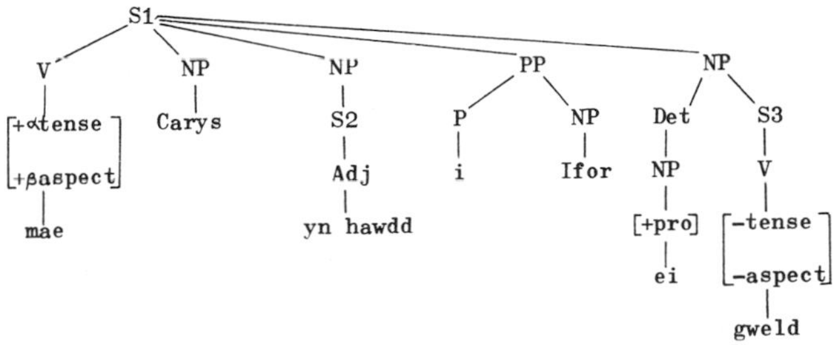

The structure of (135) is identical except for the lack of a prepositional phrase containing the deep structure subject of the embedding. T. Possessive Pronoun Deletion must apply late in the derivation of these forms. Not until the object of the embedding is copied into matrix subject position can the original object be pronominalised. And only then can the pronoun be preposed by T. Possessive Pronoun Preposing and the original pronoun following the uninflected verb deleted. The deletion rule must therefore apply when the main lines of the tree structure are as shown in (165).

Purpose phrases have the structure shown in (166), which represents the surface structure of (140). Here again T. Possessive Pronoun Deletion must apply to the tree when it is very much in this form, since it is only after the original unspecified noun phrase subject of the embedding has been removed that T. Possessive Pronoun Preposing and the following deletion rule can apply.

(166)

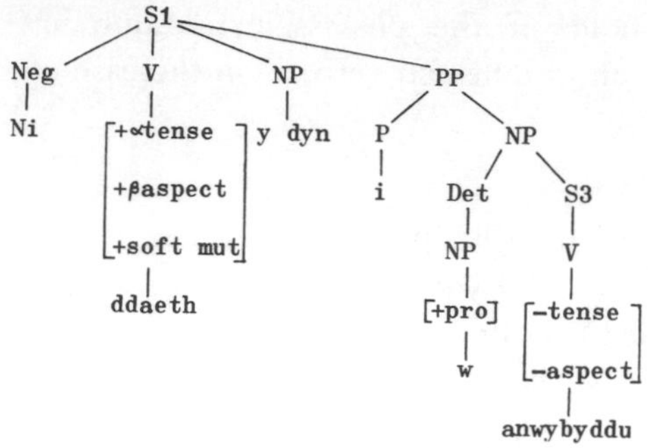

The structure of relative clauses is shown in (167), which is a representation of the surface structure of (147).

(167)

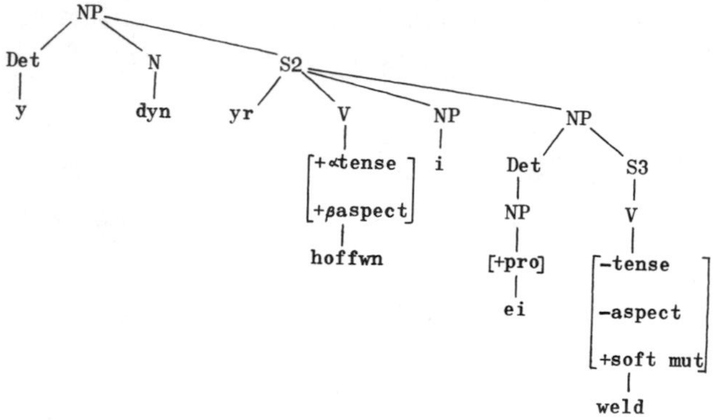

The surface structure of relatives with a lexical head noun is shown in (168) which represents (149).

(168)

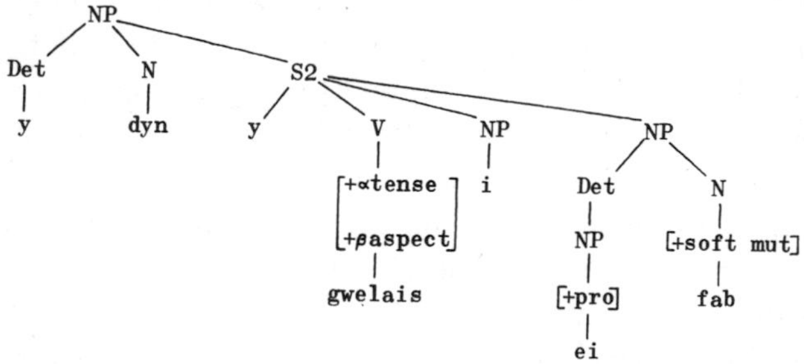

T. Possessive Pronoun Deletion must apply to the tree in more or less this form, since it is only on the cycle affecting the whole tree that the object of the embedding in the relative clause can be pronominalised on identity with the antecedent, triggering T. Possessive Pronoun Preposing and the deletion rule.

The structure of cleft sentences is very similar. (169) represents the surface structure of (152).

(169)

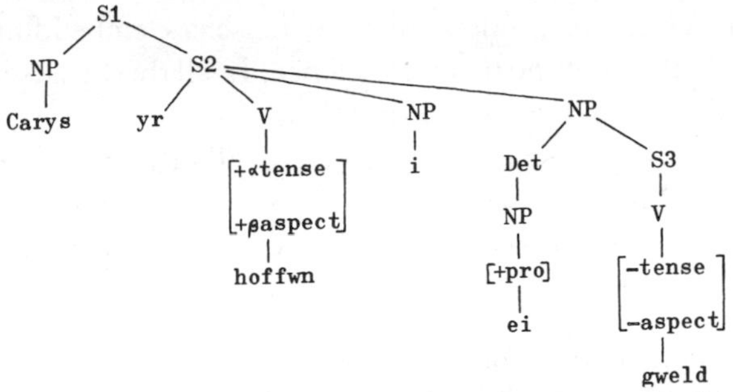

If there is a lexical head noun rather than an uninflected verb the structure is that shown in (170), which represents (155).

(170)

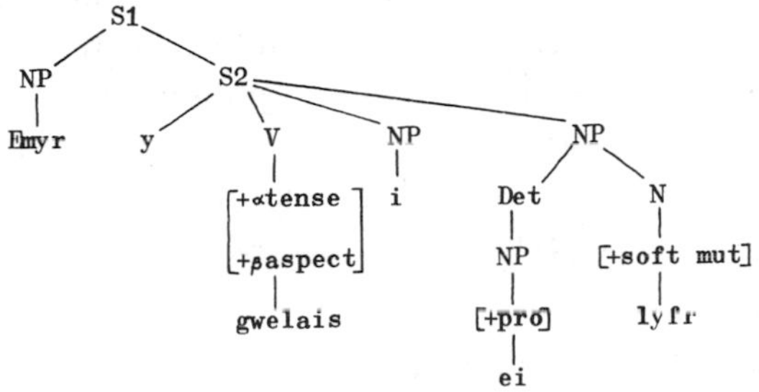

If the clefted item is already present in deep structure in sentence-initial position, then the derivation resembles that of relative clauses. If it must be copied in this position, then only after this copying rule has applied can the original noun phrase in the embedding be pronominalised. In either case, it is to a tree of this type that T. Possessive Pronoun Deletion must apply.

The structure of wh. questions is identical to that of cleft sentences, except that an interrogative pronoun appears in sentence initial position. The structure of (161) will be very similar to that shown in (169), and the structure of (163) will be very similar to that shown in (170). Here too T. Possessive Pronoun Deletion must apply late in the derivation to this type of tree.

2.6.6 Common ground It proves very difficult to see why these forms should share the restriction on possessive pronouns with the passive and other apparently similar forms should not do so.

If the 'easy' forms and the purpose phrases alone are compared with the passive, then certain similarities emerge, though they do not seem very significant as they break down when extended. In all three cases the restricted possessive pronoun is in a tenseless embedding and is identical to the subject of the matrix sentence. In all three cases it follows the uninflected verb of the embedding.

The same type of tree structure appears in other forms such as (171) where the subject of the embedding is in a tenseless sentence at this stage of the derivation (cf. section 1.5.2) and is identical to the subject of the matrix sentence.

(171) Dywedodd Ifor ei fod ef yn aros.
Said Ifor his being him in waiting.
i.e. Ifor said that he was waiting.

Clearly it is not just tree structure that is relevant, as in spite of this similarity (171) is grammatical and is not subject to the restriction. Extending the restriction to cases where the pronoun is object of the embedding only does not work either. In (172) the pronoun is the object of the tenseless embedding, and is identical to the subject of the matrix, but the sentence is grammatical.

(172) Dymunai Ifor i ni ei weld ef.
Wanted Ifor for us his seeing him.

This too is a false generalisation then. That this should be the case is in fact predicted by the VSO formalism adopted in this analysis. Since it is not possible to distinguish between subject and object noun phrases purely in terms of tree structure without knowing something of the derivational history, a restriction to object noun phrases would not be expected. In terms of this formalism the failure of (171) to show the restriction is just as odd as the failure of (172).

It is perhaps not so surprising that a simple generalisation fails to emerge when even these forms show some unexpected restrictions. For instance, in the 'easy' forms the subject of the embedding may be overt or an unspecified noun phrase. But in the case of purpose phrases it is only if the subject of the embedding is unspecified that the restriction emerges.

The partial parallelism found between these three forms is undermined by the quite different patterns found in the other restricted forms. Relatives, cleft sentences, and wh. questions may have the pronoun as the object of a tenseless embedding as before, but it is identical to the antecedent of the clause, which is separated from the pronoun by an intervening sentence containing an inflected verb. Further it is not only the object of an uninflected verb that is affected here but also the possessive with a lexical head noun, at least in the case of the cleft sentences and wh. questions.

This whole problem needs to be explored in more detail. All that it has been possible to do here is point out the existence of the restriction on other forms besides the passive, and show some of the problems of establishing the cause of its appearance in just these cases.

2.6.7 Pronoun deletion rules There are several rules in Welsh which delete pronouns, besides T. Possessive Pronoun Deletion. Two of them have been discussed already. They are T. Pronoun Subject Deletion and T. Pronoun Prepositional Object Deletion. The first relates pairs of sentences like (173) and (174).

(173) Gwelais i y llyfr.
Saw I the book.
(174) Gwelais y llyfr.
Saw (I) the book.

The second relates pairs like (175) and (176).

(175) Rhoddais i y llyfr iddo ef.
Gave I the book to him.
(176) Rhoddais i y llyfr iddo.
Gave I the book to (him).

The third rule which deletes pronouns has been briefly alluded to in section 1.2.3. It was mentioned that the pronoun object of an inflected verb may precede the verb and also follow it, as in (177), or precede it only, as in (178).

(177) Fe'i gwelais ef.
Assertion: him saw (I) him.
(178) Fe'i gwelais.
Assertion: him saw (I).

The third rule, which will be referred to as T. Pronoun Object Deletion, relates (177) and (178).

These three rules and T. Possessive Pronoun Deletion, which relates such pairs as (179) and (180), have certain characteristics in common.

(179) Gwelais i ei lyfr ef.
Saw I his book him.

(180) Gwelais i ei lyfr.
Saw I his book.

In each case, although the pronoun is deleted there is some indication left in the tree of which pronoun it was. No information is lost. And in each case, the deleted pronoun was to the right of the mark remaining in the tree. In the case of T. Possessive Pronoun Deletion and T. Pronoun Object Deletion there is another pronoun in the sentence, to the left of the deleted pronoun, which is still there to indicate which pronoun was deleted. In the case of the other two rules there is no extra pronoun but instead an inflection, on a verb and a preposition respectively, to indicate which pronoun was deleted.

It may be possible to collapse all four rules into one single rule to show this parallelism. If so, it will be necessary to devise a formula whereby instances of pronouns and instances of inflections, which for this purpose are equivalent, can be identically represented. One way of doing this is to alter the agreement rules which give the inflections on verbs and prepositions so that not only the features for number, person and gender are copied but also the feature [+pro]. This feature will then be present on both pronouns and items inflected to agree with pronouns, and the deletion rule can be formulated as in (181) to refer to the feature [+pro].

(181) T. Pronoun Deletion (unified) (optional)

```
SD. (X     A        Y      NP       )
           |               |
        [+pro  ]        [+pro  ]
        [αno   ]        [αno   ]
        [βpers ]        [βpers ]
        [γgend ]        [γgend ]

    1      2        3      4

SC. Delete 4.
```

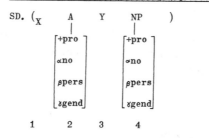

Various problems arise on this formulation. For instance, it is necessary to restrict much more closely the range over which it operates, so that it will not apply to (182) converting it to (183).

(182) Gwelais fy llyfr.
Saw (I) my book.

(183) Gwelais lyfr.
Saw I (a) book.

On the formulation given in (181) this is quite possible. Since the rules it subsumes apply to a full sentence, a noun phrase and a prepositional phrase respectively, this will lead to difficulties.

2.6.8 Morphological parallels It is necessary to refer to this set of structural descriptions elsewhere in the grammar, in order to generate the correct morphological forms of pronouns. All those pronouns which may be deleted by one of the four rules mentioned above are of the type known as *rhagenwau ategol* (confirming pronouns). These always appear in contexts where there is a previous mention of the pronoun, which these pronouns then 'confirm'. In other contexts where there is no previous mention of the pronoun, a different morphological form is found, *rhagenwau annibynnol* (independent pronouns).[9]

In some person/number forms the two forms are identical, but in the 1sg they are distinct. The confirming pronoun is *i* and the independent pronoun is *fi*. Compare the confirming form in (184) to (187) with the independent form in (188).

(184) Gwelodd Ifor fy llyfr i.
Saw Ifor my book me.
(185) Anfonodd Mair lythyr wrthyf i.
Sent Mair (a) letter to me
(186) Gwelais i y llyfr.
Saw I the book.
(187) Fe'm gwelodd i.
Assertion: me saw (he) me.
(188) Gwelodd fi.
Saw (he) me.

In (188) there is only one mention of the pronoun and so the independent form is used.

The parallelism between these pronoun forms and the possibility of deletion also appears in prepositional forms. Where the preposition inflects to agree with the pronoun object, as in (185) above, the confirming pronoun is found. But not all prepositions can inflect in this way. For instance the preposition *â* (with) does not inflect to agree with a pronoun object, as can be seen from (189) and (190).

(189) Mae Emyr yn chwarae â ni.
Is Emyr playing with us.

(190) Mae Emyr yn chwarae â hi.
Is Emyr playing with her.

Although the person and number of the pronoun change the preposition remains the same. In this instance it is the independent pronoun form which is found, as in (191).

(191) Mae Emyr yn chwarae â fi.
Is Emyr playing with me.

It cannot be deleted, so that (192) is ungrammatical.

(192) *Mae Emyr yn chwarae â.
Is Emyr playing with.

If the two sets of rules are treated as quite separate with structural descriptions in common only by accident, then a generalisation is lost. Instead it could be assumed that the morphological rules apply first and the deletion rules apply only to pronouns already marked as confirming pronouns. This will require the generalisations discussed above to be expressed by the morphological rules rather than directly by the deletion rules. The problems of specifying the joint structural description remain.

It can be seen from the data given in the last two sections that T. Possessive Pronoun Deletion is not an isolated rule but part of a complex of rules relating to pronoun deletion and pronoun form. At first sight this complicates the problem of accounting for the exceptional behaviour of T. Possessive Pronoun Deletion in the passive and the other constructions discussed above. But it also raises the possibility that this set of forms may be related to a more general restriction affecting the deletion and morphological rules as a whole.

2.7 Conclusions

We find here, as in Chapter 1, that there is no simple tie-up between semantics and syntax. The active and corresponding passive are synonymous, but they differ considerably in syntax. The passive in each case contains an extra layer of embedding, the sentence with *cael* (get), which is not present in the active. Even if the active is a simple sentence, the passive is a complex sentence. From the syntactic point of view the passive resembles the periphrastic active and embeddings below lexical verbs, particularly object embeddings. It has the same type of deep structure and most of the rules in its derivation are also needed in deriving these active embeddings. It differs from them only in the identity relations between the noun phrases in the matrix sentence and the embedding. In the passive the matrix subject and the object of the embedding must be identical, while in the other forms any restrictions are between the two subject noun phrases. As a result of this difference a different rule is needed to remove the subject of the embedding in the passive, T. Agent Postposing instead of T. Equi-Subject Deletion or T. Subject Raising. Yet the passive has no close semantic link with these other embedded forms. Syntactic and semantic groupings seem to be quite independent of each other.

3 *More passives*

Only straightforward active-passive pairs were discussed in the last chapter, and it was possible to assume that the rule ordering given in (94) was the ordering of rules within the cycle. In sections 3.1 to 3.3 of this chapter some more complicated passives will be considered, where other rules interact with the passive rules. And in section 3.4 their implications will be discussed. It appears that many of the rules involved in the derivation of the passive are postcyclic or last-cyclic rather than cyclic as was assumed till now.

3.1 Sentence conjunction

In most cases a sentence containing a conjoined noun phrase can be related to two simple sentences each containing a nonconjoined noun phrase. For instance, (1) is equivalent to (2) and (3) together.

(1) Gwelodd Ifor y dyn a'r ddynes.
Saw Ifor the man and the woman.

(2) Gwelodd Ifor y dyn.
Saw Ifor the man.

(3) Gwelodd Ifor y ddynes
Saw Ifor the woman.

It is normally assumed that a sentence such as (1) is derived from a deep structure of the type shown in (4), where (2) and (3) are conjoined.[1]

(4)

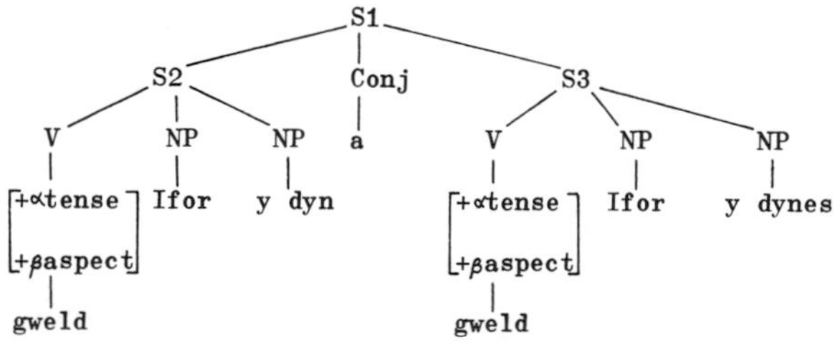

At some stage in the derivation T. Conjunction Reduction applies, converting (4) into (5), which is the surface structure of (1).

(5)

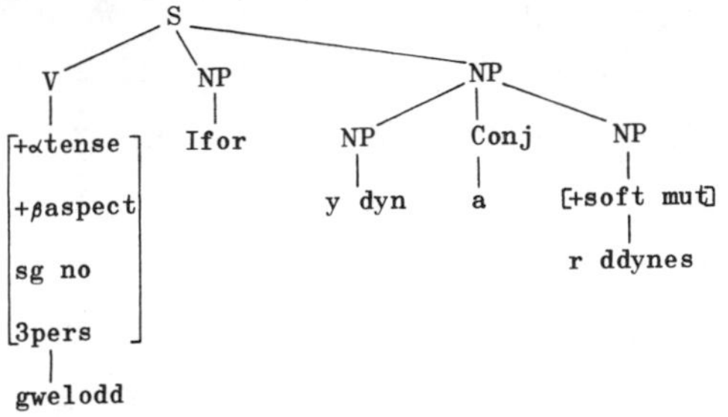

At this point only the noun phrases which differed in (4) are conjoined. Note that T. Conjunction Reduction must not apply before the S1 cycle if it is to have both the conjoined sentences in its scope.

In the same way it is possible to derive the passive form (6) from a conjunction of (7) and (8).

(6) Cafodd Wyn ei rybuddio gan Ifor ac Emyr.
Got Wyn his warning by Ifor and Emyr.

(7) Cafodd Wyn ei rybuddio gan Ifor.
Got Wyn his warning by Ifor.

(8) Cafodd Wyn ei rybuddio gan Emyr.
Got Wyn his warning by Emyr.

The deep structure is shown in (9).

(9)

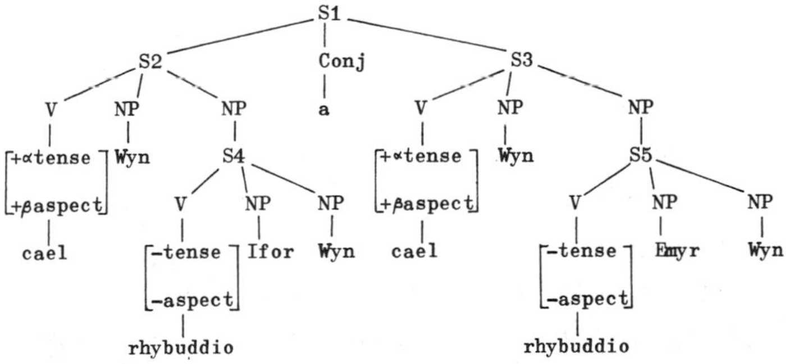

At some stage in the derivation, but not before the S1 cycle when both conjoined sentences are in its scope, T. Conjunction Reduction applies. If all the rules of the passive are cyclic, then they will by this stage have applied to S2 and S3, and the input to T. Conjunction Reduction is (10).

(10)

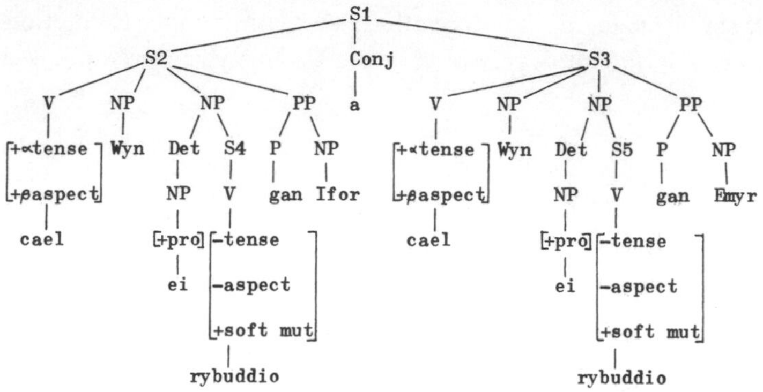

T. Conjunction Reduction converts (10) into (11) where there is a conjoined noun phrase in the prepositional agent phrase.

(11)

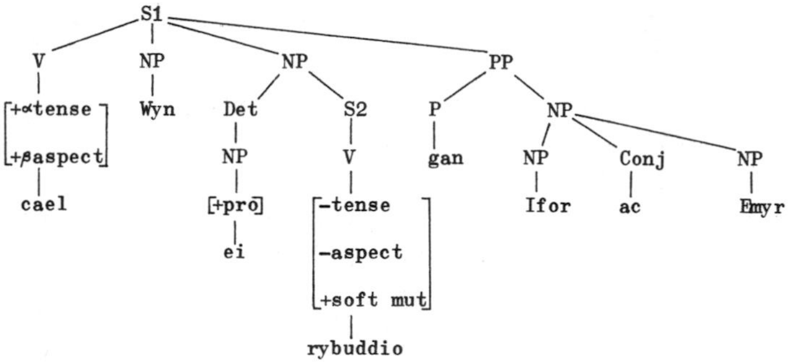

There are no difficulties in this case.

The problems arise in the case of (12) where the conjoined noun phrase is the subject of the passive rather than the agent.

(12) Cafodd Wyn ac Ifor eu rhybuddio gan Emyr.
Got Wyn and Ifor their warning by Emyr.

This can be related to the two simple forms (13) and (14).

(13) Cafodd Wyn ei rybuddio gan Emyr.
Got Wyn his warning by Emyr.

(14) Cafodd Ifor ei rybuddio gan Emyr.
Got Ifor his warning by Emyr.

(12) can be derived from the deep structure (15).

(15)

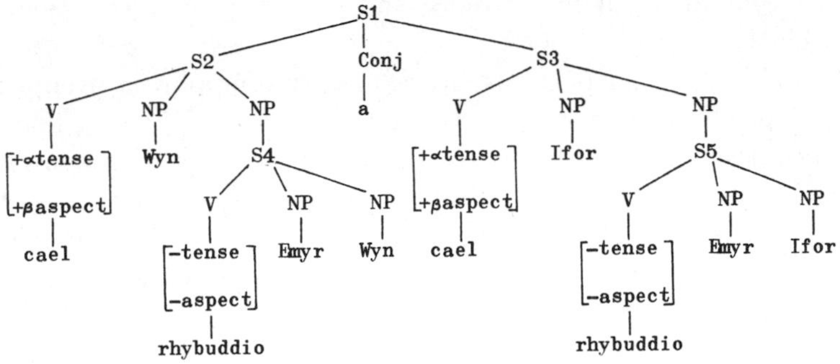

If the passive rules are cyclic then they will have already applied to S2 and S3 before the S1 cycle where T. Conjunction Reduction applies. The input to this rule will be as shown in (16).

(16)

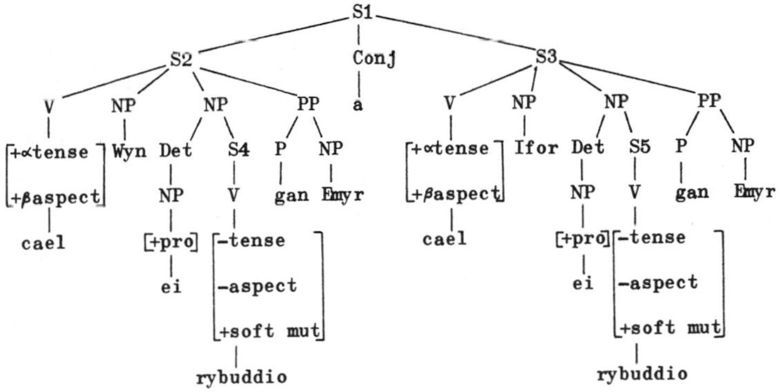

T. Conjunction Reduction converts this into the structure (17), and it is here that the problems arise.

(17)

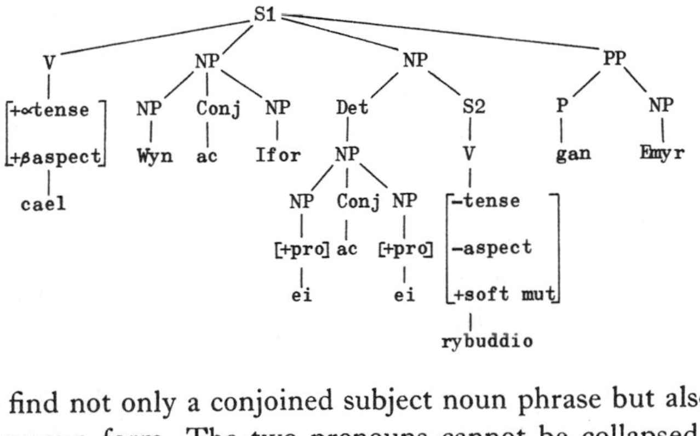

Here we find not only a conjoined subject noun phrase but also a conjoined pronoun form. The two pronouns cannot be collapsed as they

are not identical in reference any more than the two nouns in the subject.[2]

This problem does not arise if the assumption is dropped that all the passive rules are cyclic. It will be shown in section 3.4 that T. Agent Postposing must be cyclic and this is not the source of the problem here. What is needed is for T. Pronominalisation to apply after T. Conjunction Reduction. If this is the case, T. Conjunction Reduction will take as its input (18), where T. Agent Postposing has applied to S2 and S3.

(18)

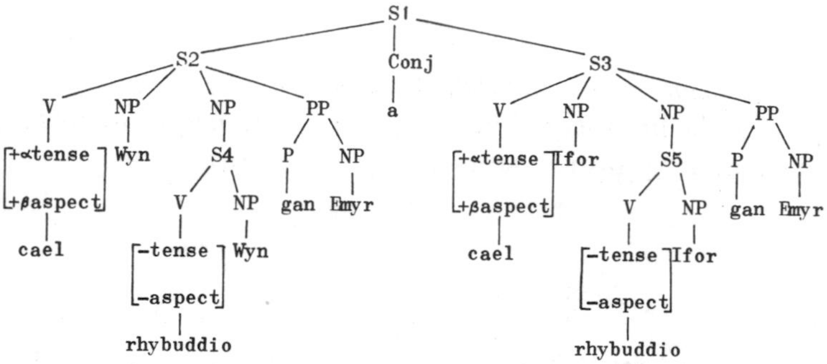

The output of T. Conjunction Reduction will be (19) on this analysis.

(19)

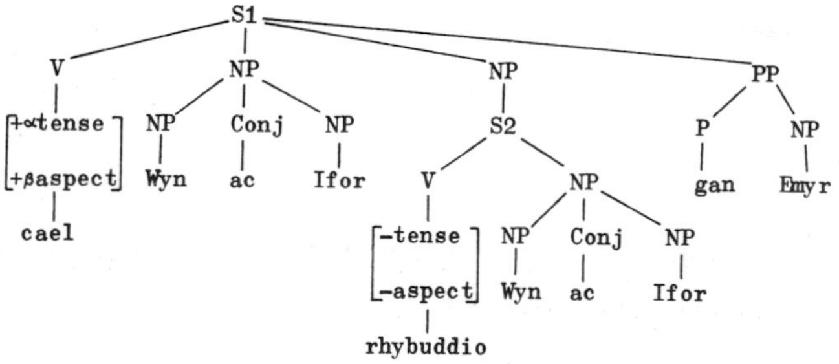

T. Pronominalisation applies to this tree, pronominalising the conjoined object of the embedding on identity with the conjoined subject of the matrix sentence.[3] The rules which are triggered by the pronoun form, such as T. Possessive Pronoun Preposing, will then follow.

On this analysis T. Pronominalisation and the rules which are triggered by it are no longer cyclic rules. They do not apply on the S2 and S3 cycles although the appropriate structural description is present. Instead they apply at a later stage in the derivation, either on the last cycle or postcyclically. It is not clear which of these is correct.

It is possible that in this case reordering is not necessary. A rule could be formulated to collapse the two pronoun forms in (17) to give the correct *eu* (their) form. Such a solution however involves an additional, unmotivated rule, and it is made more unattractive by the need to adopt the rule ordering solution in the two other cases that will be discussed in sections 3.2 and 3.3.

3.2 Phrasal conjunction

3.2.1 Deep structure conjoined noun phrases Not all sentences containing a conjoined noun phrase can be related to two sentences containing a nonconjoined noun phrase. For instance, (20) contains a conjoined noun phrase but the two simple sentences (21) and (22) are ungrammatical.

(20) Cyfarfu Ifor ac Emyr.
Met Ifor and Emyr.
(21) *Cyfarfu Ifor.
Met Ifor.
(22) *Cyfarfu Emyr.
Met Emyr.

The relation between (20) and (21) and (22) is not the same then as that between (1), (2) and (3) where all three forms were grammatical. In (20) the conjoined noun phrase is in subject position. The same pattern can be found with the conjoined noun phrase in object position, as in (23) to (25).

(23) Cymysgodd Catrin flawd a halen.
Mixed Catrin flour and salt.
(24) *Cymysgodd Catrin flawd.
Mixed Catrin flour.
(25) *Cymysgodd Catrin halen.
Mixed Catrin salt.

In all of these cases the form with a conjoined noun phrase is grammatical but not the forms with a nonconjoined noun phrase.

Lakoff and Peters (1969) suggest for similar forms in English that while such forms as (1) may be derived from a conjunction of two simple sentences as in (4), a different deep structure is needed for (20) and (23). These are simple sentences in deep structure but with a conjoined noun phrase already present. On this analysis the deep structure of (20) is (26), and the deep structure of (23) is (27).

(26)

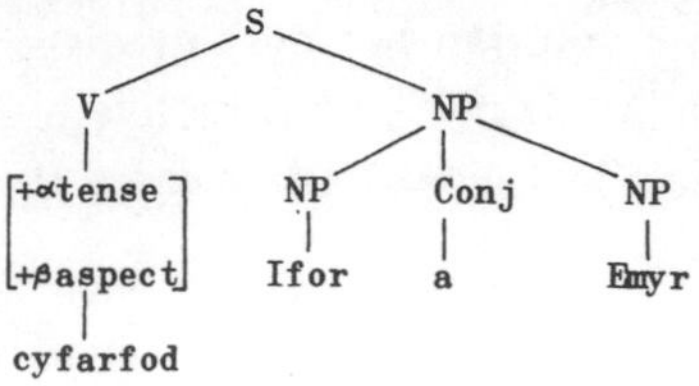

(27)

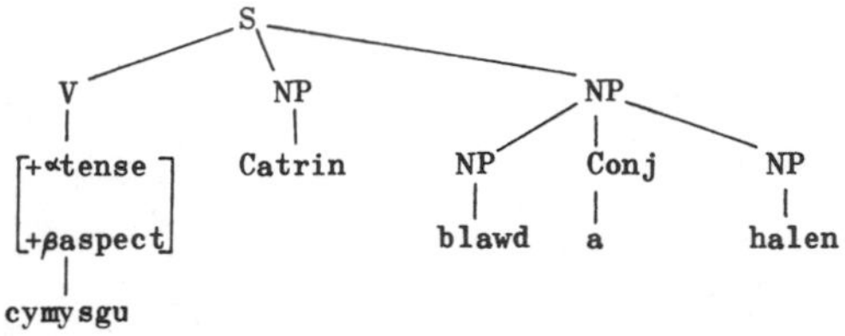

They suggest that (20) is related to (28) by an optional rule T. Conjunct Splitting that moves the second noun phrase to the end of the sentence as the object of a preposition. (23) is similarly related to (29).

(28) Cyfarfu Ifor ag Emyr.
Met Ifor with Emyr.

(29) Cymysgodd Catrin flawd â halen.
Mixed Catrin flour with salt.

This analysis seems plausible for Welsh too. Problems arise however in the case of periphrastic sentences.

3.2.2 Problems with periphrastic forms Conjoined forms of this type appear not only with a simple inflected verb but also with periphrastic forms of the verb, as in (30).

(30) Mae Ifor ac Emyr wedi cyfarfod.
Is Ifor and Emyr after meeting.

The split noun phrase too can appear in a periphrastic sentence.

(31) Mae Ifor wedi cyfarfod ag Emyr.
Is Ifor after meeting with Emyr.

The deep structure representation of (30) is (32). On the S1 cycle T. Equi-Subject Deletion applies, giving (33).

(32)

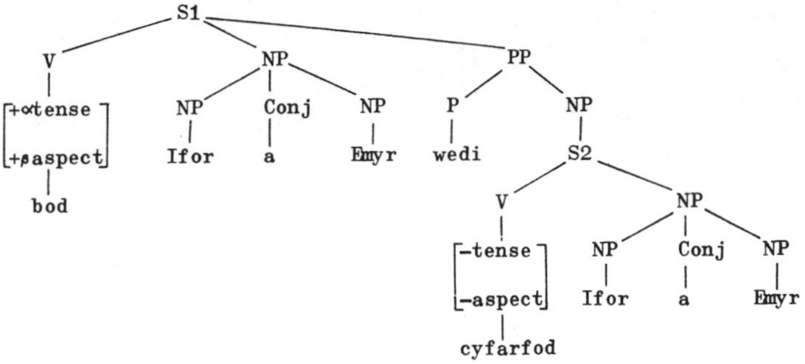

(33)

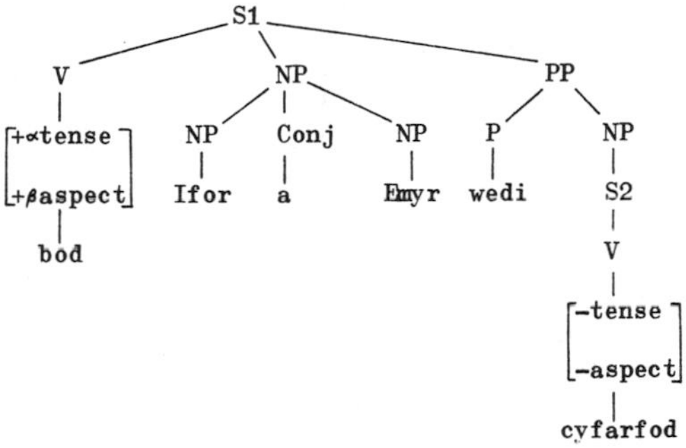

If forms like (31) with a split noun phrase should be derived from an underlying conjoined noun phrase then (32) should be the deep structure of (31) too. In order to derive (31) on the S1 cycle T. Equi-Subject Deletion applies, to give (33). Later T. Conjunct Splitting applies to convert (33) into (34).

(34)

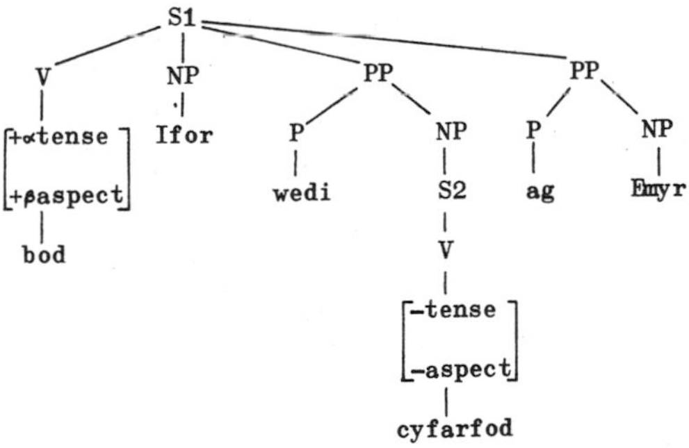

On this analysis of (31) only T. Conjunct Splitting is new and it remains an optional rule, since either (30) or (31) is a grammatical output. Any other derivation causes problems. For instance, if T. Conjunct Splitting applies on the S2 cycle, then the output of this rule is (35).

(35)

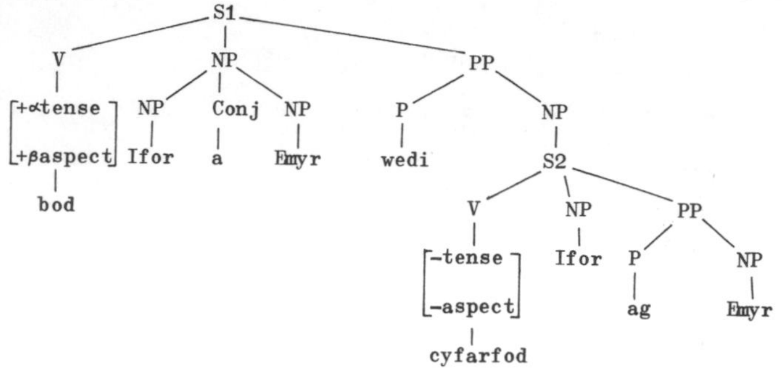

In order to generate (31) from this it is necessary for T. Conjunct Splitting to apply again on the S1 cycle and for the prepositional phrase in the embedding to be deleted on identity with the prepositional phrase in the matrix sentence. Thus the rule is no longer optional but is obligatory in certain circumstances, and an extra rule is needed to delete the lower prepositional phrase. This rule is otherwise unnecessary.

These complications suggest that T. Conjunct Splitting cannot be an optional cyclic rule. It must not apply on the S2 cycle at all. One way of avoiding this is to restrict it to apply only where there is a verb marked for tense and aspect. This will give the right results in the case of (31) where it applies on the S1 cycle only and that is the only cycle where the verb is marked for tense and aspect. It does not however allow for such forms as (36), where the conjoined noun phrase has been split in a tenseless embedding.

(36) Hoffwn i Ifor gyfarfod ag Emyr.
Should like (I) for Ifor meeting with Emyr.

But if the rule can apply in (36), why not in (31)?

One way to ensure that T. Conjunct Splitting applies only to the correct forms and remains optional is for it to be postcyclic rule. In (31) after the cyclic rules have applied the subject noun phrase of the embedding has been deleted, and it is only the subject noun phrase of the matrix that is still available for splitting. In the case of (36) however, the subject noun phrase of the embedding is still overt and so can be split. T. Conjunct Splitting can be formalised as in (37).

(37) T. Conjunct Splitting (optional) (postcyclic)

SD. $(_S$ X $(_{NP}$ NP a NP) Y)

1 2 3 4 5 6 7

SC. Adjoin 6 as right daughter of 1, in a prepositional phrase as object of the preposition â.

Delete 5.

This rule may be last-cyclic rather than postcyclic. It is not clear which is correct, and although throughout the discussion in this chapter rules will be referred to as postcyclic, the possibility exists that they are in fact last-cyclic. The important point is that there is a split between the cyclic rules and another set of rules which do not apply on each cycle.

The formulation in (37) was made general in order to allow it to apply to object noun phrases as well as subjects. It will relate such forms as (23) and (29), or the periphrastic forms (38) and (39).

(38) Mae Catrin wedi cymysgu blawd a halen.
Is Catrin after mixing flour and salt.

(39) Mae Catrin wedi cymysgu blawd â halen.
Is Catrin after mixing flour with salt.

In the case of object noun phrases too the rule must not be limited to tensed sentences, in order to allow for the periphrastic form (39) and the embedded form (40).

(40) Bwriadai Catrin gymysgu blawd â halen.
Intended Catrin mixing flour and salt.

In this the subject and object forms are the same. There is no evidence from object forms for deciding between a cyclic and a postcyclic application of the rule, but postcyclic application as required for subjects is certainly compatible with object forms. It is assumed therefore that the same rule is involved in both cases.

3.2.3 Passives Splitting the noun phrase must be postcyclic in the case of passive forms. The conjoined noun phrase may still be conjoined as subject of the passive, as in (41), or split, as in (42).

(41) Cafodd blawd a halen eu cymysgu gan Catrin.
Got flour and salt their mixing by Catrin.

(42) Cafodd blawd ei gymysgu gan Catrin â halen.
Got flour its mixing by Catrin with salt.[4]

This is true not only for passives where *cael* (get) is inflected, but also for passives where there is a periphrastic form of the verb, as in (43) and (44).

(43) Mae blawd a halen wedi cael eu cymysgu gan Catrin.
Is flour and salt after getting their mixing by Catrin.

(44) Mae blawd wedi cael ei gymysgu can Catrin â halen.
Is flour after getting its mixing by Catrin with salt.

Unless T. Conjunct Splitting is postcyclic here too then the same problems arise in the derivation of (44) as did in the derivation of the periphrastic active (31), over the conjoined subject.

There is also evidence in the passive that the rule splitting the object noun phrase must be postcyclic. The deep structure of (42) is shown in (45).

(45)

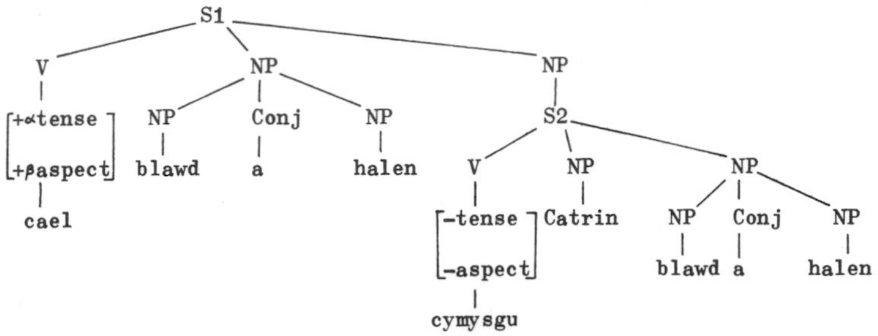

In order for T. Agent Postposing to apply on the S1 cycle it is necessary for the subject of the matrix sentence and the object of the embedding to be identical. Either both must be conjoined or both must be split. It has already been pointed out in section 3.2.2 that T. Conjunct Splitting must be postcyclic in the case of subject noun phrases, and it will be argued that T. Agent Postposing is a cyclic rule in section 3.4. It therefore follows that the noun phrase subject of the matrix sentence has not yet been split when T. Agent Postposing applies. And so the object of the embedding too must still be conjoined at this stage. The S2 cycle has already been passed, and so T. Conjunct Splitting cannot be a cyclic rule in the case of object noun phrases either.[5]

3.2.4 Postcyclic rules The fact that T. Conjunct Splitting is a postcyclic rule causes problems for the passive. After T. Agent Postposing has applied to (45), its structure is (46).

(46)

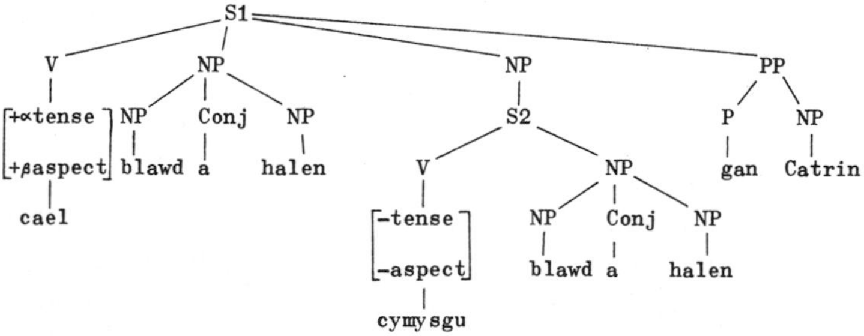

The derivation of (41) is straightforward. The object of the embedding is pronominalised on identity with the subject of the matrix, and the other rules apply as expected to give (41). In the derivation of (42), however, T. Conjunct Splitting applies. The noun phrase is split, and it is with the remaining half of the conjunction that the pronoun agrees. T. Pronominalisation must therefore follow T. Conjunct Splitting, and so too must the rules which are triggered by T. Pronominalisation. This includes T. Possessive Pronoun Preposing, T. Possessive Pronoun Deletion and the morphological and mutation rules required to give the correct forms. Since T. Conjunct Splitting is postcyclic, this means that these other rules must also be postcyclic not cyclic. This backs up the ordering suggested in section 3.1, where it was argued that T. Pronominalisation and the following rules must be postcyclic.

The position is not completely satisfactory here however. T. Pronominalisation will only apply if the two noun phrases are identical. This means that if the subject of the matrix sentence is split, then the object of the embedding must also be split. T. Conjunct Splitting has applied twice to the tree, giving (47).

(47)

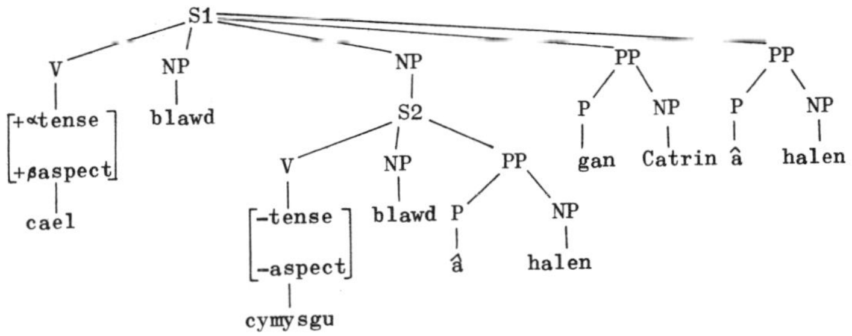

T. Pronominalisation now applies to pronominalise the noun *blawd* (flour) in the embedding. It becomes necessary however to formulate an extra rule to delete the prepositional phrase in the embedding which results from the application of T. Conjunct Splitting. This rule is otherwise unmotivated, and may be an indication that the analysis suggested here is wrong in some way. No better alternative has emerged however so it will be retained. The output of T. Pronominalisation and this extra deletion rule is (48).

The two rules which cause the verb to agree with the subject must also follow T. Conjunct Splitting, since the verbal inflection varies according to whether this rule has applied or not. If it has applied then the

(48)

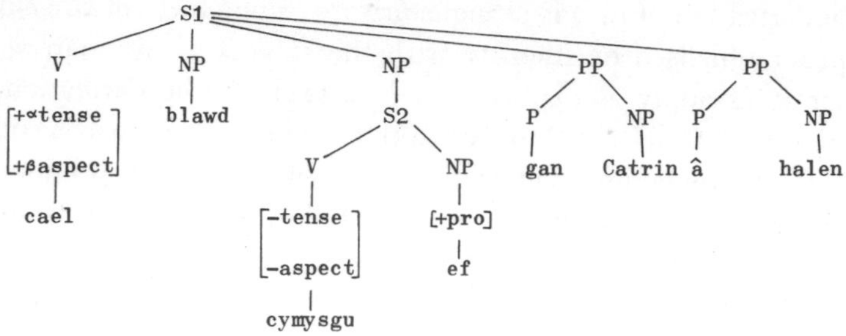

verb agrees with the noun phrase left in subject position, as in (49) and (50).

(49) Cyfarfum i â Wyn.
Met I with Wyn.
(50) Cyfarfu Wyn â fi.
Met Wyn with me.

If the rule has not applied, then the verb takes the 3sg form with the conjoined noun phrase, as in (51).

(51) Cyfarfu Wyn a fi.
Met Wyn and I.

The same pattern appears in passives.

(52) Cefais i fy nghymharu â Wyn.
Got I my comparing with Wyn.
(53) Cafodd Wyn ei gymharu â fi.
Got Wyn his comparing with me.
(54) Cafodd Wyn a fi ein cymharu.
Got Wyn and I our comparing.

The two verbal agreement rules must therefore be postcyclic too. And so must the rules which follow them: T. Soft Mutation of Direct Object, T. Pronoun Subject Deletion, and morphological rules.

Further, at least some of the rules which affect prepositional phrases must follow T. Conjunct Splitting, as this rule produces an extra prepositional phrase which must be given the correct form. It will undergo T. Prepositional Object Mutation and the appropriate phonological rules, since *â* (with) triggers aspirate mutation of a following form.

This has not appeared in any of the forms discussed so far since the nouns involved have had initial sounds which are not subject to aspirate mutation. In (55) this can be seen, where *chath* is the aspirate mutation form of *cath* (cat).

(55) Cyfarfu'r ci â chath.
Met the dog with (a) cat.

There is no evidence in these forms if T. Preposition Agreement and T. Pronoun Prepositional Object Deletion are also postcyclic, since *â* (with) does not inflect to agree with a following pronoun (cf. section 2.6.8) and so the pronoun cannot be deleted.

3.3 Tensed embeddings

3.3.1 Subject embeddings It was pointed out in section 1.5.2 that certain embeddings appear to be marked for tense and aspect in deep structure. These include forms such as (56) where there is an inflected verb in surface structure and forms such as (57) where the uninflected form of *bod* (be) is found.

(56) Cyhoeddodd y cadeirydd y byddai angen mwy o arian.
Announced the chairman that would be need (of) more of money.

(57) Cyhoeddodd y cadeirydd fod angen mwy o arian.
Announced the chairman being need (of) more of money.

Such forms may appear as the subject of a passive, though only in a position to the right of the rest of the sentence.

(58) Cafodd ei chyhoeddi gan y cadeirydd y byddai angen mwy o arian.
Got its announcing by the chairman that would be need (of) more of money.

(59) Cafodd ei chyhoeddi gan y cadeirydd fod angen mwy o arian.
Got its announcing by the chairman being need (of) more of money.

These forms are not completely acceptable to all informants, though they are accepted by some. The objections of those who do not accept them seem to be based on the length of these forms. All informants however reject passives where the embedding appears in normal subject position, rather than postposed to the end of the sentence.

(60) *Cafodd y byddai angen mwy o arian ei chyhoeddi gan y cadeirydd.
Got that would be need (of) more of money its announcing by the chairman.

(61) *Cafodd fod angen mwy o arian ei chyhoeddi gan y cadeirydd.
Got being need (of) more of money its announcing by the chairman.

This restriction also appears in active forms. These embeddings may appear postposed to the right as in (62) and (63).

(62) Synnodd bawb y byddai angen mwy o arian.
Surprised everyone that would be need (of) more of money.

(63) Synnodd bawb fod angen mwy o arian.
Surprised everyone being need (of) more of money.

But the embedding may not appear in normal subject position.

(64) *Synnodd y byddai angen mwy o arian bawb.
Surprised that would be need (of) more of money everyone.

(65) *Synnodd fod angen mwy o arian bawb.
Surprised being need (of) more of money everyone.

If the verb of the matrix is inflected, as in the examples (56) to (65) above, then there is nothing in normal subject position. If the embedding is within a periphrastic sentence however, there may either be nothing in subject position, as in (66) and (67), or there may be the pronoun *hi* (she), as in (68) and (69).

(66) Mae wedi cael ei chyhoeddi gan y cadeirydd y bydd angen mwy o arian.
Is after getting its announcing by the chairman that will be need (of) more of money.

(67) Mae wedi cael ei chyhoeddi gan y cadeirydd fod angen mwy o arian.
Is after getting its announcing by the chairman being need (of) more of money.

(68) Mae hi wedi cael ei chyhoeddi gan y cadeirydd y bydd angen mwy o arian.
Is it after getting its announcing by the chairman that will be need (of) more of money.

(69) Mae hi wedi cael ei chyhoeddi gan y cadeirydd fod angen mwy o arian.
Is it after getting its announcing by the chairman being need (of) more of money.

This pronoun is ungrammatical with an inflected matrix verb, as in (70) and (71).

(70) *Cafodd hi ei chyhoeddi gan y cadeirydd y byddai angen mwy o arian.
Got it is announcing by the chairman that would be need (of) more of money.
(71) *Cafodd hi ei chyhoeddi gan y cadeirydd fod angen mwy o arian.
Got it its announcing by the chairman being need (of) more of money.

This restriction also holds of active forms. If the matrix verb is inflected, as in (72) and (73), there may not be a pronoun in subject position.

(72) *Synodd hi bawb y byddai angen mwy o arian.
Surprised it everyone that would be need (of) more of money.
(73) *Synnodd hi bawb fod angen mwy o arian.
Surprised it everyone being need (of) more of money.

If the matrix verb is in a periphrastic form then the pronoun *hi* may appear in subject position.

(74) Mae hi wedi synnu pawb y bydd angen mwy o arian.
Is it after surprising everyone that will be need (of) more of money.
(75) Mae hi wedi synnu pawb fod angen mwy o arian.
Is it after surprising everyone being need (of) more of money.

These periphrastic forms are also grammatical without a pronoun in subject position.

(76) Mae wedi synnu pawb y bydd angen mwy o arian.
Is after surprising everyone that will be need (of) more of money.
(77) Mae wedi synnu pawb fod angen mwy o arian.
Is after surprising everyone being need (of) more of money.

The situation in active and passive forms is completely parallel. The tensed embedding may be postposed to the right of the sentence. In the case of periphrastic forms the pronoun *hi* may or may not appear in subject position. In the case of inflected forms nothing may appear in subject position.

3.3.2 The deep structure These forms can be explained if in deep structure the embedded sentence appears as the complement of a noun phrase whose head noun is the pronoun *hi*, as in (78).[6]

(78)

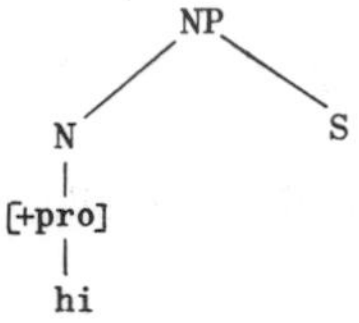

The embedded sentence is moved to the right out of the noun phrase, leaving behind the pronoun *hi*. Later another rule deletes *hi*, obligatorily if the matrix verb is inflected, optionally if the embedding is in a periphrastic sentence.

This tree structure is not yet however fully adequate for Welsh. If the possessive pronoun subject in such forms as (79) is to be accounted for by the same rule as the possessive pronoun object in tenseless embeddings, i.e. T. Possessive Pronoun Preposing, then not only must the verb be tenseless at this stage but the whole sentence must be dominated by a noun phrase node, as in (80).

(79) Synnodd bawb ei fod yn dod.
Surprised everyone his being in coming.

(80)

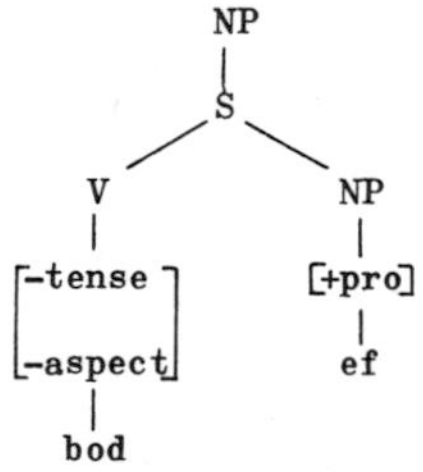

The tenselessness of the verb was discussed above in section 1.5.2, and now the dominating noun phrase node must be introduced.

If the embedding is dominated by a noun phrase node at this stage in the derivation, then it is simplest to assume that it is also dominated by this node in deep structure. This gives the deep structure representation (81).

(81)

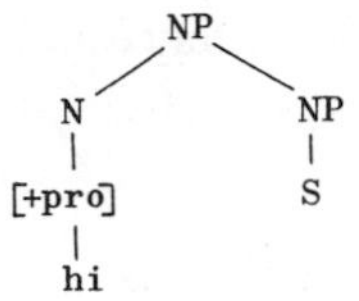

The embedded sentence is here dominated by a noun phrase node and this in turn is embedded within another noun phrase. This allows the noun phrase characteristics of the postposed sentence to be explained since not only the embedded sentence but also the noun phrase node above it is moved to the end of the sentence. If the deep structure was (78) then only the sentence would be moved and there would be no explanation for the noun phrase characteristics it displays, such as a preposed possessive pronoun.

This tree structure (81) also shows the parallelisms between the forms discussed above and embedded sentences with a lexical head noun, such as (82).

(82) Synnodd y ffaith ei fod yn dod bawb.
Surprised the fact his being in coming everyone.

The deep structure representation of (82) will be identical to (81) except that the head noun is not a pronoun.

(83)

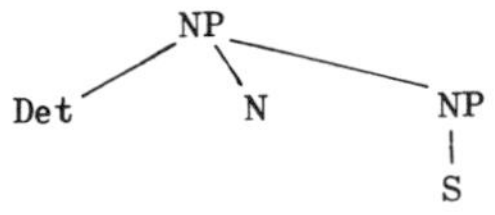

Here again the embedded sentence must be dominated by its own noun phrase node, or it will not be possible to explain the parallelism of the possessive pronoun to other forms, such as the tenseless embeddings and the possessive noun phrases. The failure of the embedding in (82) to postpose to the end of the sentence, giving (84), can be accounted for by restricting the postposing rule to forms with a pronominal head noun.

(84) *Synnodd y ffaith bawb ei fod yn dod.
Surprised the fact everyone his being in coming.

3.3.3 Sentence postposing It can be seen from the ungrammaticality of such forms as (60) and (61) or (64) and (65), where the embedded sentence has not been postposed, that T. Sentence Postposing is an obligatory rule. If it fails to apply then the output is ungrammatical.

This causes problems in cases where the matrix sentence is itself embedded in a periphrastic form, as in (85).

(85) Mae hi wedi synnu pawb fod Emyr yno.
Is it after surprising everyone being Emyr there.

The deep structure representation of (85) is (86).

(86)

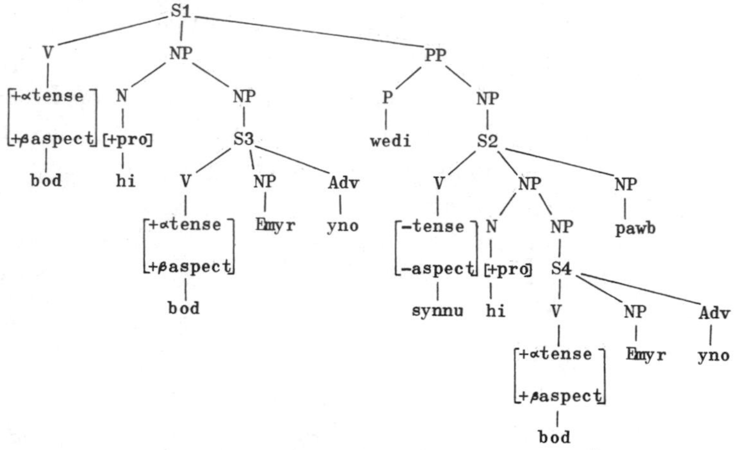

If the obligatory rule T. Sentence Postposing is a cyclic rule, then it applies on the S2 cycle, to give the tree (87).

(87)

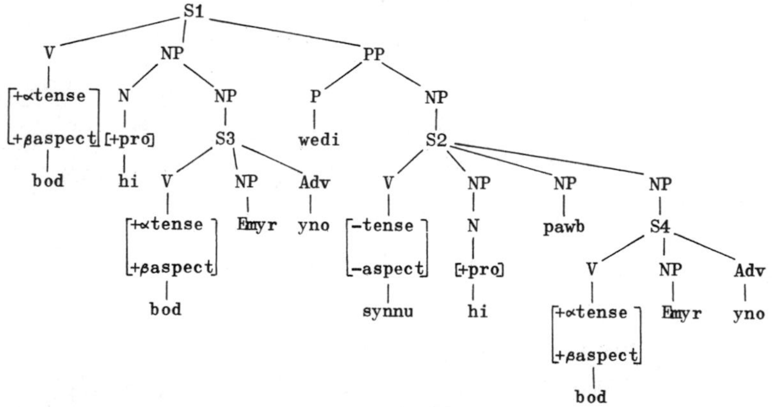

T. Equi-Subject Deletion cannot apply to this tree as the subject of S1 is not identical to the subject of S2. It can only apply after T. Sentence Postposing has applied on the S1 cycle too, to give the tree (88) with a pronoun only in subject position in each case.

(88)

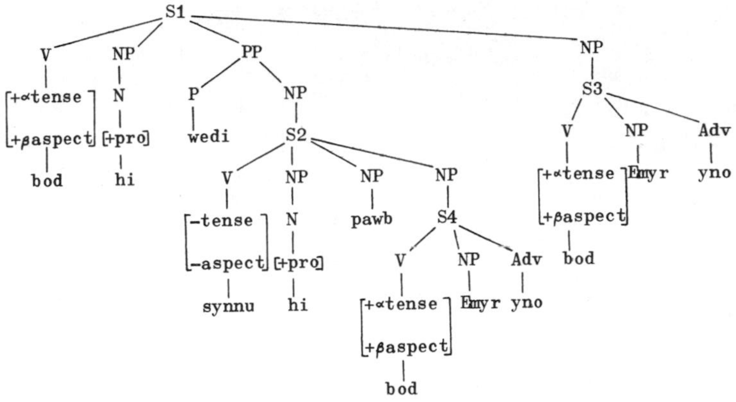

Now T. Equi-Subject Deletion can apply, but in order to generate the correct surface structure forms another rule is needed to delete the lower instance of the postposed embedded forms. This rule is otherwise unnecessary.

This further complication can be avoided if T. Sentence Postposing does not apply on the S2 cycle. In this case the embedded sentence which is the subject of S2 is deleted by T. Equi-Subject Deletion, and then T. Sentence Postposing applies to move the embedding out of the subject of the matrix sentence. No additional rules are needed on this analysis.

How is this restriction of T. Sentence Postposing to the S1 cycle to be achieved? One way of doing this is to restrict it to applying only if the matrix verb is marked for tense and aspect. In the case of (85) this gives the right results, since the matrix verb on the S2 cycle is not marked for tense and aspect, but on the S1 cycle it is marked for these features. This solution however fails to account for forms such as (89).

(89) Bwriadai Emyr iddi synnu pawb ei fod yn dod.
Intended Emyr for it surprising everyone his being in coming.

The matrix verb *synnu* (surprise) here is not marked for tense and aspect, but T. Sentence Postposing has applied.

It appears that T. Sentence Postposing must be a postcyclic rule. In this way it can be restricted to apply only on the S1 cycle in deriving (85), since after the cyclic rules have applied only the embedded subject of S1 is still available to be postposed. It can also on this view apply to (89), since after the cyclic rules have applied the subject embedding here is still overt. The rule can be formalised as in (90).

(90) T. Sentence Postposing (obligatory) (postcyclic)

```
SD. (S V (NP N (NP (S X      V          Y ) ) ) Z )
             |               |
             hi         [+αtense  ]
                        [+βaspect ]

     1  2  3  4  5  6 7      8          9         10

SC. Adjoin 5 as right daughter of 1.
```

If the deep strutcure (86) undergoes T. Equi-Subject Deletion on the S1 cycle, and then T. Sentence Postposing, the output tree is (91).

(91)

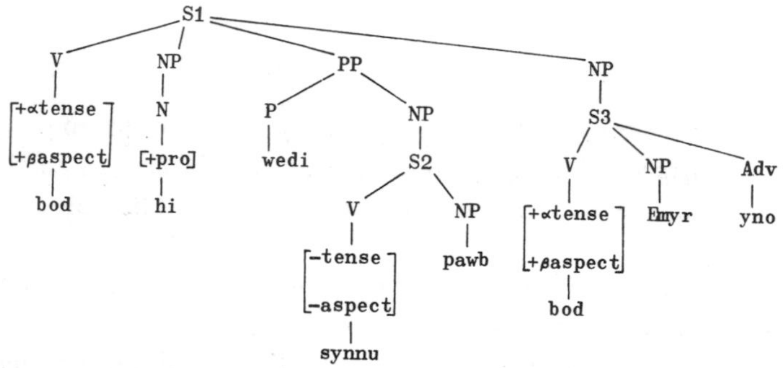

The rule deleting the pronoun *hi* must also be postcyclic as it must follow T. Sentence Postposing. It is optional if the matrix verb is *bod* (be), and obligatory if the matrix verb is anything else. If the matrix verb is itself a tenseless embedding as in (89) the pronoun is not deleted. This set of rules, or single rule with complicated conditions, will not be formalised here, as the details are not directly relevant. It will be referred to as T. Hi-Subject Deletion.

3.3.4 Object embeddings It seems that embeddings of this type must also be postposed from object position. (92) with the embedding in normal object position is ungrammatical, but (93) where it has been postposed is grammatical.

(92) *Dywedodd Ifor y byddai angen mwy o arian i Wyn.
Said Ifor that would be need (of) more of money to Wyn.

(93) Dywedodd Ifor i Wyn y byddai angen mwy o arian.
Said Ifor to Wyn that would be need (of) more of money.

In such forms the pronoun *hi*, which sometimes appears in subject position, is never found. (93) without the pronoun is grammatical, but not (94) where it is present.

(94) *Dywedodd Ifor hi i Wyn y byddai angen mwy o arian.
Said Ifor it to Wyn that would be need (of) more of money.

If these forms are to be treated as parallel to the subject embeddings discussed in the last section, then T. Sentence Postposing must be generalised to cover object embeddings too. This is done in (95).

(95) <u>T. Sentence Postposing (obligatory) (postcyclic)</u>[2]

```
SD. (S W (NP N (NP (S X      V         Y ) ) )  Z  )
             |               |
             hi         [+αtense ]
                        [+βaspect]

    1   2  3   4  5   6  7   8       9          10
```

SC. Adjoin 5 as right daughter of 1.

There is in fact no evidence from active forms if postposing object embeddings should be cyclic or postcyclic. Postcyclic application is compatible with them however, and required in the case of the passives, as will be shown in section 3.3.5. T. Hi-Subject Deletion must be extended to cover obligatory deletion of the pronoun in object position, and will now be termed T. Hi Deletion.

3.3.5 Passives The deep structure of (96) is shown in (97).

(96) Cafodd ei chyhoeddi gan Emyr fod Wyn yno.
Got its announcing by Emyr being Wyn there.

(97)

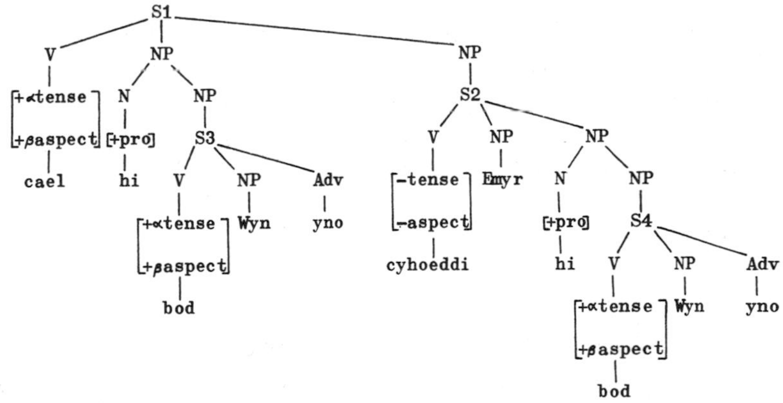

At the point in the derivation where T. Agent Postposing applies, the subject of S1 and the object ot S2 must be identical. It will be argued that T. Agent Postposing is a cyclic rule in section 3.4. T. Sentence Postposing has been shown to be postcyclic where subject embeddings are concerned. It has therefore not yet applied to the subject at the point when T. Agent Postposing applies. It is therefore necessary that it should not yet have applied either to the object embedding in S2. Since the S2 cycle has already been passed, this means that T. Sentence Postposing must also be postcyclic with respect to object embeddings. The output of T. Agent Postposing is (98).

(98)

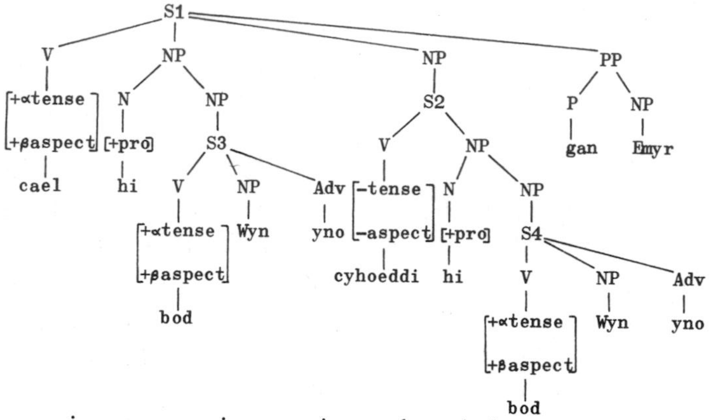

The possessive pronoun in a passive such as (96) agrees with the 3sg fem pronoun *hi* which is the subject of the sentence after the embedded sentence has been postposed. There are two ways in which this output may be generated, each having rather different implications.

One possibility is that T. Sentence Postposing applies first and then T. Pronominalisation applies to the pronoun left in the noun phrase position as subject of the matrix and object of the embedding. This explains why it is the pronoun that is crucial in the pronominalisation rule, with no effect from the embedding. On this approach, T. Sentence Postposing gives the output (99) here when applied to (98).

(99)

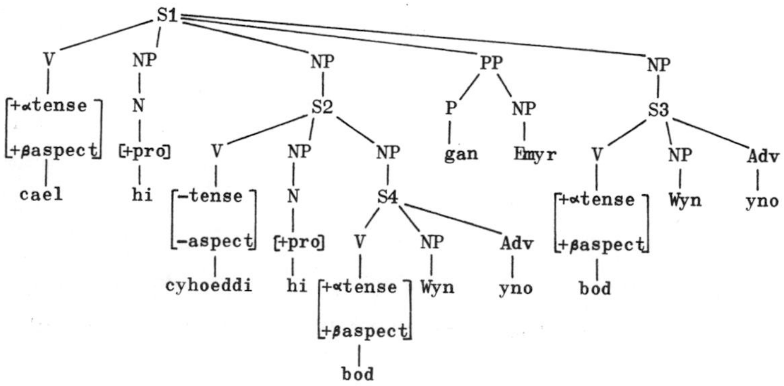

T. Pronominalisation applies to this tree (vacuously), and is now a postcyclic rule as it follows another postcyclic rule. And so the rules which follow T. Pronominalisation must also be postcyclic, such as T. Possessive Pronoun Preposing, T. Possessive Pronoun Deletion, and the morphological and mutation rules involved.

There is a difficulty here however. In order to have an identical noun phrase in subject position in the matrix and object position in the embedding for T. Pronominalisation, it is necessary for T. Sentence Postposing to have operated on both the subject of S1 and the object of S2. This in turn means that an extra rule is needed to delete the lower postposed embedding to give the correct output. This rule is otherwise unnecessary. It is the same type of problem as arose in the discussion of phrasal conjunction in section 3.2.4 and it may again be an indication that there is something wrong with the analysis.

In the case of phrasal conjunction there was no alternative analysis. Here however there is an alternative view of the pronominalisation rule. The pronoun *hi* is the head noun of the noun phrase which contains the embedding. In other cases where there is a head noun and some other element in a noun phrase, it is the head noun which governs the type of pronoun which appears in place of the whole noun phrase. For instance, in the passive form (100) the subject of the passive is a noun phrase consisting of the head noun yr hanes (the story) and an embedding. The possessive pronoun agrees with the head noun, and is 3sg masc.

(100) Cafodd yr hanes fod Wyn yno ei gyhoeddi gan Emyr.
Got the story being Wyn there its announcing by Emyr.

Here T. Sentence Postposing has not applied and so pronominalisation has affected the noun phrase as a whole.

It is possible then that T. Pronominalisation precedes T. Sentence Postposing in the derivation of (96), applying to the tree (98). The object of S2 is pronominalised as a whole to agree with the head of the subject of S1, giving the tree (101).

(101)

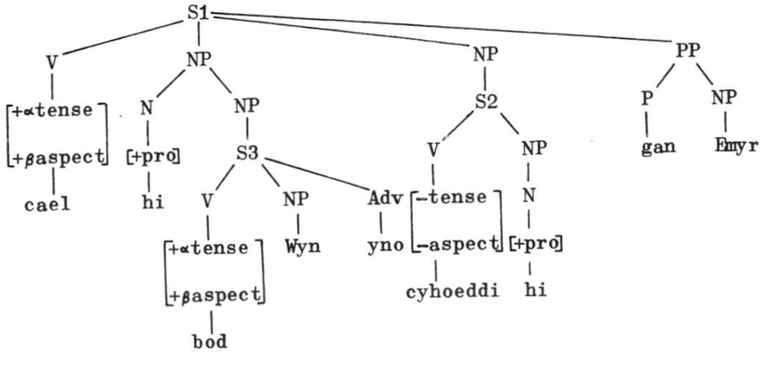

T. Sentence Postposing applies later when only the embedding in the subject of S1 is still available. On this account no extra rules are required.[7]

This second account does not require postcyclic application of T. Pronominalisation. If it precedes T. Sentence Postposing it may be cyclic or postcyclic but ordered before T. Sentence Postposing. These embedded forms then are not decisive evidence in favour of T. Pronominalisation being postcyclic but they are certainly compatible with this view. And this is true too of the rules which must follow T. Pronominalisation.

3·4 Cyclic and postcyclic rules

3·4·1 Cyclic rules It was assumed in Chapter 2 that all rules were cyclic and that the order in which they applied to the passive reflected their ordering within the cycle. It has become clear however in this chapter that this is an oversimplified view, and that while some rules are indeed cyclic others must be postcyclic.

Only two rules seem to be clearly cyclic. These are T. Equi-Subject Deletion and T. Agent Postposing. It is necessary for T. Equi-Subject Deletion to be a cyclic rule in order for complex embedded forms such as (102) to be generated.

(102) Mae Ifor wedi bod yn canu.
Is Ifor after being in singing.

The deep structure of this form is (103).

(103)

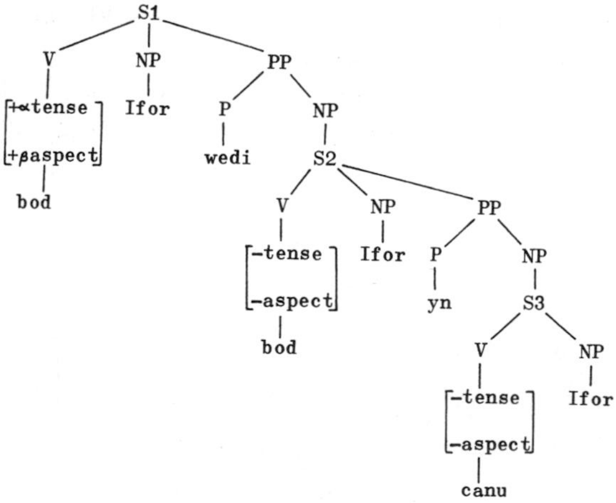

If T. Equi-Subject Deletion applies cyclically, deleting first the subject of S3 and then the subject of S2, the sentence (102) may be derived without difficulty. If however the rule does not apply cyclically, and deletes first the subject of S2, then it can no longer apply to delete the subject of S3 as its structural description is no longer met.

It was pointed out in section 2.4.1 that T. Equi-Subject Deletion must not apply to a passive deep structure such as (104).

(104)

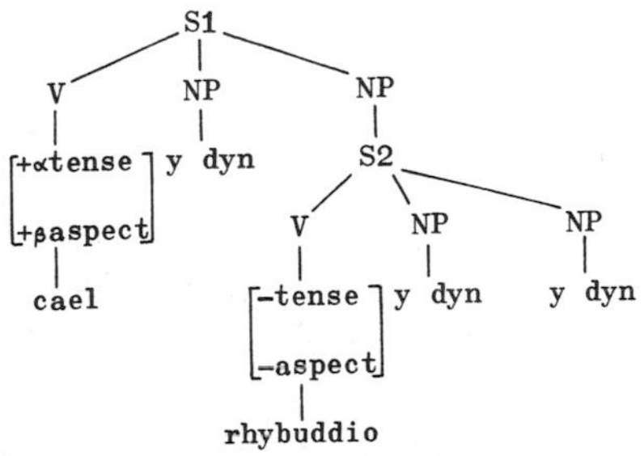

If T. Equi-Subject Deletion does apply then it generates (105) which has a different interpretation from (104).

(105) Cafodd y dyn ei rybuddio.
Got the man his warning.

In order to generate the passive with the interpretation of (104), T. Agent Postposing must apply to give (106).

(106) *Cafodd y dyn ei rybuddio ganddo ef ei hun.[8]
Got the man his warning by himself.

This can be ensured by ordering T. Agent Postposing before T. Equi-Subject Deletion. But if T. Equi-Subject Deletion is a cyclic rule then in order to precede it on every occasion T. Agent Postposing must be cyclic too.

This is compatible with the ordering required to generate complex passives such as (107).

(107) Mae Ifor wedi cael ei rybuddio gan Wyn.
Is Ifor after getting his warning by Wyn.

The deep structure of this form is shown in (108). T. Agent Postposing must apply on the S2 cycle, and then T Equi-Subject Deletion on the S1 cycle. Reverse ordering destroys the structural description of T. Agent Postposing. An example of the reverse ordering with T. Equi-Subject

(108)

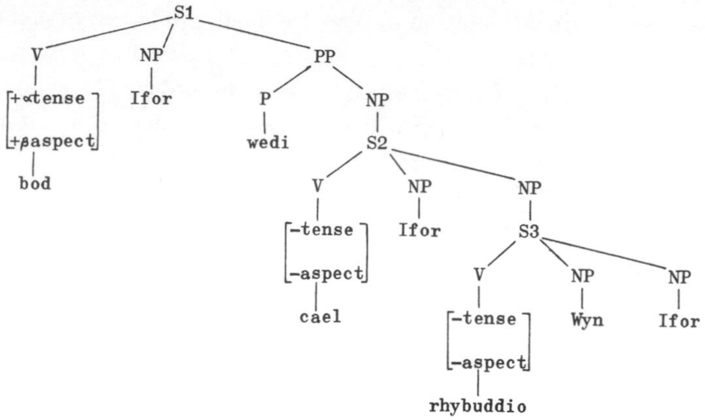

Deletion applying on an earlier cycle than T. Agent Postposing is given in section 4.2.2 below. Only if both rules apply in the cycle can all these forms be generated.

It appears then that both these rules are cyclic, applying in the order shown in (109).

(109) T. Agent Postposing
↓
T. Equi-Subject Deletion

3.4.2 Postcyclic rules It has been suggested in sections 3.1 to 3.3 that certain rules are postcyclic. These are T. Conjunct Splitting, T. Sentence Postposing and T. Hi Deletion. There are problems with the analyses suggested, and these were pointed out in the relevant sections, but it is still true that postcyclic application of these rules gives a simpler account of certain forms than does cyclic application. T. Hi Deletion must follow T. Sentence Postposing, but T. Conjunct Splitting is not ordered relative to these two rules.

If these rules are postcyclic, then certain other rules must also be postcyclic. For instance, it was pointed out in section 3.2.2 that T. Conjunct Splitting can apply to the subject noun phrase of a tenseless embedding such as (110).

(110) Bwriadai Ifor i Ann gyfarfod â Wyn.
Intended Ifor for Ann meeting with Wyn.

In such forms the subject noun phrase of the embedding is raised into a prepositional phrase in the matrix sentence as the object of the preposition *i* (for), as was shown in section 1.4.4. Does T. Conjunct Splitting apply to this noun phrase before it is raised into a prepositional phrase or after this has happened? There is some evidence that the noun phrase must be split while it is still subject of the embedding, before it is raised by T. Subject Raising. The object of the preposition *i* in (111) is a conjoined noun phrase, and it is an example of phrasal conjunction since (111) is not equivalent to (112) and (113). The gift is a joint one to both boys at once.

(111) Rhoddodd Ifor y llyfr i Wyn ac Emyr.
Gave Ifor the book to Wyn and Emyr.
(112) Rhoddodd Ifor y llyfr i Wyn.
Gave Ifor the book to Wyn.
(113) Rhoddodd Ifor y llyfr i Emyr.
Gave Ifor the book to Emyr.

The noun phrase cannot be split to give (114).

(114) *Rhoddodd Ifor y llyfr i Wyn ag Emyr.
Gave Ifor the book to Wyn with Emyr.

This suggests that T. Conjunct Splitting does not apply to the subject of the embedding in (110) after it has been raised into the prepositional phrase. T. Subject Raising must therefore follow T. Conjunct Splitting and be a postcyclic rule. This means that the rules which must follow T. Subject Raising are also postcyclic. The rules concerned are those which affect prepositional phrases, since T. Subject Raising creates a new prepositional phrase in the matrix sentence. They include T. Preposition Agreement, T. Pronoun Prepositional Object Deletion, T. Preposition Object Mutation, and the various morphological and phonological rules needed to give the correct inflections and mutation forms.

In the case of T. Sentence Postposing on the other hand it appears that the rule can apply to tensed embeddings which are the object of a prepositional phrase. It seems likely that in deep structure (115) has the tensed embedding as the object of the preposition *am* (about) in order to parallel (116) where the verb takes a prepositional object throughout the derivation.

(115) Soniodd Ifor wrth Emyr fod angen mwy o arian.
Mentioned Ifor to Emyr being need (of) more of money.
(116) Soniodd Ifor am ei wyliau.
Mentioned Ifor about his holidays.

It is therefore possible that T. Subject Raising has already applied before T. Sentence Postposing. Later T. Hi Deletion applies to delete the pronoun left behind. This leaves the preposition *am* with no noun phrase object and it is deleted by T. Preposition Deletion (cf. section 2.5.3) which must also be a postcyclic rule now.

It was also pointed out in sections 3.1 to 3.3 that certain rules involved in the passive must be postcyclic to allow for the derivations discussed there. T. Pronominalisation must be postcyclic to allow for the derivation of both sentence conjunction forms and phrasal conjunction forms. As a result the rules which are triggered by T. Pronominalisation must also be postcyclic. The tensed embeddings that undergo T. Sentence Postposing are at the least compatible with this view. In addition, the rules which give verbal agreement with the subject of the sentence must follow T. Conjunct Splitting and so be postcyclic, as must be the rules which follow verbal agreement. And some of the rules which affect prepositional phrases must follow T. Conjunct Splitting.

The ordering of these postcyclic rules is shown in (117). Rules that are crucially ordered are linked by arrows.

(117)
T. Conjunct Splitting
↓
T. Subject Raising

T. Sentence Postposing
↓
T. Hi Deletion
↓
T. Preposition Deletion

→T. Preposition Agreement
↓
T. Pronoun Prepositional Object Deletion

→Morphological Rules for Pronoun and Preposition Forms

→T. Prepositional Object Mutation

→T. Pronominalisation
↓
T. Possessive Pronoun Preposing
↓
Morphological Rules for Preposed Pronoun Form
↓
T. Preposed Pronoun Mutation

→T. Possessive Pronoun Deletion

→T. Subject-Verb Agreement (Noun)

→T. Subject-Verb Agreement (Pronoun)

T. Soft Mutation of Direct Object
↓
→T. Pronoun Subject Deletion

→Morphological Rules for Verb Forms

→Phonological Rules for Mutations

There remain a few rules which are not clearly postcyclic or cyclic. They may be either. These are T. Cael Deletion, and T. Unspecified Noun Phrase Deletion and T. Conjunction Reduction. These rules are ordered relative to some of the rules discussed above. T. Unspecified Noun Phrase Deletion must follow T. Agent Postposing and precede T. Preposition Deletion. T. Cael Deletion must follow T. Agent Postposing. T. Conjunction Reduction must precede T. Pronominalisation. Thus these rules follow cyclic rules and precede postcyclic rules, and they may be late cyclic rules or early postcyclic rules.

3.5 Conclusions

The rules which were established to account for the passive in Chapter 2 are adequate also for these more complicated forms. It is necessary however to divide them into two sets, one set of cyclic rules and another set of noncyclic rules, in order to account for their interrelation with other rules which must also be divided into cyclic and noncyclic sets.

4 *Restrictions on the passive*

Not all active sentences have a grammatical passive equivalent. In this chapter these restrictions on passives will be described and an attempt made to explain why they should appear. Section 4.1 concerns cases where the lack of a passive seems to be due to a restriction on the verb of the active sentence. Sections 4.2 to 4.5 concern cases where the lack of a passive seems to be due to a restriction on the subject or object of the active appearing as agent or subject of the passive.

4.1 Restrictions on the verb

4.1.1 Defective verbs Some verbs are defective. They can appear only with a very few inflections, and lack the uninflected form of the verb completely. Such verbs are clearly not able to appear in the passive construction, or any other tenseless embedding, where the uninflected form of the verb is required for the verb of the embedded sentence. Examples of such verbs are *dylai* (ought he), which appears only in the imperfect[1] or pluperfect forms, *meddai* (said he) which appears only in the present and imperfect forms, and *moes* (take) which appears only in the imperative.

Some of these verbs will be excluded on other grounds too. For instance, *dylai* takes a tenseless embedding as direct object, as in (1). Such forms are discussed in sections 4.2.1 and 4.2.2.

(1) Dylai Mair ddychwelyd.
Ought Mair returning.

And *meddai* takes a quotation from direct speech as direct object, as in (2). Such forms are discussed in section 4.2.6.

(2) 'Mae'n hwyr' meddai Mair.
'Is late' said Mair.

4.1.2 Nonagentive and stative verbs The passive equivalent (4) of the active sentence (3) is generally felt to be ungrammatical.

(3) Mae Emyr yn adnabod Catrin.
Is Emyr in knowing Catrin.
(4) *Mae Catrin yn cael ei hadnabod gan Emyr.
Is Catrin in getting her knowing by Emyr.

There is an uninflected form of the verb *adnabod* (know) available, and the subject and object of the active can appear as agent and subject of the passive with a different verb, as in (5).

(5) Cafodd Catrin ei rhybuddio gan Emyr.
Got Catrin her warning by Emyr.

The ungrammaticality of (4) must therefore be due to some other reason. Other verbs which are restricted in the same way are *hoffi* (like) and *casáu* (dislike). In each case the passive containing this verb is ungrammatical though there is an uninflected form of the verb, and nothing odd about the subject and object of the active.

These verbs fit all the criteria but one suggested by Lakoff (1966) as characterising stative verbs. For instance, they cannot appear in imperative forms, as in (6).

(6) *Adwaen y plant!
Know the children!

Nor can they appear embedded below the verbs *atgofio* (remind) and *darbwyllo* (persuade), as in (7) and (8).

(7) *Atgofiais Wyn i adnabod y plant.
Reminded (I) Wyn for knowing the children.
i.e. I reminded Wyn to know the children.
(8) *Darbwyllais Wyn i adnabod y plant.
Persuaded (I) Wyn for knowing the children.

They do not appear as the focus of a pseudocleft sentence, as in (9).

(9) *Yr hyn a wnaeth Wyn oedd adnabod y plant.
That which did Wyn was knowing the children.
i.e. What Wyn did was know the children.

They may not appear with manner adverbials.

(10) *Adnabu Wyn y plant yn ofalus.
Knew Wyn the children carefully.

Verbs such as *rhybuddio* (warn) on the other hand, which can appear in the passive, can also appear in all of these constructions. Examples corresponding to (6) to (10) are given in (11) to (15).

(11) Rhybuddiwch y plant!
Warn the children!

(12) Atgofiais Wyn i rybuddio'r plant.
Reminded (I) Wyn for warning the children.

(13) Darbwyllais Wyn i rybuddio'r plant.
Persuaded (I) Wyn for warning the children.

(14) Yr hyn a wnaeth Wyn oedd rhybuddio'r plant.
That which did Wyn was warning the children.

(15) Rhybuddiodd Wyn y plant yn ofalus.
Warned Wyn the children carefully.

One of the tests used by Lakoff, whether a verb can appear with a progressive auxiliary or not, cannot be used in Welsh since the equivalent periphrastic forms with the aspect marker *yn* (in) are not restricted in this way. An equivalent test seems to be the possibility of co-occurrence with the auxiliary verb of past punctual aspect *darfu* (happened). Verbs such as *adnabod* (know) cannot be embedded below *darfu* as in (16), but the verbs which can appear in the passive like *rhybuddio* (warn) can be embedded in this position as in (17).

(16) *Darfu i Wyn adnabod y plant.
Happened for Wyn knowing the children.
i.e. Wyn knew the children.

(17) Darfu i Wyn rybuddio'r plant.
Happened for Wyn warning the children.

It appears then that stative verbs should be excluded from passives. It is not clear though how this should be done. There are two possibilities, both corresponding to types of restriction already needed in the grammar. The rule T. Agent Postposing, the only rule limited to the derivation of passives and appearing in the derivation of all passives, could be constrained to apply only to nonstatives. The verb in the embedding on this view is marked as [–stative] and the rule is sensitive to this feature in the same way as it is already sensitive to the features [–tense] and [–aspect] on the verb of the embedding. The second possibility is that there should be selection restrictions on what types of verb can be embedded below *cael*, with only nonstative verbs possible in this position. Such restrictions on embedding are needed in other cases to account for the difference in grammaticality between such forms as (16) and (17). There does not seem to be any way of deciding between these two possibilities. Some evidence in favour of the first is given in Chapter 5 and some in favour of the second in Chapter 6.

It is not only verbs which can be defined as stative by these tests which seem ungrammatical in passives. Other verbs such as *gweld* (see), *clywed* (hear), and *cael* (get) are felt to be ungrammatical in passives by many informants. They resemble the stative verbs in failing to appear in imperatives as in (18), embedded below *atgofio* (remind) and *darbwyllo* (persuade) as in (19) and (20), in a pseudocleft sentence as in (21), and with manner adverbials as in (22).

(18) *Gwelwch y plant!
See the children!

(19) *Atgofiais Wyn i weld y plant.
Reminded (I) Wyn for seeing the children.

(20) *Darbwyllais Wyn i weld y plant.
Persuaded (I) Wyn for seeing the children.

(21) *Yr hyn a wnaeth Wyn oedd gweld y plant.
That which did Wyn was seeing the children.

(22) *Gwelodd Wyn y plant yn ofalus.
Saw Wyn the children carefully.

These verbs differ from stative verbs however in that they can appear embedded below *darfu* (happened) as in (23).

(23) Darfu i Wyn weld y plant.
Happened for Wyn seeing the children.

The two sets of verbs can be related if the restrictions are reinterpreted. All the tests except the possibility of being embedded below *darfu* can be interpreted as indicating if a verb is agentive or not. Agentive verbs can appear in these constructions, and nonagentive verbs cannot. Only the ability of a verb to appear embedded below *darfu* is a test of the feature [± stative]. On this view *adnabod* (know) is nonagentive and stative, and *gweld* (see) is nonagentive and nonstative.

While verbs which are nonagentive and stative are rejected by everyone in the passive, there is less certainty about verbs which are nonagentive and nonstative. Passives with *gweld* (see) are accepted by some informants. For those who reject all of these forms the restriction refers to the feature [− agentive], and for those who reject *adnabod* (know) but accept *gweld* (see) the restriction refers to the feature [+stative]. The degree of overlap between the two sets of verbs referred to makes this type of variation understandable.

4.2 Restrictions on embeddings

4.2.1 Tenseless embeddings as subject Tenseless embeddings which may appear as object of the active as in (24) may not appear as subject of the passive as in (25).

(24) Ceisiodd Ifor ddarllen y neges.
Tried Ifor reading the message.
(25) *Cafodd darllen y neges ei geisio gan Ifor.
Got reading the message its trying by Ifor.

Since the matrix verb of the active form (24) is neither nonagentive nor stative, as can be seen from (26) and (27), the ungrammaticality of the passive form (25) must be due to some other factor.

(26) Ceisiwch ddarllen y neges!
Try reading the message.
(27) Darfu i Ifor ddarllen y neges.
Happened for Ifor reading the message.

In (24) and (25) the embedding has no overt subject noun phrase. In (28) and (29) the subject noun phrase of the embedding is overt.

(28) Dymunai Wyn i Ifor ddarllen y neges.
Wanted Wyn for Ifor reading the message.
(29) *Câi i Ifor ddarllen y neges ei ddymuno gan Wyn.
Was getting for Ifor reading the message its wanting by Wyn.

Here too the passive is ungrammatical. But in this case, and it seems in the case of all verbs which can take an object embedding with an overt subject in surface structure, the matrix verb is both nonagentive and stative, according to the tests discussed in the last section. It is to be expected therefore that the passive will be ungrammatical on this ground alone and it is not possible to tell if a passive with such an embedding as subject would be ungrammatical with a more suitable matrix verb.

4.2.2 A natural explanation There is no general restriction on subjectless tenseless embeddings in subject position, as can be seen from the active form (30).

(30) Mae mynd yno wedi tristáu pawb.
Is going there after saddening everyone.

The explanation must therefore be found in some other factor.

It may in fact be possible to account for the ungrammaticality of (25) as a simple consequence of the analysis of the passive set up in Chapters 2 and 3. The deep structure of (25) is (31).

(31)

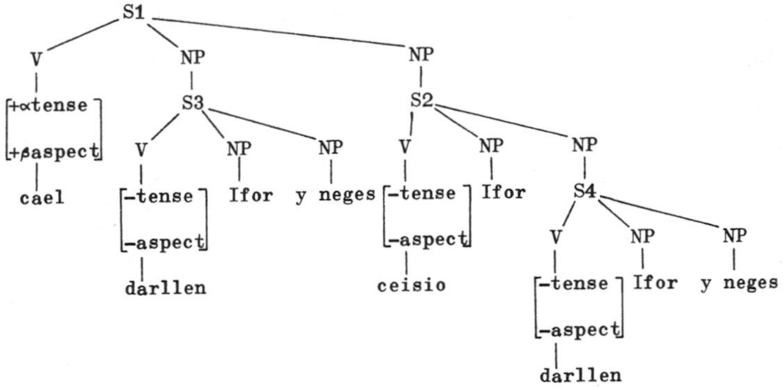

In the S2 cycle T. Equi-Subject Deletion applies, deleting the subject of S4 on identity with the subject of S2. The output of this rule is the tree (32).

(32)

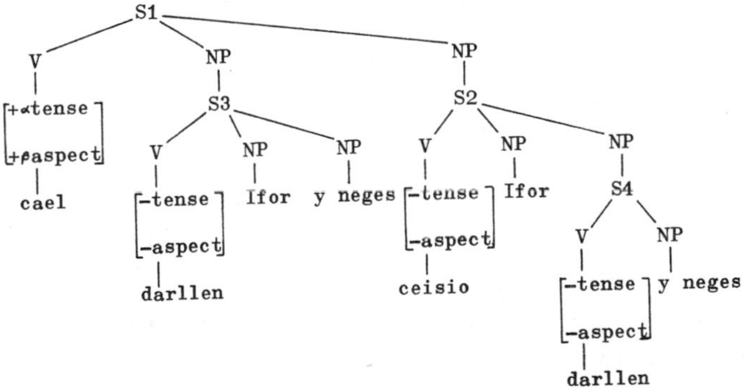

When the S1 cycle is reached and T. Agent Postposing should apply, it is blocked as the subject of the matrix is no longer identical to the subject of the embedding and so the structural description of the rule is no longer met. The embedding which is the subject of S1 is intact with its subject still present, but the embedding which is the object of S2 has lost its subject.

If this is the reason why (25) is ungrammatical, then there is no reason why (29) where the subject of the embedding is overt and T. Equi-Subject Deletion does not apply, should be ungrammatical given a suitable matrix verb. The subject of the embedding here is eventually moved into a prepositional phrase by T. Subject Raising but it was shown in section 3.4.2 that this is a postcyclic rule. At the point then where T. Agent Postposing, a cyclic rule, applies nothing has happened to the embedding. The deep structure (33) is still unchanged as the input to T. Agent Postposing and the two embeddings S3 and S4 are still identical.[2]

(33)

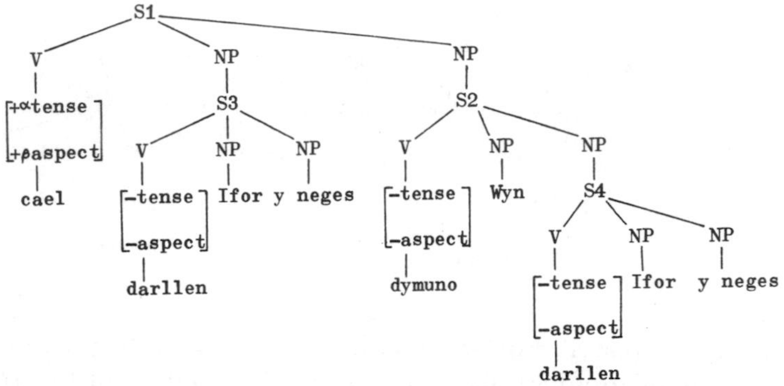

4.2.3 Tenseless embeddings as agent Tenseless embeddings may not appear as the agent of the passive. This is true of embeddings without an overt subject as in (34) and (35), and of embeddings with an overt subject as in (36) and (37).

(34) Mae mynd yno wedi cyffroi pawb.
Is going there after angering everyone.

(35) *Cafodd pawb eu cyffroi gan fynd yno.
Got everyone their angering by going there.

(36) Mae wedi cyffroi pawb iddo fynd yno.
Is after angering everyone for him going there.

(37) *Cafodd pawb eu cyffroi gan iddo fynd yno.
Got everyone their angering by for him going there.

The verb *cyffroi* (anger) is neither nonagentive nor stative, as can be seen from (38) and (39).

(38) Cyffrowch bawb!
Anger everyone!

(39) Darfu iddo gyffroi pawb.
Happened for him angering everyone.

Indeed it can appear in the passive if the agent is different, as in (40).

(40) Cafodd y plant eu cyffroi gan yr hanes.
Got the children their angering by the story.

It seems that the ungrammaticality of (35) and (37) is due to the fact that the agent is a tenseless embedding.

The restriction can easily be enforced by restricting T. Agent Postposing to noun phrases not containing a tenseless embedding. But it is not clear why such a restriction should exist since it does not reflect a general restriction on tenseless embeddings as object of a preposition. Such forms as (41) and (42) are fully grammatical. There is no overt subject in the embedding in (41), but there is in (42).

(41) Hiraethai Wyn am ddychwelyd.
Longed Wyn for returning.

(42) Hiraethai Wyn am i Ann ddychwelyd.
Longed Wyn for for Ann returning.[3]

4.2.4 Tensed embedding as subject Some informants find passives with a tensed embedding as subject of the passive grammatical, and these forms were discussed above in section 3.3 on this basis. Other informants find these forms ungrammatical, and for them the passive must be suitably restricted. It is not clear how best to do this. One possibility is to restrict T. Agent Postposing so that it will not move the subject noun phrase over an embedding which contains a tensed verb. An alternative possibility is that there be a selection restriction on *cael* to prevent it having a tensed embedding as subject.

Even to those informants who find the examples discussed in section 3.3 grammatical, other examples with a different matrix verb are less acceptable. For example, if the matrix verb is *gofyn* (ask) or *dweud* (say) as in (43) and (44), then the passive is less acceptable than if the matrix verb is *cyhoeddi* (announce), as in section 3.3.

(43) *Cafodd ei gofyn gan Ifor a oedd pawb yno.
Got its asking by Ifor whether was everyone there.

(44) *Cafodd ei dweud gan Ifor fod pawb yno.
Got its saying by Ifor being everyone there.

The problem with these forms seems to be partly a matter of the individual verbs involved and partly a matter of the tensed embedding. It appears however that it is more a question of the embedding than the verb, since (45) and (46) where the verbs *gofyn* (ask) and *dweud* (say) are found with a nonembedded subject in the passive, are better than (43) and (44).

(45) Cafodd y cwestiwn ei ofyn gan Ifor.
Got the question its asking by Ifor.

(46) Cafodd yr ateb ei ddweud gan Ifor.
Got the answer its saying by Ifor.

Even for those speakers who find all passives with a tensed embedding as subject ungrammatical, the bulk of the analysis in sections 3.3 and 3.4 still holds. T. Sentence Postposing must still be a postcyclic rule in order to account for the periphrastic active forms. And so rules which follow it must also be postcyclic.

4.2.5 Tensed embeddings as agent Tensed embeddings, like tenseless embeddings, may not appear as the agent of the passive.

(47) *Cafodd pawb eu cyffroi gan nad oedd Ifor wedi dod.
Got everyone their angering by not was Ifor after coming.
i.e. Everyone was angered by that Ifor had not come.

(48) *Cafodd pawb eu cyffroi gan fod Ifor wedi dod.
Got everyone their angering by being Ifor after coming.

In section 3.4.2 it was suggested that tensed embeddings can be postposed out of a prepositional phrase, with the preposition being eventually deleted. In the case of the passive forms, if the tensed embedding is postposed out of the agent prepositional phrase and the preposition is deleted the output is as shown in (49) and (50).

(49) *Cafodd pawb eu cyffroi nad oedd Ifor wedi dod.
Got everyone their angering not was Ifor after coming.

(50) *Cafodd pawb eu cyffroi fod Ifor wedi dod.
Got everyone their angering being Ifor after coming.

These forms are ungrammatical however. It seems that the tensed embedding cannot have been moved into the prepositional phrase by T. Agent Postposing in the first place. In section 4.2.3 T. Agent Postposing was restricted so that it would not move a noun phrase subject dominating a tenseless embedding. This restriction must now be extended to noun phrases dominating a tensed embedding. This is in fact a simplification, since it is now only the presence of an embedding which matters, not its internal composition.

4.2.6 Direct speech as subject Direct speech quotations may appear as the object of the active, but not as the subject of an equivalent passive, as in (51) and (52).

(51) Cyhoeddodd Emyr 'Mae pawb yn dod'.
Announced Emyr 'Is everyone in coming'.

(52) *Cafodd 'Mae pawb yn dod' ei chyhoeddi gan Emyr.
Got 'Is everyone in coming' its announcing by Emyr.

Nor may the question appear as subject of the passive if it is postposed to the right as in (53).

(53) *Cafodd ei chyhoeddi gan Emyr 'Mae pawb yn dod'.
Got its announcing by Emyr 'Is everyone in coming'.

For those who find tensed embeddings ungrammatical as subject of the passive it may be possible to extend this restriction to direct speech forms too, since they are in a way tensed embeddings.

This is not possible for those who find tensed embeddings grammatical as subject of the passive. There is evidence however that though direct speech quotations may be tensed embeddings, they nevertheless differ from the tensed embeddings considered in section 4.2.4. Quite how they differ is not clear, but they do undergo certain rules which do not affect tensed embeddings which are not quotations. For instance, quotations can be preposed to the left to sentence-initial position as in (54), but non-quotations cannot.

(54) 'Mae pawb yn dod' cyhoeddodd Emyr.
'Is everyone in coming' announced Emyr.

(55) *Fod pawb yn dod cyhoeddodd Emyr.
Being everyone in coming announced Emyr.

Similarly, in the case of quotations the verb and subject of the matrix sentence can be inserted in the middle of the quotation, as in (56). This is not possible in the case of other tensed embeddings.

(56) 'Mae pawb', cyhoeddodd Emyr, 'yn dod'.
'Is everyone', announced Emyr, 'in coming'.

(57) *Fod pawb, cyhoeddodd Emyr, yn dod.
Being everyone, announced Emyr, in coming.

It is necessary therefore to distinguish between quotations and other tensed embeddings in order to account for the difference in grammaticality between the forms (54) and (55) and the forms (56) and (57).

This difference can also be invoked to account for the difference in grammaticality between passives with quotations as subject and passives with other tensed embeddings as subject. The restriction here too must either prevent T. Agent Postposing from moving a noun phrase subject over this type of object, or prevent *cael* from having this type of subject.

This latter restriction seems to be the more independently motivated here, since quotations never appear as subject of an active transitive verb. As a result the question of quotations appearing as agent of the passive does not arise.

4.2.7 Embeddings summarised Embeddings then are very strongly restricted in the passive, both as subject and agent. No embeddings may appear as agent of the passive and the T. Agent Postposing must be appropriately constrained.

The position over subject embeddings is less clear cut. Quotations from direct speech seem ungrammatical to all speakers, as do tenseless subjectless embeddings. It is not possible to say how tenseless embeddings with an overt subject would be judged. Tensed embeddings are differently judged by different informants, with some people finding all of them ungrammatical, and others accepting at least some.

For those who reject all tensed embeddings in passive subject position a blanket restriction may be postulated which applies to all embeddings in this position. This covers tensed, tenseless and quotation forms. It makes individual restrictions on such forms as tenseless subjectless embeddings unnecessary, and implies that tenseless embeddings with an overt subject will be ungrammatical as subject of the passive even given a suitable matrix verb. The restriction may either limit the application of T. Agent Postposing or impose a selection restriction on *cael* (get) to rule out subject embeddings.

For those who do accept at least some tensed embeddings in passive subject position, a more piecemeal approach is needed on the lines of the restrictions suggested above in sections 4.2.1 to 4.2.6.

4.3 Restrictions on pronouns

4.3.1 Reflexive pronouns as subject The subject of the passive may not be a reflexive pronoun, as in (58).

(58) *Cafodd ef ei hun ei rybuddio gan Wyn.
Got himself his warning by Wyn.

This can be explained as a straightforward consequence of the way T. Reflexivisation operates. In a sentence such as (59) where there are two identical noun phrases, T. Reflexivisation turns the rightmost one of the two into a reflexive pronoun to give (60).

(59)

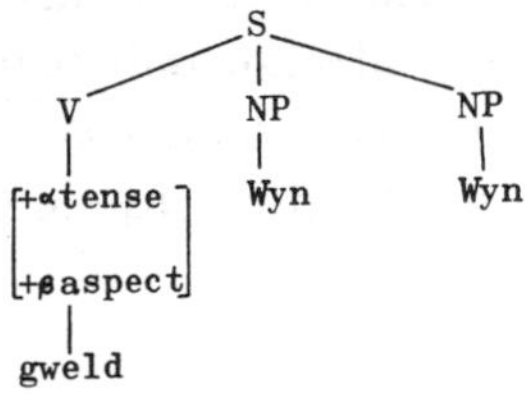

(60) Gwelodd Wyn ef ei hun.
Saw Wyn himself.

It may not operate in the reverse direction, giving the output (61) with the subject as a reflexive pronoun.

(61) *Gwelodd ef ei hun Wyn.
Saw himself Wyn.

The passive (58) is ruled out in the same way as the active (61). It could only be generated by allowing T. Reflexivisation to apply backwards to the underlying form (62).

(62)

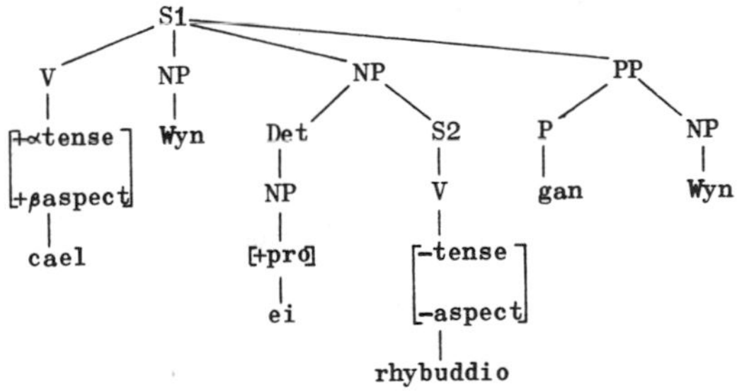

No new constraints are needed here.

4.3.2 Reflexive pronouns as agent A reflexive pronoun may not appear either as agent of the passive, as in (63).

(63) *Cafodd Wyn ei rybuddio ganddo ef ei hun.
Got Wyn his warning by himself.

Here it appears that T. Reflexivisation has applied normally, pronominalising the rightmost noun phrase. This is therefore no explanation for the ungrammaticality of (63). This ungrammaticality can however be explained as a result of another aspect of the normal operation of T. Reflexivisation.

It appears that this rule should apply cyclically, since this gives the simplest formulation. It can be formulated as affecting only pairs of noun phrases within one simple sentence, pronominalising the second of these two noun phrases. It can thus apply to the structure (64) to give (65).

(64)

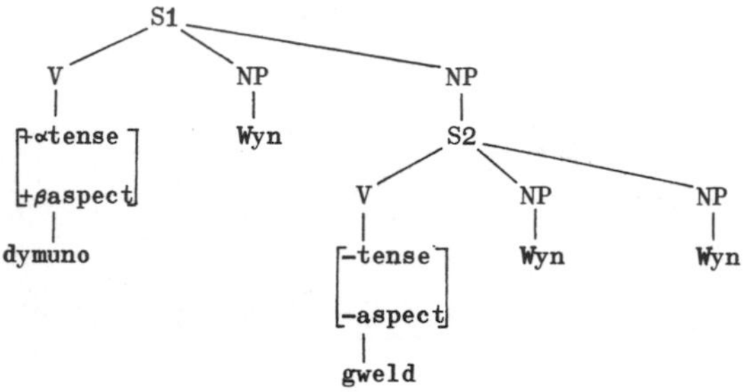

(65) Dymuna Wyn ei weld ei hun.
Wants Wyn his seeing himself.

On the S2 cycle there are two identical noun phrases within the S2 simple sentence. It cannot however apply to the structure (66) to give (67), since the two identical noun phrases are not within the same simple sentence. One is in S2 and one in S1.

(66)

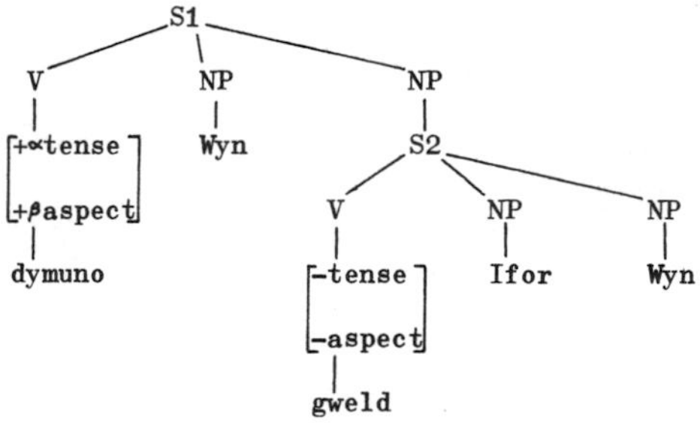

(67) *Dymuna Wyn i Ifor ei weld ei hun.
Wants Wyn for Ifor his seeing him.

The correct surface structure realisation of (66) is (68) where there is no reflexive pronoun.

(68) Dymuna Wyn i Ifor ei weld ef.
Wants Wyn for Ifor his seeing him.

If T. Reflexivisation applies postcyclically on the other hand, it becomes more difficult to distinguish between cases like (65) and cases like (68). T. Equi-Subject Deletion has already applied to convert (64) into (69), where the two remaining noun phrases are not in the same simple sentence.

(69)

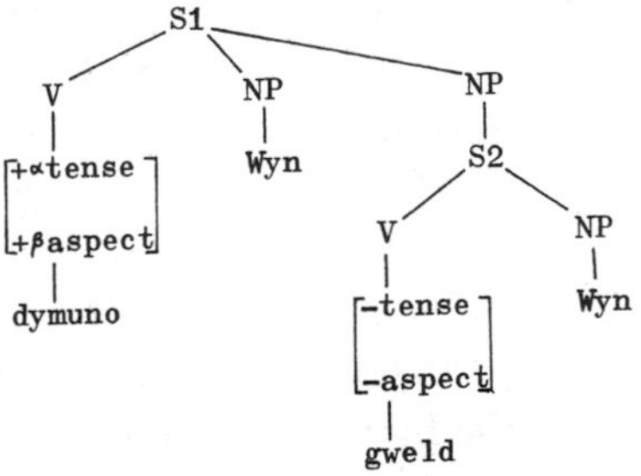

There is no obvious way now of distinguishing between (69) which underlies (65) and (66) which underlies (68). In both the two noun phrases are in different simple sentences. Yet they must be differently affected by T. Reflexivisation, which must apply in the case of (69) but not in the case of (66). This problem is avoided if T. Reflexivisation is a cyclic rule.

An explanation may now be offered for the ungrammaticality of the passive form (63). The deep structure of this passive is (70).

(70)

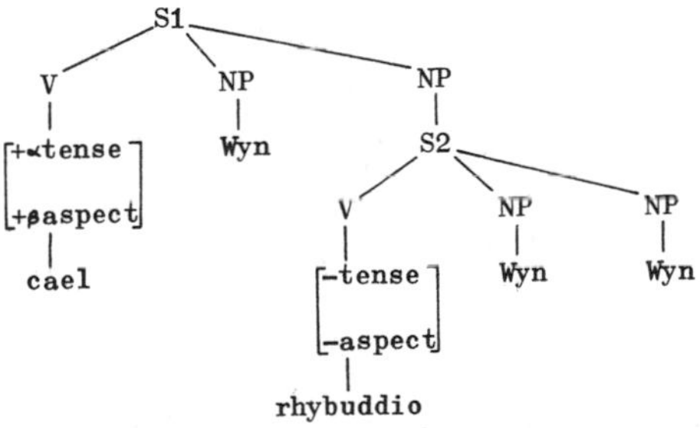

On the S2 cycle T. Reflexivisation applies, converting (70) into (71) with a reflexive pronoun as object of the embedding.

(71)

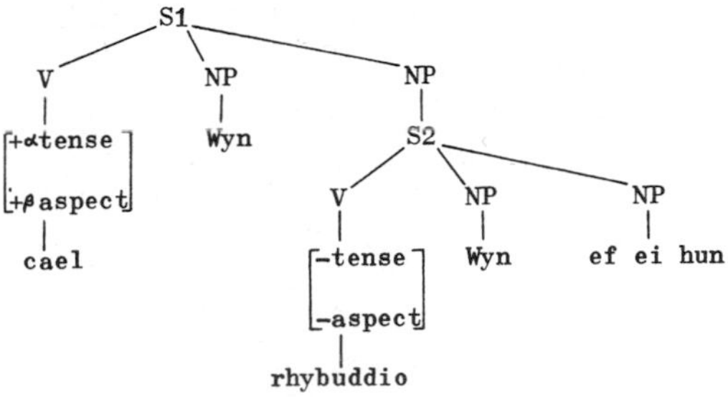

When the S1 cycle is reached and T. Agent Postposing should apply, the subject of the matrix sentence is no longer identical to the object of the embedding, and the structural description of this rule is not met. It cannot apply and so no passive output can appear in surface structure. (63) is therefore ruled out.

This derivation in fact casts further light on the ungrammatical form (58) with the reflexive pronoun in subject position. This form too must be derived from the deep structure (70), with T. Reflexivisation applying on the S2 cycle to give (71). Here too then T. Agent Postposing rule is blocked and the passive cannot be generated. It was pointed out in section 4.3.1 that T. Reflexivisation must apply backwards to the tree (62) to generate (58). Now it is clear that the tree (62) itself cannot be generated because of the block on T. Agent Postposing. (58) is therefore doubly ungrammatical. It is blocked in the same way as (63), and in addition involves backwards application of T. Reflexivisation on the tree which has been ruled out.[4]

4.3.3 An alternative reflexive form Some verbs can be reflexivised in two different ways. Either the object noun phrase is changed into a reflexive pronoun as in the examples discussed so far, or a different rule is applied. This converts (72) into (73).

(72)

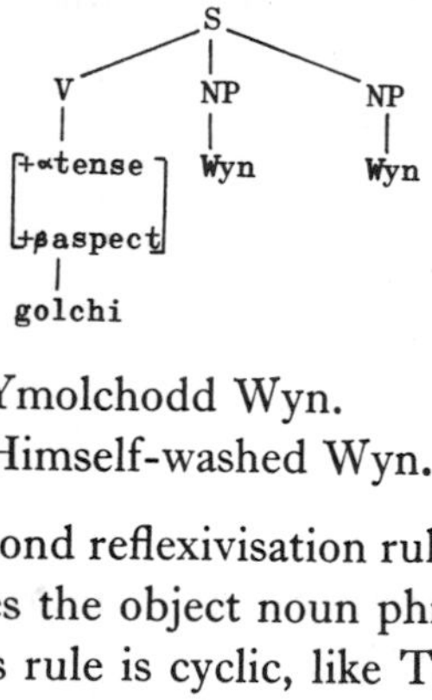

(73) Ymolchodd Wyn.
Himself-washed Wyn.

This second reflexivisation rule applies only to a small number of verbs. It deletes the object noun phrase and adds the prefix *ym-* to the verb.

If this rule is cyclic, like T. Reflexivisation, then the failure of such forms to appear in the passive can be explained simply. The deep structure of the passive is (74).

(74)

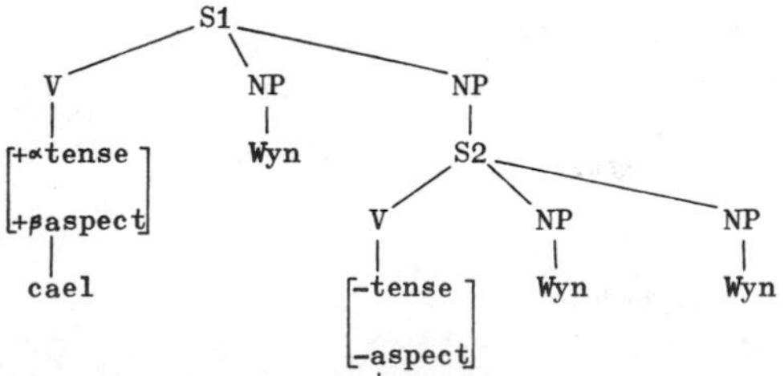

On the S2 cycle the reflexivising rule applies to give (75).

(75)

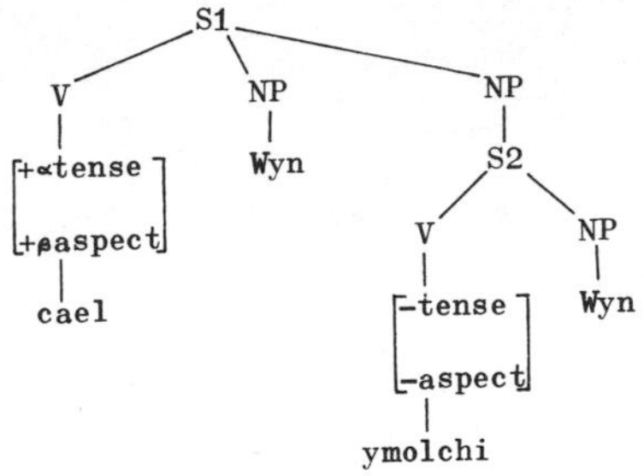

When T. Agent Postposing is reached on the S1 cycle it is blocked, as there is no object noun phrase in the embedding to be identical to the subject of the matrix.

4.3.4 Reciprocal pronouns as subject The subject of the passive may not be a reciprocal pronoun, as in (76).

(76) *Cafodd ei gilydd eu rhybuddio gan Wyn ac Ifor.
Got each other their warning by Wyn and Ifor.

This is the passive equivalent of (77).

(77) Rhybuddiodd Wyn ac Ifor ei gilydd.
Warned Wyn and Ifor each other.

As in the case of reflexive subjects, the ungrammaticality of the passive (76) can be explained as a result of the way T. Reciprocalisation operates. It derives (77) from (78), by turning the rightmost noun phrase into a reciprocal pronoun.

(78)

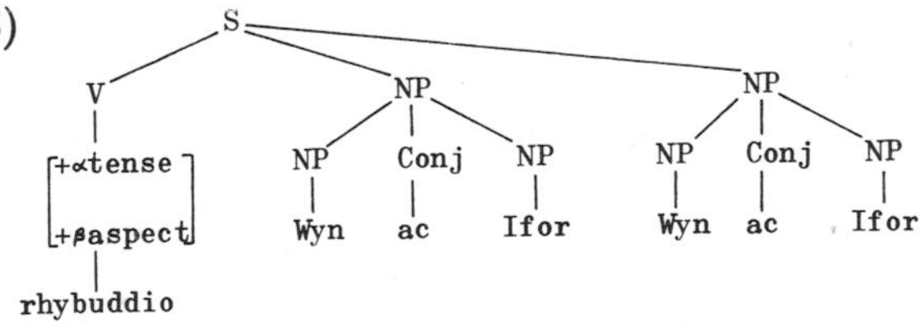

It may not operate in the other direction to give (79) with a reciprocal pronoun as subject.

(79) *Rhybuddiodd ei gilydd Wyn ac Ifor.
Warned each other Wyn and Ifor.

In order to derive the passive (76) T. Reciprocalisation would have to apply backwards to the tree (80).

(80)

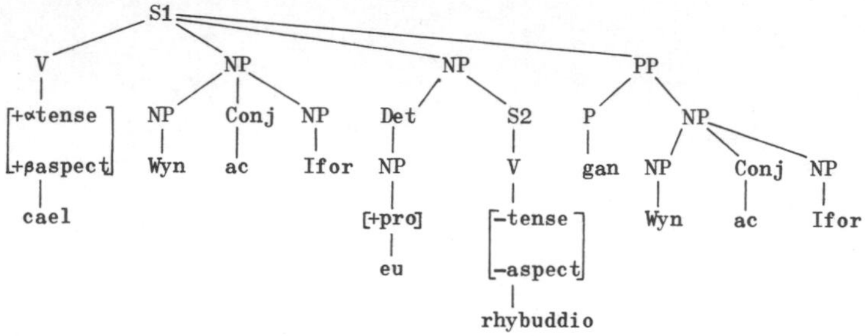

It is ungrammatical in the same way as the active (79) is ungrammatical.

4.3.5 Reciprocal pronouns as agent A reciprocal pronoun cannot appear, either, as agent of the passive, as in (81), which also corresponds to the active (77).

(81) *Cafodd Wyn ac Ifor eu rhybuddio gan ei gilydd.
Got Wyn and Ifor their warning by each other.

Again as in the case of reflexive agents, it is not possible to explain the ungrammaticality of this form so easily since T. Reciprocalisation applies in the correct direction, pronominalising the rightmost noun phrase.

It may be possible to extend the parallelism between reflexive and reciprocal forms to account for this form too. This depends on the assumption that at some point in the derivation of (81) the tree structure is (82).

(82)

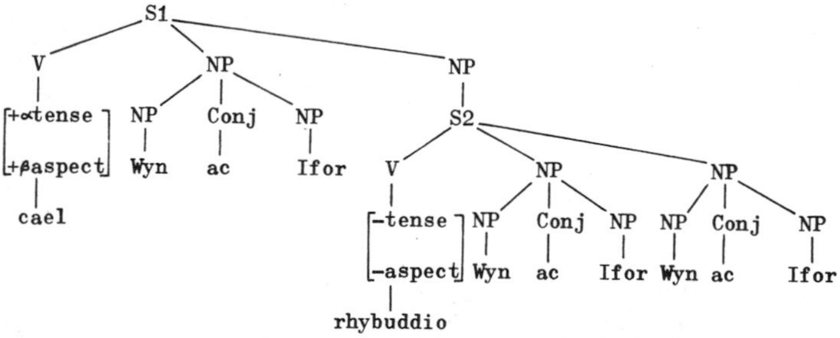

It appears that T. Reciprocalisation should be a cyclic rule, like T. Reflexivisation, and for similar reasons. If it is a cyclic rule then it can be formulated as applying to pairs of noun phrases within a simple sentence, pronominalising the second of the two. For instance, it applies to (83) to give (84).

(83)

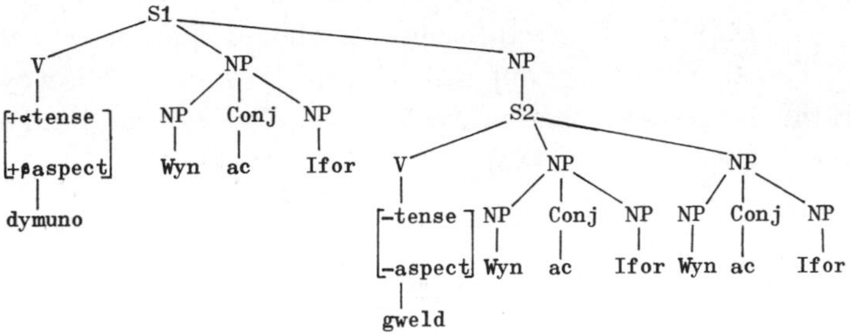

(84) Dymuna Wyn ac Ifor weld ei gilydd.
Want Wyn and Ifor seeing each other.

On the S2 cycle of (83)there are two suitable noun phrases within a simple sentence. There is no such pair within a simple sentence in (85).

(85)

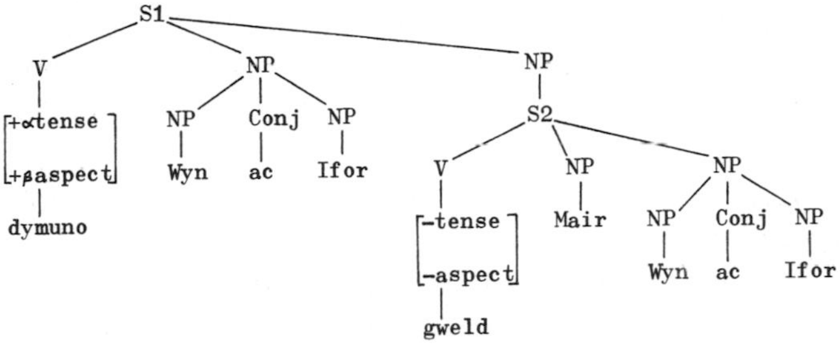

T. Reciprocalisation cannot apply to give (86) with a reciprocal pronoun as object of the embedding.

(86) *Dymuna Wyn ac Ifor i Mair weld ei gilydd.
Want Wyn and Ifor for Mair seeing each other.

The correct output from (85) is (87) with no reciprocal pronoun.

(87) Dymuna Wyn ac Ifor i Mair eu gweld.
Want Wyn and Ifor for Mair their seeing.

On a cyclic view of T. Reciprocalisation the difference between (83) and (85) is easily expressed.

If T. Reciprocalisation is a postcyclic rule, however, problems arise in distinguishing between these forms. T. Equi-Subject Deletion has already converted (83) into (88).

(88)

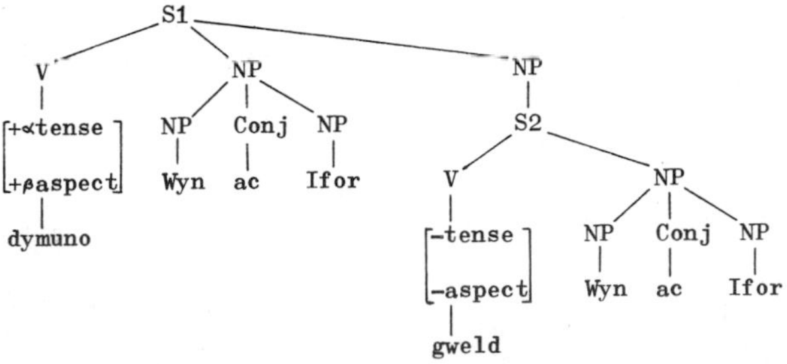

The two relevant noun phrases are now in different simple sentences just as in (85). Yet T. Reciprocalisation should apply to (88) and not to (85). This difficulty does not arise if T. Reciprocalisation is a cyclic rule.

If this is the case then, on the S2 cycle, T. Reciprocalisation applies to the passive structure (82), giving the output (89).

(89)

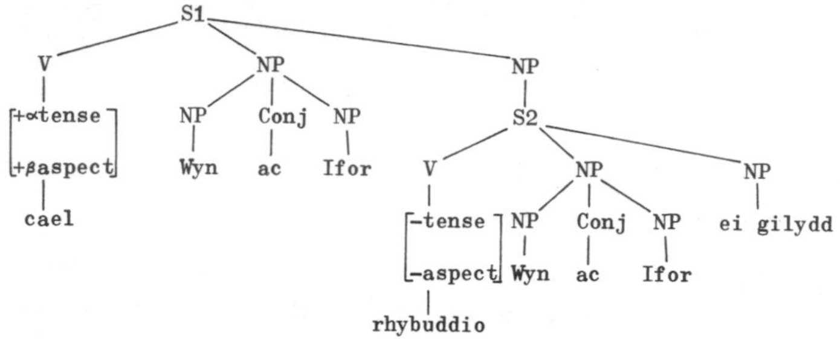

The subject of the matrix and the object of the embedding are no longer identical and on the S1 cycle T. Agent Postposing is blocked. The passive (81) cannot be derived.

This analysis of T. Reciprocalisation has in turn implications for the passive form (76) where the reciprocal pronoun is the subject. It has already been pointed out in section 4.3.4 that this form involves backwards application of T. Reciprocalisation to the tree (80). Now however it becomes clear that (80) itself cannot be generated. The structure of the passive (76) is (82). This is converted by T. Reciprocalisation into (89). At this point T. Agent Postposing is blocked, so the passive tree (80) cannot be derived. There is here a double violation then, with a rule applying in the wrong way to a tree that cannot be derived.[5]

4.3.6 Pronouns summarised The position over reflexive and reciprocal forms is very similar then. In each case the restrictions on the passive follow naturally from the application of the pronominalisation rule. The cyclic application of this rule prevents the passive being realised since it blocks T. Agent Postposing. The reflexive and reciprocal pronoun therefore do not appear in agent position. They are excluded from subject position not only by this general constraint but also because this would require backwards application of T. Reflexivisation and T. Reciprocalisation.

4.4 Additional syntactic restrictions

4.4.1 Prepositional objects Some verbs take a prepositional object rather than a direct object, such as in (90).

(90) Gofalodd y ci am y defaid.
Looked the dog after the sheep.

The passive equivalents of such forms are felt in some cases to be marginally grammatical, though reactions vary. The passive (91) is one of the more acceptable forms.

(91) Cafodd y defaid eu gofalu amdanynt gan y ci.
Got the sheep their looking after them by the dog.

Such passives can be derived in a very similar way to normal passives. The deep structure of (91) is that shown in (92).

(92)

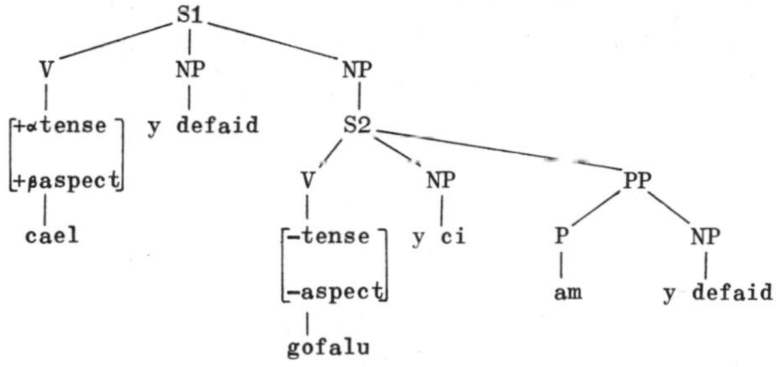

This is identical to the deep structure of the normal passive except that the subject of the matrix sentence is identical to the prepositional object of the embedding rather than the direct object. T. Agent Postposing applies here too, with its structural description generalised to allow for a prepositional object, to give (93).

(93)

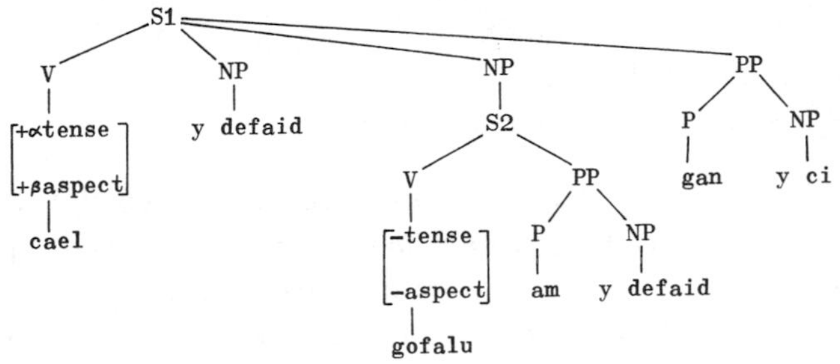

The prepositional object is pronominalised on identity with the subject of the matrix, and the preposition is inflected to agree with the pronoun object, as in such active forms as (94).

(94) Dymuna Ifor i bawb sôn amdano.
Wants Ifor for everyone speaking about him.

T. Possessive Pronoun Preposing applies to give a copy of the pronoun to the left of the uninflected verb, and the pronoun in the original position is obligatorily deleted. (95) where the pronoun is still overt is ungrammatical.

(95) *Cafodd y defaid eu gofalu amdanynt hwy gan y ci.
Got the sheep their looking after them by the dog.

Morphological and mutation rules apply as usual. These forms differ from normal passives then only in the addition of rules to give the correct form of the prepositional phrase. They differ however from other prepositional phrase forms. In no other such form is the pronoun object preposed as it is here. (96) where the pronoun has been preposed is ungrammatical.

(96) *Dymuna Ifor i bawb ei sôn amdano ef.
Wants Ifor for everyone his speaking about him.

It may be this attempt to combine the structure of the passive with the rather different structure characteristic of a prepositional phrase that makes these forms so marginal.

Even informants who accept some prepositional objects in passives reject others however. For instance the passive (97) which corresponds to the active (98) seems to be generally rejected.

(97) *Câi'r canu ei wrando arno gan Ifor.
Was getting the singing its listening to it by Ifor.

(98) Gwrandawai Ifor ar y canu.
Was listening Ifor to the singing.

It is not clear why there should be a difference in acceptability between *gofalu am* (look after) and *gwrando ar* (listen to). Otherwise they seem to be identical in syntax. For those informants who reject all prepositional objects the restriction is easily handled by limiting T. Agent Postposing to verbs taking direct objects.

4.4.2 Adverbs Some verbs take a noun phrase which appears in normal object position and undergoes soft mutation like a direct object, but yet cannot be the subject of an equivalent passive. For instance (99), the passive equivalent of (100), is ungrammatical.

(99) *Cafodd milltiroedd eu cerdded gan Luned.
Got miles their walking by Luned.

(100) Cerddodd Luned filltiroedd.
Walked Luned miles.

The verb here is agentive and nonstative, as can be seen from (101) and (102). Some other reason must therefore be found for the ungrammaticality of (99).

(101) Cerddwch filltiroedd!
Walk miles!

(102) Darfu i Luned gerdded filltiroedd.
Happened for Luned walking miles.

One possible alternative explanation is that these noun phrases should be analysed as a type of adverb. If so they will not meet the structural description of T. Agent Postposing and the passive will not be generated. This view is supported by the fact that the same verbs as take this type of noun phrase, such as *cerdded* (walk), can also take adverbs of degree freely as in (103).

(103) Cerddodd Luned yn bell.
Walked Luned far.

These adverbs may not co-occur with the noun phrases as in (104), suggesting that the two are instances of the same category.

(104) *Cerddodd Luned filltiroedd yn bell.
Walked Luned miles far.

Similarly, prepositional phrases which can alternate with adverbs of place, direction and so on may not appear in passive equivalents, even for those informants who accept passive forms with *gofalu am* (look after). For instance the prepositional phrase in (105) alternates with the adverb in (106).

(105) Rhedodd Wyn at y tŷ.
Ran Wyn to the house.

(106) Rhedodd Wyn yno.
Ran Wyn there.

They cannot co-occur as in (107), suggesting that they are instances of the same category.

(107) *Rhedodd Wyn at y tŷ yno.
Ran Wyn to the house there.

The passive equivalent of (105) is ungrammatical.

(108) *Cafodd y tŷ ei redeg ato gan Wyn.
Got the house its running to it by Wyn.

If the prepositional phrase is an adverb then here too the lack of a passive can be explained, as the structural description of T. Agent Postposing is not met.

4.5 Idioms

Idiomatic forms are very strongly constrained and do not appear freely in passive forms. In this they differ from their literal equivalents.

For instance, if an idiom is formed of a verb and its direct object as in (109) then it may not appear in the passive form as in (110).

(109) Mae Ifor wedi rhoi'r ffidil yn y tô.
Is Ifor after putting the fiddle in the roof.
i.e. Ifor has given up.
(110) *Mae'r ffidil wedi cael ei rhoi yn y tô gan Ifor.
Is the ffiddle after getting its putting in the roof by Ifor.

(110) is grammatical in its literal meaning but not in its idiomatic meaning. Similarly, if the idiom is formed of a verb, its object and a preposition, with the object of the preposition not in the idiom, then the object of the verb cannot be the subject of a passive form. An example of this is (111), whose passive form (112) is ungrammatical.

(111) Mae Huw wedi achub y blaen ar Wyn,
Is Huw after saving the front on Wyn.
i.e. Huw has beaten Wyn.
(112) *Mae'r blaen wedi cael ei achub ar Wyn gan Huw.
Is the front after getting its saving on Wyn by Huw.

Since this idiom has no literal meaning (112) is meaningless.

Lakoff (1971) discusses the failure of idioms to appear in the *get* passive in English, as in the pair (113) and (114).

(113) The police kept tabs on John.
(114) *Tabs got kept on John by the police.

She suggests (p. 153) a very similar structure for these *get* passives to the one suggested here for *cael* passives in Welsh. She explains the ungrammaticallity of such forms as (114) as being due to the isolation of the subject noun phrase from the rest of the idiom in deep structure and its failurc to get a correct idiomatic interpretation. There is then a conflict between the literal interpretation of the subject noun phrase and the idiomatic interpretation of the embedding. This explanation seems to work for the Welsh forms too, and in making the restriction a semantic one it avoids the problem of specifying syntactically that any unit is an idiom. There does not seem to be any way of telling if a sentence is an idiom or a literal form on the purely syntactic level.

Another factor which may be involved is also semantic. In the idiomatic forms (109) and (111) the object noun phrase is not a separate unit as in a normal sentence, but is rather part of the verbal form. For instance in (109) the verb and object together are equivalent to a simple intransitive verb *gorffen* (finish), and in (111) the verb and object and preposition together are equivalent to a simple transitive verb *curo* (beat). It is not clear how this data should be formalised, especially since the object noun phrase is treated just like a normal noun phrase object for many rules such as mutation. Nor is this carried to the logical conclusion as it is in English. If the verb and object and preposition are equivalent to a transitive verb, then one might expect the prepositional object to resemble the object of a transitive verb and to appear as subject of the passive. This is grammatical in English in such forms as (115).

(115) John got kept tabs on by the police.

But in Welsh the equivalent passive of (111) is ungrammatical.

(116) *Cafodd Wyn ei achub y blaen arno gan Huw.
Got Wyn his saving the front on him by Huw.

The same restrictions appear in the case of sentences containing a dummy verb and an object noun phrase related to another verb. For instance, the dummy verb and object of (117) are equivalent to the verb of (118).

(117) Mae hi'n bwrw glaw.
Is it in throwing rain.

(118) Mae hi'n glawio.
Is it in raining.

And in (119) the verb, object and preposition of the sentence are equivalent to the verb and preposition of (120).

(119) Mae Ifor yn talu sylw i'r plant.
Is Ifor in paying attention to the children.
(120) Mae Ifor yn sylwi ar y plant.
Is Ifor in attending to the children.

Neither (117) nor (119) has a passive equivalent.

(121) *Mae glaw yn cael ei fwrw ganddi.
Is rain in getting its throwing by it.
(122) *Mae sylw yn cael ei dalu i'r plant gan Ifor.
Is attention in getting its paying to the children by Ifor.

These forms do not seem idiomatic to the same degree as those discussed above, since there is a regular link between the verb of the one sentence and the object of the other. The dummy verb however is to some extent given an idiomatic reading in forms like (117) and (119).

4.6 Conclusions

The restrictions discussed in this chapter vary in type. Some follow naturally from the analysis of passives given in Chapters 2 and 3. Examples are the lack of verbs with no uninflected form, the lack of verbs taking a prepositional object or an adverb, and the lack of idiomatic forms. Other restrictions follow from the interaction of the passive analysis with the application of other rules. In this way the lack of tenseless subjectless embeddings as subject of the passive can be explained as due to the interaction of the passive and T. Equi-Subject Deletion, and the lack of reflexive and reciprocal pronouns can be explained by the interaction of the passive and T. Reflexivisation and T. Reciprocalisation.

Other restrictions cannot be explained in this way and it proves necessary to add further restrictions to the passive. In this way it is ensured that the passive is limited to verbs which are [+agentive] and [−stative]. And it is in this way too that tensed embeddings are ruled out as subject or agent of the passive, and tenseless embeddings are ruled out as agent. Some of these additional restrictions can be formulated in one of two ways, as a restriction on T. Agent Postposing or as a selectional restriction on the verb *cael* (get). Some evidence in favour of the first possibility will be presented in Chapter 5, section 5.2.2 and some in favour of the second possibility in Chapter 6, section 6.2.2.

5 *Other agent transformations*

It was pointed out in section 2.7 that most of the rules required in the derivation of the passive are independently needed in the derivation of other forms. In this chapter the possibility is explored that T. Agent Postposing is also independently needed. Three constructions are examined where it appears that the subject noun phrase is postposed into a prepositional phrase as object of the preposition *gan* (by). These are impersonal passives, certain adjectival constructions, and certain nominal constructions. In each case the movement transformation is formulated and compared with T. Agent Postposing.

5.1 Impersonal passives

5.1.1 Impersonal passives Just as there are pairs of synonymous active and passive sentences, so there are also pairs of synonymous active and impersonal passive sentences. Examples are given in (1) to (6).

(1) Rhybuddiodd y dyn y plant.
Warned the man the children.
(2) Rhybuddiwyd y plant gan y dyn.
Warned the children by the man.
(3) Rhybuddiai'r dyn y plant.
Was warning the man the children.
(4) Rhybuddid y plant gan y dyn.
Was warning the children by the man.
(5) Rhybuddia'r dyn y plant.
Warns the man the children.
(6) Rhybuddir y plant gan y dyn.
Warns the children by the man.

In fact the impersonal passives are traditionally considered equivalent to the *cael* passives though stylistically superior to them.[1]

In each case, the impersonal passive form consists of an inflected verb corresponding to the verb of the active, followed by a noun phrase identical to the object noun phrase of the active, and a prepositional phrase consisting of the preposition *gan* (by) and a noun phrase identical to the subject of the active. The inflection of the verb in the impersonal passive is different from that of the active but still varies for tense and aspect. This relation is summarised in (7), where identical items are marked with the same subscript number.

(7)

Active	V_1 (inflection$_4$)	NP_2	NP_3	
Impersonal Passive	V_1 (inflection$_5$)	NP_3	gan	NP_2

The selection restrictions on the noun phrases in the active and impersonal passive are identical. Where the subject and object noun phrases are acceptable in the active, they are also acceptable in the corresponding impersonal passive, as in (1) to (6). Where they are not acceptable in the active then they are not acceptable either in the impersonal passive, as in (8) to (11).

(8) *Rhybuddiodd y bwrdd y plant.
Warned the table the children.
(9) *Rhybuddiwyd y plant gan y bwrdd.
Warned the children by the table.

(10) *Rhybuddiodd y dyn y llyfr.
Warned the man the book.
(11) *Rhybuddiwyd y llyfr gan y dyn.
Warned the book by the man.

The noun phrase *bwrdd* (table) is unacceptable as subject of the active (8) and also following *gan* in the impersonal passive (9). The noun phrase *llyfr* (book) is unacceptable as object of the active form (10) and also in the impersonal passive (11).

This identity of selection restrictions and the regular formal correspondence of the active and the impersonal passive can be explained if they are transformationally related. If the deep structure of the impersonal passive is the same as the active then the identical selection restrictions follow. In order to account for the reversed ordering of the impersonal passive, a movement transformation is needed to move the subject noun phrase to the right of the object into a prepositional phrase as object of *gan* (by). But in order to formulate this movement transformation it is necessary to consider in more detail the surface structure of the impersonal passive.

5.1.2 The surface structure In the case of the *cael* (get) passive forms the object noun phrase of the active appears as subject of the passive equivalent. Is this also the case in the impersonal passive? It might at first sight appear so since the noun phrase corresponding to the object of the active appears in the impersonal passive immediately following the verb, that is in the normal subject position. There are however problems with this analysis of the noun phrase.

It was shown in section 1.1.2 that the verb normally agrees with a following pronoun subject in person and number. In the impersonal passive no such agreement is found between the verb and the immediately following noun phrase, as can be seen from (12) to (14).

(12) Rhybuddiwyd fi gan y dyn.
Warned me by the man.
(13) Rhybuddiwyd ni gan y dyn.
Warned us by the man.
(14) Rhybuddiwyd chwi gan y dyn.
Warned you by the man.

In these forms the noun phrase following the verb is a pronoun varying in person and number. (12) and (13) differ in number, while (13) and (14) differ in person. Yet the verbal inflection remains the same in each case.

While this would be exceptional if the noun phrase following the verb was the subject of the sentence, it would be normal if this noun phrase was the object. In (15) to (17) the object of the active is a pronoun which varies in number and person, but the verbal inflection remains the same in spite of this variation.

(15) Gwelais ef.
Saw (I) him.
(16) Gwelais hwy.
Saw (I) them.
(17) Gwelais chwi.
Saw (I) you.

In this then the noun phrase following the verb in the impersonal passive resembles an object rather than a subject.

This noun phrase displays another pattern characteristic of a pronoun object. It may appear following the verb as in (12) or both preceding and following it as in (18).

(18) Fe'm rhybuddiwyd i gan y dyn.
Assertion: me warned me by the man.

Further, the pronoun following the verb may be missing, giving the form (19) with only a pronoun preceding the verb.

(19) Fe'm rhybuddiwyd gan y dyn.
Assertion: me warned by the man.

It was pointed out in section 1.2.3 that this pattern is found only with the object of the inflected verb following the assertion marker *fe*.

There are also morphological parallelisms between the pronoun object here and the object of an active sentence. Both are independent pronouns rather than confirming pronouns. (12) with an independent pronoun is grammatical, but (20) with a confirming pronoun is not.

(20) *Rhybuddiwyd i gan y dyn.
Warned me by the man.

Compare these two with the active forms (21) and (22).

(21) Gwelodd y dyn fi.
Saw the man me.

(22) *Gwelodd y dyn i.
Saw the man me.

The subject pronoun of the active is however a confirming pronoun, as in (23).

(23) Gwelais i y dyn.
Saw I the man.

This parallelism is not however very important. When the distinction between the two types of pronoun was pointed out in section 2.6.8, it was shown that the choice of which type appears in a particular environment depends on whether there has been a previous mention of the pronoun. The choice of an independent pronoun in the impersonal passive merely reflects the fact already mentioned that the verb does not agree with the following noun phrase. There is therefore no previous mention of the pronoun in the sentence and so the independent form of the pronoun is chosen. There is here no new evidence for an object analysis. Significantly, in (18) where there is a preposed pronoun form of the object, the pronoun following the verb is a confirming pronoun.

There is a problem however in the object analysis, which arises in the case of nouns. It is normally the case that a direct object noun phrase appears in soft mutation form if its initial sound is subject to this change, as was said in section 1.1.3. In (24) the noun *plant* (children) is mutated to *blant*.

(24) Rhybuddiodd y dyn blant Ifor.
Warned the man (the) children (of) Ifor.

In the corresponding impersonal passive however the noun retains its isolation form.

(25) Rhybuddiwyd plant Ifor gan y dyn.
Warned (the) children (of) Ifor by the man.

In this lack of mutation then the noun resembles the subject of an active rather than the object.

It might be suggested that although a noun object does not appear in soft mutation form, a pronoun object does so. There are two possible forms of the independent pronoun which might be subject to mutation. The 1sg has the two forms *mi* and *fi*, and the 2sg has the two forms *ti* and *di*. In each case the second form might be seen as the soft mutation form of the first, and it is the second form which appears following the verb in the impersonal passive in (26).

(26) Rhybuddiwyd fi gan y dyn.
Warned me by the man.

If the pronoun forms are in fact mutated as object of the verb, then the difficulties of accounting for the failure of nouns to mutate are multiplied.

However pronouns do not follow the same regularities as nouns over mutation. Watkins (1961 p. 162) points out that the independent pronoun form *fi* appears in many places where a noun would not be in soft mutation form. For instance, *fi* appears following the preposition *gyda* (with) though a noun in this environment appears in aspirate mutation form.

(27) Daeth yma gyda fi.
Came (he) here with me.

(28) Daeth yma gyda phlant Ifor.
Came (he) here with (the) children (of) Ifor.

Similarly, the pronoun *fi* appears as the focus in cleft sentences though a noun retains its isolation form here.

(29) Fi sydd yn iawn.
Me that is right.
i.e. It's me that is right.

(30) Plant Ifor sydd yn iawn.
(The) children (of) Ifor that is right.

In (28) *plant* appears in aspirate mutation form *phlant* and in (30) it retains its isolation form. Clearly there are different factors involved in the choice of independent pronoun forms and the mutation of nouns, and it is not necessary to assume that the forms *fi* and *di* are mutated forms of *mi* and *ti*.

In favour of an object analysis of the noun phrase following the verb of the impersonal passive then are two facts, the lack of verbal agreement and the possibility of a preposed pronoun form. The presence of independent pronoun forms and the soft mutation of some of them are irrelevant. And the lack of soft mutation of noun forms must be explained if the object analysis is to be adopted.

5.1.3 Unspecified noun phrase subject If the noun phrase following the verb is indeed the object, what is the subject of the impersonal passive? It is not possible to say that there is no subject noun phrase, because of the problems that this causes over agreement rules. If there is no subject noun phase present at the point where the agreement rules apply then it will not be possible to show that the noun phrase discussed above is object and not subject. The agreement rules will treat this noun phrase as subject and cause the verb to agree with it. Since this is not the case, it must be possible to show that the noun phrase is object, and this requires the presence of another noun phrase subject between the verb and the object.[2]

In order to establish what this subject noun phrase is, it is necessary to consider other forms which have the same verbal inflections as the impersonal passives. These are intransitive forms like (31).

(31) Rhedwyd yno.
Ran there.

In these forms there is no overt subject noun phrase, and no subject can be interpreted from the verbal inflection as can be done in the case of actives like (32).

(32) Rhedais yno.
Ran (I) there.

All that is known of the subject is what can be interpreted from the selection restrictions of the verb, here for instance that the subject must be animate and have legs. The subject is otherwise completely unspecified.

If it is assumed that the subject of (31) is an unspecified noun phrase, then it is possible to account for certain aspects of the syntax of these sentences. There is only one inflection of the verb for each tense and aspect combination because the verb is in each case agreeing with the same subject noun phrase, the unspecified noun phrase. This unspecified noun phrase is later deleted, never appearing in the surface structure as it is not a full lexical item. The unspecified noun phrase is represented here as a noun phrase node dominating the symbol ∅, as in (33) which is the structure of the intransitive (31).

(33)

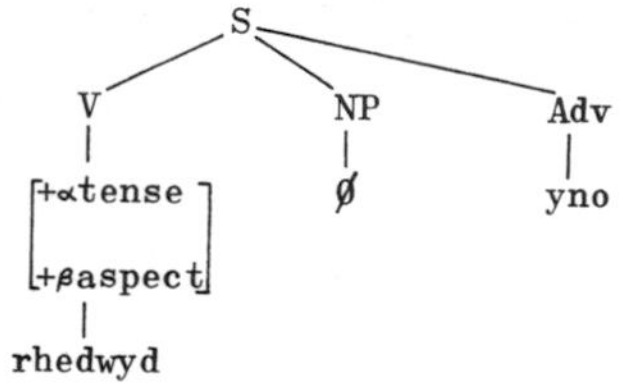

If the inflection of the impersonal passive is to be accounted for in a parallel way, then the impersonal passive too must have an unspecified noun phrase subject at some point in the derivation. It must be present when the agreement rules apply, and later deleted. The structure of the impersonal passive before the unspecified noun phrase is deleted is as shown in (34) on this analysis.

(34)

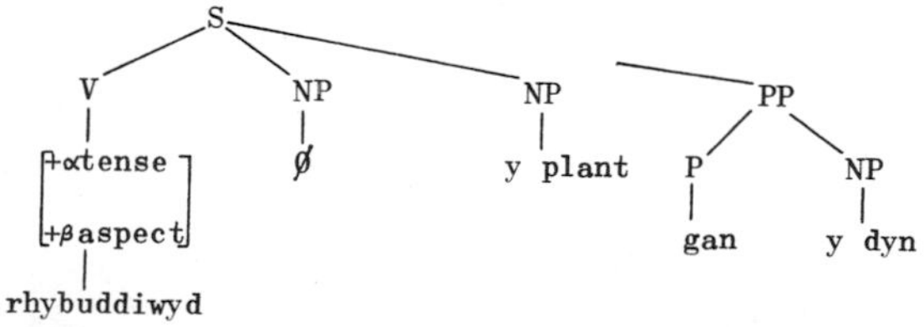

It is now possible to explain the lack of soft mutation of the object noun. If the rule deleting the unspecified noun phrase subject applies before T. Soft Mutation of Direct Object then the tree structure (34) is converted into (35).

(35)

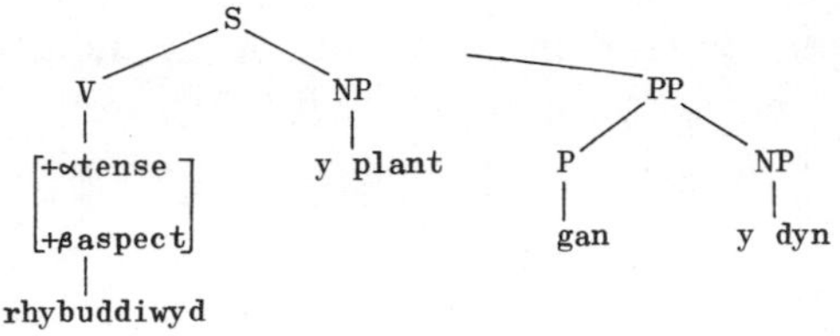

This is identical to the tree structure of an intransitive form with only one noun phrase following the verb. It does not meet the structural description of T. Soft Mutation of Direct Object which requires two noun phrases following the verb. The confusion between subject and object interpretation which it was necessary to avoid in the case of the agreement rules above, is here an essential part of the analysis.[3]

The rule ordering needed here is shown in (36). It is possible that the two new rules are postcyclic as it was shown in section 3.4.2 that the other agreement rules and T. Soft Mutation of Direct Object are postcyclic.

(36) T. Subject-Verb Agreement (Unspecified Noun Phrase)
↓
T. Unspecified Subject Deletion
↓
T. Soft Mutation of Direct Object

5.1.4 Phrase structure In the tree structure (35) above, the prepositional phrase containing the noun phrase corresponding to the subject of the active is not attached to any node in the tree. The final question in examining the surface structure of the impersonal passive, is where this prepositional phrase should be attached.

It may be the focus of a cleft sentence, as in (37).

(37) Gan y dyn y rhybuddiwyd y plant.
By the man that warned the children.

According to the test discussed above in section 2.2.2 this indicates that the prepositional phrase should be attached directly to the sentence node, as in (38), which appears to be the structure of the impersonal passive before the unspecified noun phrase is deleted.

(38)

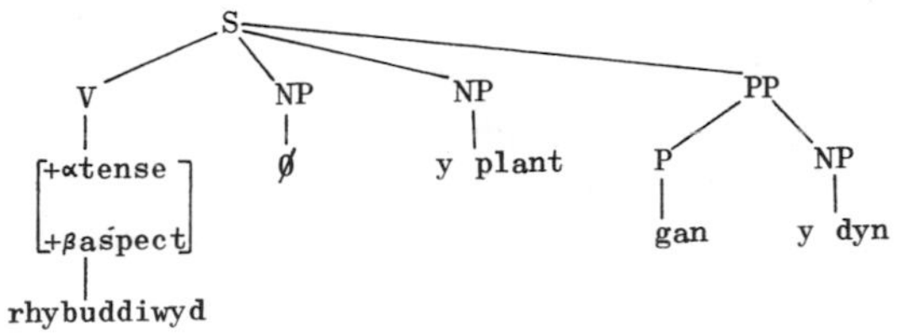

5.1.5 Impersonal agent postposing The movement transformation deriving the impersonal passive form from a deep structure active can be formulated as in (39). It must be an optional rule since the active may remain as a fully grammatical form.

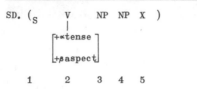

(39) T. Impersonal Agent Postposing (optional)

```
SD. (S   V              NP  NP  X  )
         |
      [+αtense ]
      [+βaspect]

    1    2              3   4   5
```

SC. Adjoin 3 as right daughter of 1, in a prepositional phrase as object of the preposition gan.

Leave an unspecified noun phrase node in the position of 3.

In the derivation of the impersonal passive form (40), this rule converts the active deep structure (41) into the structure (42).

(40) Darllenwyd y llyfr gan bawb.
Read the book by everyone.

(41)

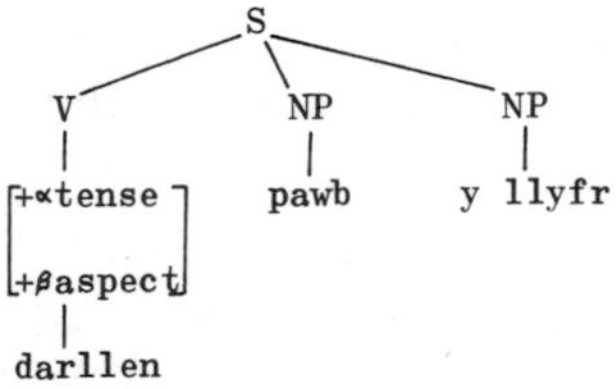

(42)

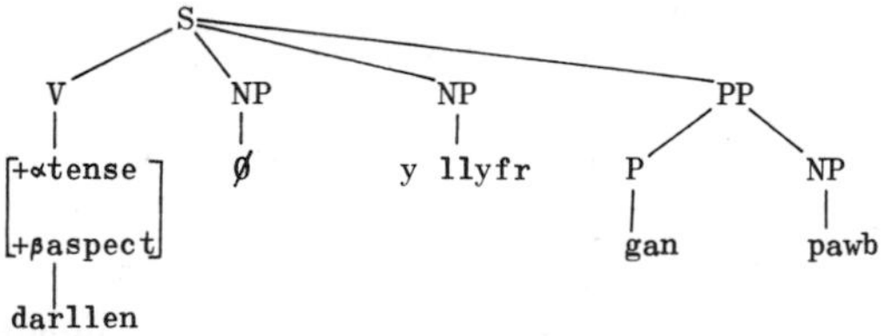

It also applies in the derivation of longer examples, where there is material to the right of the object noun phrase, such as (43).

(43) Rhoddwyd y llyfr i'r plentyn gan yr athro.
Gave the book to the child by the teacher.

The variable in the structural description of the rule covers the extra prepositional phrase in this case.

5.1.6 Agentless forms Impersonal passives are also possible without an overt agent phrase, as in (44).

(44) Rhybuddiwyd y plant.
Warned the children.

In this case, as with the intransitive forms discussed above in section 5.1.3, the subject of the deep structure active sentence is unspecified, and can be interpreted only from the selection restrictions of the verb. This deep structure is shown in (45).

(45)

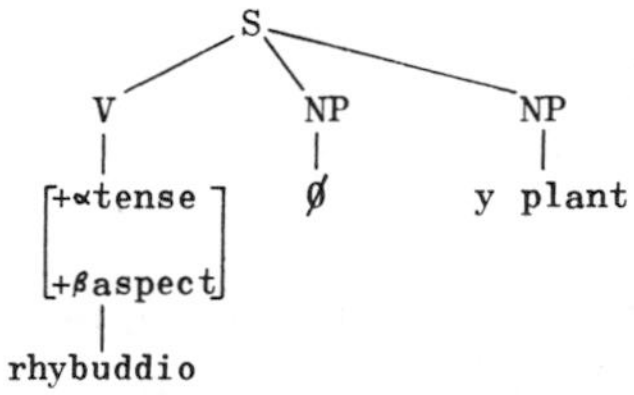

A problem arises here. Should T. Impersonal Agent Postposing apply in the derivation of such forms as (44) or not?

The formulation of the rule given in (39) allows it to apply in these cases too. It converts the deep structure (45) into (46).

(46)

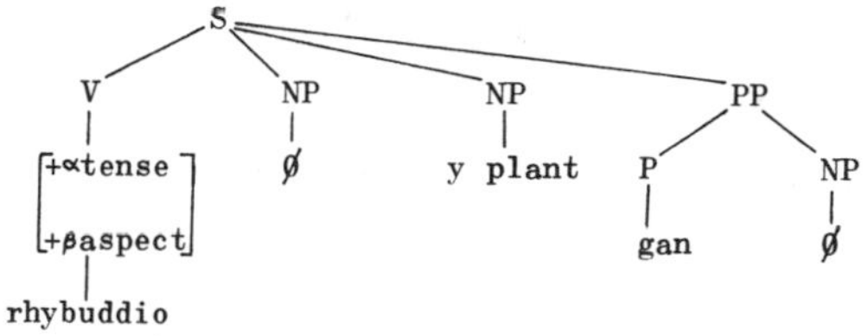

As in the case of agentless *cael* passives discussed above in section 2.5.3, further rules apply to (46) to delete the unspecified noun phrase object of *gan* and then the preposition *gan* itself. It is not necessary however for the movement transformation to apply in the case of (44) since there is already an unspecified noun phrase in subject position. The correct verb form can be derived as in the intransitive forms without postposing this noun phrase and introducing another one.

There is in fact some evidence that T. Impersonal Agent Postposing does not apply in the case of these agentless forms. This evidence is based on restrictions which are found with impersonal passives where there is an overt agent but not with forms where there is no overt agent. For instance, if the object of the verb is a tenseless embedding, then an impersonal passive with an agent is found ungrammatical by most informants as in (47).

(47) *Gellid mynd yno gan Ifor.
Could going there by Ifor.

The form without an overt agent is however fully grammatical.

(48) Gellid mynd yno.
Could going there.

Similarly, stative, nonagentive verbs are more acceptable if there is no agent.

(49) *Gwyddys yr ateb gan bawb.
Knows the answer by everyone.

(50) Gwyddys yr ateb.
Knows the answer.

The difference in grammaticality between these forms can be explained if it is due to the application of the transformation in the case of one member of each pair but not in the case of the other. No other explanation seems to be available to cover this difference.

If this is true then the movement rule must be restricted to actives having a full lexical item as subject, as in (51).

(51) <u>T. Impersonal Agent Postposing (optional)</u>[2]

```
SD. (S     V        NP  NP  X )
           |
      [+αtense ]
      [+βaspect]

    1      2        3   4   5
```

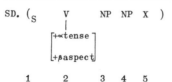

Condition. 3 is a full lexical item.

SC. Adjoin 3 as right daughter of 1, in a prepositional phrase as object of the preposition <u>gan</u>.

Leave an unspecified noun phrase node in the position of 3.

It appears that the intransitive impersonal forms such as (31) should resemble these agentless transitive forms in not having a modified version of T. Impersonal Agent Postposing apply in the course of the derivation. The form of the verb here too is conditioned by the deep structure unspecified noun phrase subject. In the case of the intransitives this view is further supported by the ungrammaticality of all forms such as (52) with an overt agent.

(52) *Rhedwyd yno gan Ifor.
Ran there by Ifor.

If T. Impersonal Agent Postposing applies at all to the intransitives, it is confined to those forms which have an unspecified noun phrase subject in deep structure – the very cases where it is not needed in order to generate the correct surface forms.

The formulation given in (51) with the subject specified as a full lexical item and the rule limited to transitive sentences seems therefore to be justified.

5.1.7 Periphrastic forms Impersonal forms may appear in periphrastic sentences as well as simple sentences, though the periphrastic forms are less often used and seem more old fashioned. They are found with both transitive and intransitive verbs, as in (53) and (54).

(53) Yr ydys wedi darllen y llyfr.
Is after reading the book.

(54) Yr ydys wedi rhedeg yno.
Is after running there.

These periphrastic forms may not have an overt agent as in (55) and (56). This is true of both transitive and intransitive forms.

(55) *Yr ydys wedi darllen y llyfr gan Ifor.
Is after reading the book by Ifor.

(56) *Yr ydys wedi rhedeg yno gan Ifor.
Is after running there by Ifor.

These forms are excluded by the formulation of T. Impersonal Agent Postposing given in (51), since this specifies a tensed simple sentence. The rule cannot apply to the periphrastic forms on the cycle of the embedded sentence, since a tensed verb is required. On the cycle of the matrix sentence the sentence is not transitive.

5.2 The relationship with the passive

5.2.1 Formulation There are some clear similarities between T. Impersonal Agent Postposing as formulated in (51) and the T. Agent Postposing of the *cael* (get) passive. This latter rule is presented again here for ease of reference.

(57) T. Agent Postposing (obligatory)

SD. ($_S$ V NPx ($_{NP}$ ($_S$ V NP NPx X)))

cael [−tense −aspect]

1 2 3 4 5 6 7 8 9

SC. Adjoin 7 as right daughter of 1, in a prepositional phrase as object of the preposition gan.

Both rules move the subject of a transitive sentence to the right into a prepositional phrase as object of the preposition *gan*. In both cases the prepositional phrase is immediately dominated by the highest available sentence node, as right daughter to it.

One apparent difference in the formulation of the two rules appears on consideration to be unimportant. It is essential for T. Impersonal Agent Postposing to leave an unspecified noun phrase node behind in subject position in order to account for the verbal inflection, but it is not necessary for T. Agent Postposing to do so. There is however no reason why T. Agent Postposing could not be reformulated to leave an unspecified noun phrase in subject position in the embedded sentence, giving as output of the rule the tree (58) in the derivation of (59).

(58)

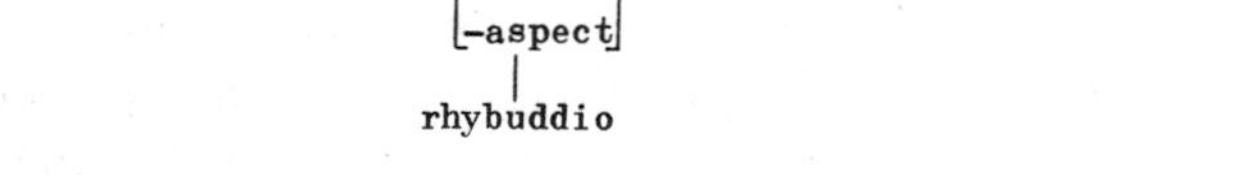

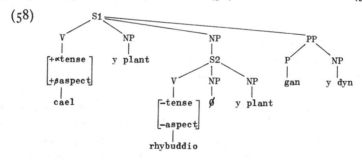

(59) Cafodd y plant eu rhybuddio gan y dyn.
Got the children their warning by the man.

The unspecified noun phrase subject of the embedded sentence must be deleted at a later stage of the derivation to give the tree (60) which is identical to the output of T. Agent Postposing under the original formulation, so allowing such rules as T. Possessive Pronoun Preposing to apply as before.

(60)

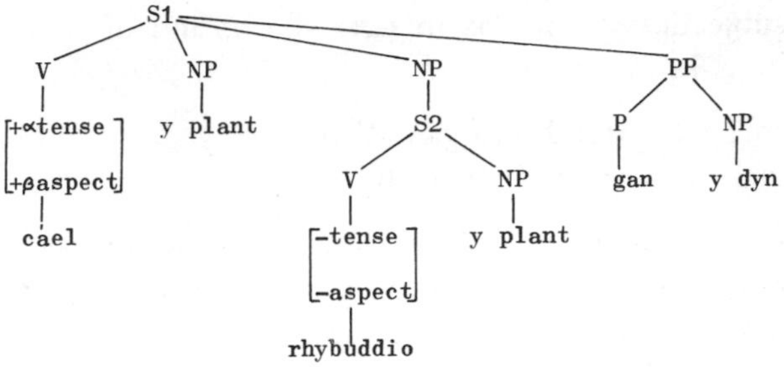

The unspecified noun phrase may even be deleted by the same rule as is needed in the derivation of the impersonal passive. Since it has been shown already in section 3.4.2 that T. Possessive Pronoun Preposing and other following rules are postcyclic, there is no problem in their following another postcyclic rule.

It may be necessary to modify T. Agent Postposing as shown in (61) in order to bring out the similarity between it and T. Impersonal Agent Postposing.

(61) <u>T. Agent Postposing (obligatory)</u>[2]

SD. ($_S$ V NPx ($_{NP}$ ($_S$ V NP NPx X)))

1	2 (cael)	3	4	5	6 ([−tense, −aspect])	7	8	9

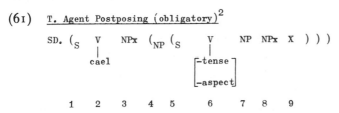

SC. Adjoin 7 as right daughter to 1, in a prepositional phrase as object of the preposition <u>gan</u>.

Leave an unspecified noun phrase node in the position of 7.

5.2.2. Restrictions Some of the restrictions which affect the *cael* passive also affect impersonal passives. These include restrictions on the verbs involved and on the noun phrases. Note that restrictions on the subject of a *cael* passive correspond to restrictions on the object of an impersonal passive.

It was pointed out above in section 5.1.6 that stative, nonagentive verbs are not acceptable to most people if there is an overt agent in the impersonal passive. Compare these forms with the similarly ungrammatical *cael* passives in section 4.1.2.

The same restrictions appear on embeddings as were found in the case of *cael* embeddings in section 4.2. Tenseless embeddings may not appear as object of an impersonal passive with an overt agent. This is true of subjectless forms, as in (47) above, and of forms with an overt subject as in (62).

(62) *Hoffid i Ifor fynd yno gan Wyn.
Liked for Ifor going there by Wyn.

Embeddings with an overt subject however only appear with non-agentive, stative matrix verbs, so that the impersonal passive will be ungrammatical if only because of the verb. It is not possible to tell the effect of the embedding independently. The same problem arises in the case of *cael* passives. Tenseless embeddings, with or without an overt subject, are also ungrammatical as the agent of an impersonal passive.

(63) *Synnwyd pawb gan weld yr olygfa.
Surprised everyone by seeing the view.
(64) *Synnwyd pawb gan iddo weld yr olygfa.
Surprised everyone by for him seeing the view.

Tensed embeddings are grammatical as the object of the verb as long as they are postposed to the end of the sentence, as in (65) and (66).

(65) Cyhoeddwyd ganddo fod y cyngerdd wedi dechrau.
Announced by him being the concert after starting.
i.e. It was announced by him that the concert had started.
(66) Cyhoeddwyd ganddo y byddai'r cyngerdd yn dechrau.
Announced by him that would be the concert in starting.

Not all verbs are equally acceptable though. For instance *gofyn* (ask) is rather odd as in (67).

(67) *Gofynnwyd ganddo a fyddai Ifor yno.
Asked by him whether would be Ifor there.

Nor may tensed embeddings appear as the agent of the impersonal passive.

(68) *Synnwyd fi gan ei fod wedi cyrraedd.
Surprised me by his being after arriving.
(69) *Synnwyd fi gan y byddai ef wedi cyrraedd.
Surprised me by that would be he after arriving.

Direct speech quotations too seem odd as the object of the impersonal if there is an agent.

(70) *Dywedwyd gan Ifor 'Mae Wyn yno'.
Said by Ifor 'Is Wyn there'.

These last do not however seem quite as bad as the corresponding *cael* passives.

Reflexive and reciprocal pronouns are also restricted. As in the *cael* passive examples discussed in section 4.3, these pronouns may not appear either as agent or object of the impersonal passive. The reflexive examples are shown in (71) and (72).

(71) *Rhybuddiwyd ef ei hun gan Wyn.
Warned himself by Wyn.

(72) *Rhybuddiwyd Wyn ganddo ef ei hun.
Warned Wyn by himself.

Reciprocal examples are shown in (73) and (74).

(73) *Rhybuddiwyd ei gilydd gan Wyn ac Ifor.
Warned each other by Wyn and Ifor.

(74) *Rhybuddiwyd Wyn ac Ifor gan ei gilydd.
Warned Wyn and Ifor by each other.

Again impersonal passives too cannot have adverbial noun phrases if there is an overt agent as in (75).

(75) *Cerddwyd milltiroedd gan Rhian.
Walked miles by Rhian.

Prepositional objects vary but not all are acceptable, as in (76).

(76) *Gwrandawyd ar y radio gan Wyn.
Listened to the radio by Wyn.

And prepositional phrases which can be analysed as adverbs of place or direction cannot appear in these forms either.

(77) *Rhedwyd at y tŷ gan Wyn.
Ran to the house by Wyn.

The only point where impersonal passives differ from *cael* passives in the restrictions on them is in relation to idiomatic forms. While *cael* passives cannot include idioms, as was shown in section 4.5, they may appear freely in the impersonal passive.

(78) Rhoddwyd y ffidil yn y tô gan Ifor.
Put the fiddle in the roof by Ifor.
i.e. Ifor gave up.

(79) Achubwyd y blaen ar Wyn gan Ifor.
Saved the front on Wyn by Ifor.
i.e. Ifor beat Wyn.

It is interesting that it is only in the case of idioms that a semantic rather than a syntactic explanation was suggested for the restriction on the *cael* passive. There the noun phrase subject was separated from the rest of the idiom and so a semantic block developed. In the case of the impersonal passive the object is not separated in this way, and so there is no semantic block.

The only factor which the derivations of the *cael* passive and the impersonal passive seem to have in common is the presence of a rule postposing the subject. Otherwise the deep structure, surface structure and transformations of the two differ. The parallelism in constraints therefore suggests that in both cases it is the postposing rule that is the source of the constraints. Either there are two rules identically constrained or there is one rule applying in the two constructions.

For some of the restrictions this is straightforward. The lack of prepositional objects and adverbial forms is ensured by the transitive structural description given for both rules. And it has already been suggested that the restrictions on nonagentive, stative verbs, the restrictions on tensed embeddings as subject and agent, and on tenseless embeddings as agent in the case of the *cael* passives could be accounted for by restrictions on T. Agent Postposing. If the parallelism with the impersonal passive is to be fully implemented it appears that the restriction on tenseless embeddings as subject of the *cael* passive should also result from restrictions on this rule. The block to the derivation discussed for subjectless embeddings in section 4.2.2 now becomes merely one extra factor contributing to the ungrammaticality of such forms but not crucial.

A problem remains in the restrictions on reflexive and reciprocal pronouns. The explanation offered in section 4.3 related to the interaction of the cyclic pronominalisation rules and the embedded structure of the passive. The impersonal passive does not involve an embedding so this explanation is no longer available. It appears that T. Impersonal Agent Postposing may well be a cyclic rule like T. Reflexivisation and T. Reciprocalisation, so rule ordering alone will not serve to rule out both subject and agent pronouns either. If T. Impersonal Agent Postposing applies first on the cycle, then it should be possible to generate (72) and (74) with these pronouns in agent position. And if the reverse ordering holds with T. Reflexivisation and T. Reciprocalisation applying first, then it should be possible to generate (71) and (73) with the pronouns in object position. Some other source must be found for the constraint then in these cases. One possibility is to adopt the restriction originally suggested by Postal and discussed in n. 4 of Chapter 4. This involves a constraint on movement transformations preventing them moving a noun phrase over another identical noun phrase in the same simple sentence. T. Impersonal Agent Potsposing is a rule of this type and this explanation may help. The constraint may also contribute to the ungrammaticality of these forms in the *cael* passive though it is not the only source of the ungrammaticality there.

5.2.3 One rule or two? It is clear from sections 5.2.1 and 5.2.2 that the two rules T. Agent Postposing and T. Impersonal Agent Postposing are very similar in formulation and restrictions, and the possibility has been raised that we have here one rule applying in two different constructions rather than two different rules. Some further evidence will now be given that they are indeed best analysed as subcases of one single rule.

It is not possible to have an impersonal passive form of the *cael* passive, either with or without an agent derived by T. Agent Postposing. But the significance of the two forms is different.

The lack of a *cael* passive derived from the deep structure (80) is due to a morphological gap in Welsh.

(80)

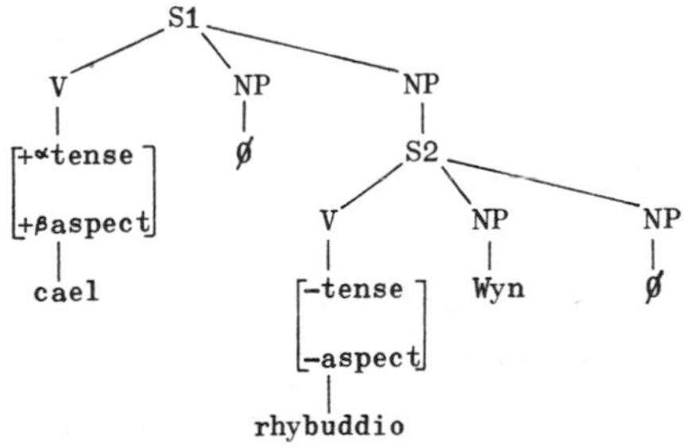

In (80) both the matrix subject and the object of the embedding are unspecified noun phrases. It is possible to have such a noun phrase in subject position in Welsh where the verbal inflection can indicate unambiguously its presence. But it is not possible to have such a noun phrase as object of an embedded sentence. There is no overt form for a possessive pronoun corresponding to an unspecified noun phrase, and the sentence (81) with a blank in this position is ungrammatical.

(81) *Cafwyd rhybuddio gan Wyn.
Got warning by Wyn.

This is not true of passives only but of other forms where there is a possessive pronoun. For instance, the object of the embedding in the deep structure (82) should appear as a possessive pronoun in surface structure. Again there is no overt form for it and a blank is not possible either.

(82)
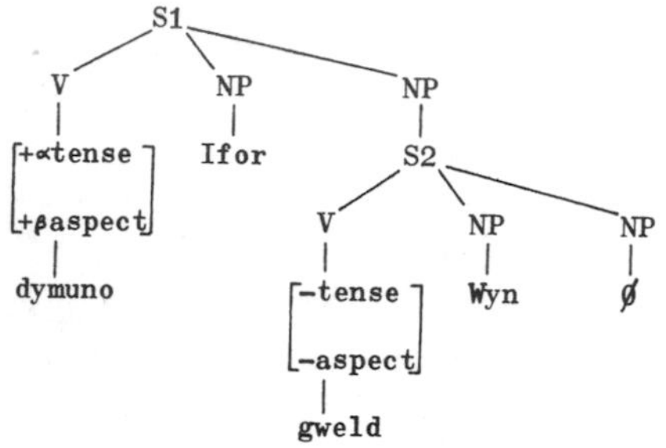

(83) *Dymuna Ifor i Wyn weld.
Wants Ifor for Wyn seeing.

That this restriction is in fact due to the lack of an overt form marking the presence of an unspecified noun phrase at some stage in the derivation and not to a deep structure constraint can be seen from the behaviour of reflexive forms. The reflexive pronoun includes a preposed possessive pronoun agreeing with the antecedent and the noun *hun* (self), as in (84).

(84) Gwelodd Wyn ef ei hun.
Saw Wyn his self.

The lack of a preposed possessive form representing the unspecified noun phrase suggests that the reflexive form of the deep structure (85) will be ungrammatical, and it can be seen that this is so from (86).

(85)
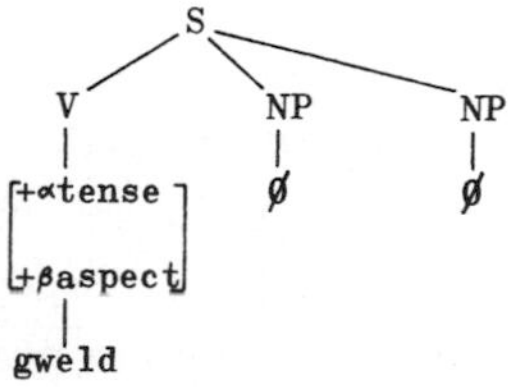

(86) *Golchwyd hun.
Washed self.

A pronominal reflexive is not possible. On the other hand, if the alternative prefixing reflexivising rule is used, as discussed in section 4.3.3, then the result is grammatical.

(87) Ymolchwyd.
Self-washed.

Had there been a deep structure constraint (87) too would have been ungrammatical.

The lack of a passive form corresponding to the deep structure (80) can be explained then by a general morphological lack of overt forms in Welsh to represent unspecified noun phrases. Here the impersonal inflection of *cael* reflects an unspecified noun phrase subject in deep structure.

More relevant to the problem of the relation of the two agent postposing rules is the lack of an impersonal *cael* passive where the unspecified noun phrase subject results from the application of T. Impersonal Agent Postposing. The deep structure of such a sentence is shown in (88).

(88)
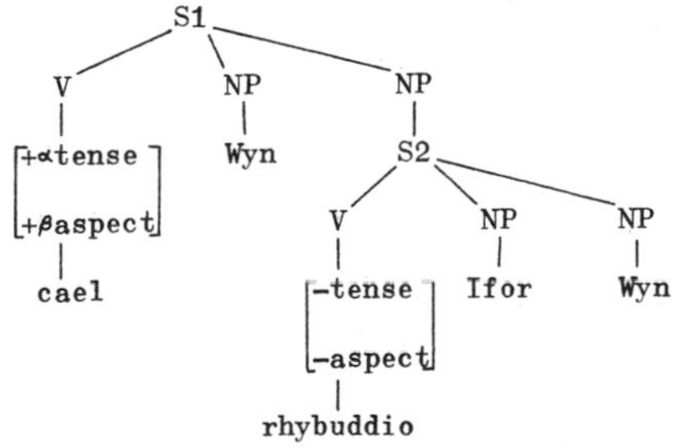

T. Agent Postposing applies first to the tree to give (89).

(89)
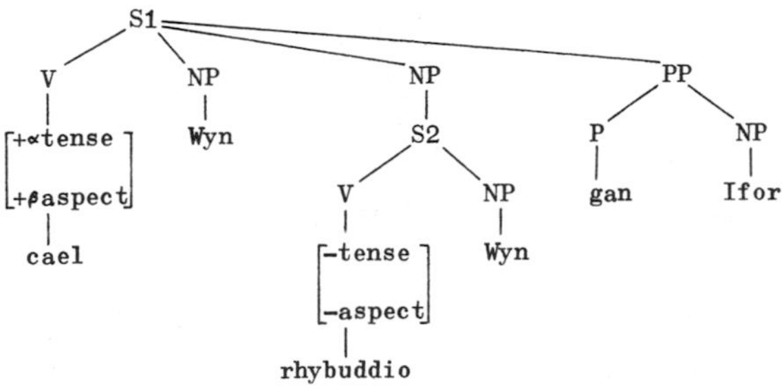

Then T. Impersonal Agent Postposing applies to give the tree (90).

(90)

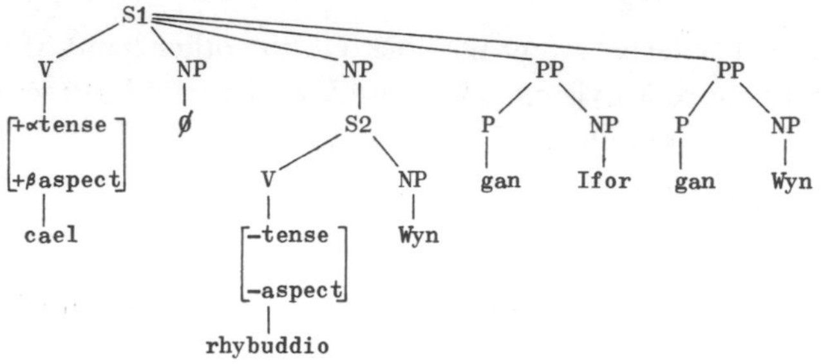

Reverse ordering will block the derivation, since application of T. Impersonal Agent Postposing to the deep structure (88) leaves a tree where the subject of the matrix is not identical to the object of the embedding and so the structural description of T. Agent Postposing is not met. The output from (90) is the ungrammatical form (91).

(91) *Cafwyd ei rybuddio gan Ifor gan Wyn.
Got his warning by Ifor by Wyn.

The ungrammaticality of (91) is due in part to the fact that the rule T. Impersonal Agent Postposing has applied to a sentence where the object of the verb is a tenseless embedding. This restriction on impersonal passives was pointed out in section 5.2.2. But the ungrammaticality is increased by the presence of two agent phrases, resulting from the application of both postposing rules in the same sentence on the same cycle. In order to prevent this some way must be found to prevent both rules applying on the same cycle. In particular some way must be found of preventing T. Impersonal Agent Postposing from applying to these forms. T. Agent Postposing alone gives the grammatical output (92).

(92) Cafodd Wyn ei rybuddio gan Ifor.
Got Wyn his warning by Ifor.

T. Impersonal Agent Postposing alone however gives the ungrammatical output (93).

(93) *Cafwyd ei rybuddio Ifor gan Wyn.
Got his warning Ifor by Wyn.

One way to prevent both rules from applying would be a global constraint of the type discussed by Lakoff (1970b). Such a constraint would state that if the two rules applied to the same simple sentence in the course of a derivation, then the output would be ungrammatical. In the case of (91) this has happened. In the case of (94) however the two rules have applied to two different simple sentences, and the output is fully grammatical.

(94) Cyhoeddwyd gan yr heddlu fod y lladron wedi cael eu dal gan y milwyr.
Announced by the police being the thieves after getting their catching by the soldiers.
i.e. It was announced by the police that the thieves had been caught by the soldiers.

T. Agent Postposing applies on the *cael* cycle, and T. Impersonal Agent Postposing applies on the *cyhoeddi* (announce) cycle.

This constraint is only needed if it is assumed that there are in fact two separate rules involved. Another way of preventing them from both applying on the same cycle is to assume that they are subcases of one single rule. This rule applies only once on each cycle and so it is not possible for both subcases to affect the same cycle. This explanation is supported by the similarities in formulation and restrictions already presented.

5.2.4 Differences There are however also differences between the two rules. T. Agent Postposing is an obligatory rule since if it is not applied to the deep structure (88) this has no grammatical output. T. Impersonal Agent Postposing on the other hand is an optional rule. If it does not apply then a fully grammatical active form is generated. Further, T. Agent Postposing applies to a complex sentence and moves a subject noun phrase from a tenseless embedding into the matrix sentence. T. Impersonal Agent Postposing applies to a simple sentence and reorders the subject noun phrase within this sentence.

Another difference between the two rules is that T. Agent Postposing was assumed in section 2.5.3 to apply to both full lexical items and unspecified noun phrases, while T. Impersonal Agent Postposing was shown in section 5.1.6 to apply only to full lexical items. The motivation for preventing T. Impersonal Agent Postposing from applying to unspecified noun phrases was that these forms were not restricted in the same way as forms which had an overt agent and had clearly undergone the rule. This difference in restrictions does not appear in the case of *cael* passive forms. (95) and (96), the one with and the other without an overt agent, are equally ungrammatical.

(95) *Cafodd Ifor ei adnabod gan Wyn.
Got Ifor his knowing by Wyn.
(96) *Cafodd Ifor ei adnabod.
Got Ifor his knowing.

There is no motivation then for a different derivation for forms with and without an agent in the *cael* passive.

The justification for having T. Agent Postposing apply in the case of unspecified noun phrase subjects in the *cael* passive was that it enabled a distinction to be drawn between passives and other embeddings. Only in the passive is there a grammatical output if the subject of the embedding is not identical to the subject of the matrix and the subject of the embedding is an unspecified noun phrase. This can be related to the fact that only in the passive does T. Agent Postposing apply. This motivation still holds.

It appears then that the two rules differ in that T. Agent Postposing applies freely, while T. Impersonal Agent Postposing does not apply to unspecified noun phrases.

5.2.5 Collapsing the rules If it is correct to regard the two rules as subcases of one rule, then it should be possible to collapse them into one transformation. The collapsed rule should allow priority to the subcase corresponding to T. Agent Postposing, so that in the case of deep structures like (88) it is this subcase that will be chosen.

An approximation to the structural description of such a collapsed rule is given in (97).

(97) T. Agent Postposing and T. Impersonal Agent Postposing (combined)

$$\text{SD.}\ \langle (_{S}\ \underset{\text{cael}}{\text{V}}\ \ \text{NPx}\ \ (_{NP}\ \rangle\ (_{S}\ \text{V}\ \ \text{NP}\ \ \text{NPx}\ \ \text{X}\ )\ \langle\ )\ )\ \rangle$$

1 2 3 4 5 6 7 8 9

The structural description subsumes the structural description of both rules. The full reading corresponds to the structural description of T. Agent Postposing. The reading without the items contained inside angled brackets corresponds to the structural description of T. Impersonal Agent Postposing. The disjunctive ordering convention ensures that the tree is scanned first for the full reading, and only if this is not met is it scanned for the lesser reading.

There are problems still, in that the structural description does not show the differing constraints on the two subrules. For instance, the verb numbered 6 in (97) must be tenseless on the reading corresponding to T. Agent Postposing, and tensed on the reading corresponding to T. Impersonal Agent Postposing. Also the differing restrictions on noun phrases must be specified.

There are also difficulties in specifying the structural change in a way which covers both cases. The subrule corresponding to T. Agent Postposing adjoins the agent phrase to the sentence node numbered 1 in (97), while the subrule corresponding to T. Impersonal Agent Postposing adjoins it to the sentence node numbered 5. It does not seem possible to express the change in a way which covers both possibilities at once. But this difficulty seems to be a result of the type of notation used here to express transformations, which relies on numbering items. As was pointed out in section 5.2.1, both rules adjoin the agent phrase to the highest available sentence node. If a different notation were adopted, where the structural change referred to constituents by name and not by number it might be possible to express this generalisation. Instructions to adjoin the agent phrase could be correctly interpreted in each case.

5.2.6 A problematic case It appears then that there are some interesting similarities between the two rules but there are also differences, and it is not clear if it is possible to collapse them into one rule. Some at least of the problems which arise in collapsing the rules seem to result from the notation used, so that this may not be a major objection. The question cannot be decided either way with any certainty, but the possibility that the two rules are really only one cannot be ruled out.

One problem remains, whichever decision is made over the two rules. This is the odd behaviour of the verb *geni* (be born). The two forms (98) and (99) are grammatical, and the form (100) does not seem to be.

(98) Cafodd Wyn ei eni.
Got Wyn his bearing.
i.e. Wyn was born.

(99) Ganwyd Wyn.
Bore Wyn.

(100) *Yr ydys wedi geni Wyn.
Is after bearing Wyn.

The *cael* passive and the impersonal passive are grammatical but not the periphrastic impersonal.

The postposing rules apply only in the case of the *cael* passive and the simple sentence impersonal, so that it might be possible to explain the pattern shown in (98) to (100) by saying that *geni* (be born) must undergo one of these rules. This would further support the collapsing of the two rules into one since such a restriction would be much easier to express if there were only one rule involved. But this in turn causes problems since it requires T. Impersonal Agent Postposing to apply to a form with an unspecified noun phrase subject, in defiance of the restriction set up on the rule in section 5.1.6. *Geni* (be born) must be restricted to unspecified noun phrase subjects since any forms derived from a deep structure with a full lexical item subject are ungrammatical. Examples are the active form (101) and the two forms (102) and (103) with an overt agent phrase.

(101) *Ganodd hi Wyn.
Bore she Wyn.
(102) *Cafodd Wyn ei eni ganddi hi.
Got Wyn his bearing by her.
(103) *Ganwyd Wyn ganddi hi.
Bore Wyn by her.

An alternative view is that the forms (98) and (99) are both grammatical because they are surface structure realisations of deep structures having an unspecified noun phrase subject. The actual derivation is irrelevant. But there are still problems on this view, since it is not possible to explain the ungrammaticality of (100).

5.3 Passive adjectives

5.3.1 Passive adjectives Some adjectives may appear in two different but synonymous constructions. Examples are given in (104) to (109).

(104) Mae Wyn yn hoff o afalau.
Is Wyn fond of apples.
(105) Mae'n hoff gan Wyn afalau.
Is fond by Wyn apples.

(106) Yr wyf i'n hoff o afalau.
Am I fond of apples.
(107) Mae'n hoff gennyf i afalau.
Is fond by me apples.

(108) Yr wyt ti'n hoff o afalau.
Art thou fond of apples.
(109) Mae'n hoff gennyt ti afalau.
Is fond by thee apples.

There is a regular relation between the sentences of each pair. The subject noun phrase of the first sentence appears in the second sentence in a prepositional phrase as object of the preposition *gan*. The prepositional object of the first sentence appears in the second in sentence-final position. The form of the adjective remains the same in both sentences, but while the verb *bod* (be) agrees with the subject in the first sentence it has no overt subject in the second and takes the 3sg inflection. This pattern is summarised in (110). Corresponding items are given the same subscript number.

(110)

Form A	Bod_1	NP_2	Adj_3	$Prep_4$	NP_5
	$inflection_2$				
Form B	Bod_1	Adj_3	gan	NP_2	NP_5
	$inflection_{3sg}$				

The selection restrictions on the noun phrases in the sentences of each pair are identical. If the subject and prepositional object of the A form are acceptable then they are also acceptable in the B form though in reverse order. Conversely, if one of the two noun phrases is not acceptable in the A form then it is not acceptable either in the B form. For instance, in (111) and (112), the subject of the A form (111) is not acceptable, and so the B form (112) is not acceptable either, where this noun phrase appears as the object of *gan* (by).

(111) *Mae'r bwrdd yn hoff o afalau.
Is the table fond of apples.
(112) *Mae'n hoff gan y bwrdd afalau.
Is fond by the table apples.

Similarly, in the A form (113) the prepositional object is not acceptable, and so the B form (114) is not acceptable either.

(113) *Mae Wyn yn edifar o'i ladrad.
Is Wyn sorry for his theft.
(114) *Mae'n edifar gan Wyn ei ladrad.
Is sorry by Wyn his theft.

The adjective *edifar* (sorry) may take only a tensed embedding as prepositional object in the A form and sentence-finally in the B form.

(115) Mae Wyn yn edifar ei fod wedi dwyn yr arian.[4]
Is Wyn sorry his being after taking the money.
(116) Mae'n edifar gan Wyn ei fod wedi dwyn yr arian.
Is sorry by Wyn his being after taking the money.

The formal parallelisms between the two adjectival forms and the identical selection restrictions they display can be explained if they are transformationally related. If they are derived from a single deep structure the identity of selectional restrictions follows. A movement transformation must be formulated in order to account for the different ordering of items in surface structure.

In this case it is necessary to decide which of the two reflects the deep structure ordering and which is the result of the movement transformation. It appears that the A form is the more basic of the two, with the B form derived by the movement transformation. In some cases the adjective in these constructions is related to a transitive verb, as *hoff* (fond) in the examples above is related to the verb *hoffi* (like). In such cases the subject of the transitive verb is identical to the subject of the adjective in the A form, and the object of the verb is identical to the prepositional object of the adjective. Compare (104) with (117).

(117) Mae Wyn yn hoffi afalau.
Is Wyn in liking apples.

Active transitive verbs have been taken as basic in this study so this parallelism suggests that the A forms of the adjectives should also be taken as basic. The A forms will now be referred to as active adjectives and the B forms as passive adjectives.

This view of which of the two forms is basic is further supported by evidence from reflexive forms. In the active the prepositional object, being the rightmost noun phrase, may reflexivise freely.

(118) Mae Wyn yn hoff ohono ef ei hun.
Is Wyn fond of himself.

In the passive however neither of the two noun phrases may be reflexivised, as in (119) and (120).

(119) *Mae'n hoff gan Wyn ef ei hun.
Is fond by Wyn himself.
(129) *Mae'n hoff ganddo ef ei hun Wyn.
Is fond by himself Wyn.

This restriction was also found on the *cael* passives and the impersonal passives in sections 4.3 and 5.2.2. In each of these cases the derivation of the restricted sentence involved a movement transformation. If the restriction on these adjectival forms is to be explained eventually in the same way, then it too must have a movement transformation in its derivation. The active form, which does not display this restriction, reflects the deep structure ordering.

5.3.2 An optional rule The movement rule which relates the active and passive adjective forms moves the subject of the active into a prepositional phrase as object of the preposition *gan* (by). This rule must now be examined in detail.

Some adjectives, such as *hoff* (fond), and *edifar* (sorry), may appear in both active and passive forms, as can be seen from the pairs (104) and (105) and also (115) and (116). For these adjectives the rule T. Adjectival Agent Postposing is optional.

Other adjectives may appear only in the passive form. Examples are *da* (good), *drwg* (bad), *gwell* (better) and *blin* (sorry). For instance, *da* may appear in the passive form (121) but not in the active form (122).

(121) Mae'n dda gan Wyn afalau.
Is good by Wyn apples.
i.e. Wyn likes apples.
(122) *Mae Wyn yn dda o afalau.
Is Wyn good of apples.

For these adjectives the transformation is obligatory.

Still other adjectives may appear only in the active form. For instance, *balch* (glad) may appear in the active form (123) but not in the passive form (124).

(123) Mae Wyn yn falch ei fod yn dod.
Is Wyn glad his being in coming.

(124) *Mae'n falch gan Wyn ei fod yn dod.
Is glad by Wyn his being in coming.

In the case of these adjectives the transformation does not apply.

The different patterns found here can be accounted for if T. Adjectival Agent Postposing is an optional rule and the adjectives are marked with rule features of the type suggested by Lakoff (1970a) to show if they behave normally with respect to it or if they are exceptional in some way. The adjectives which optionally undergo the rule are the normal case. Those which must undergo it are obligatory exceptions and those which do not undergo it are negative exceptions.

5.3.3 A tentative derivation In surface structure the prepositional phrase containing the deep structure subject is to the left of the deep structure object. The simplest formulation of the transformation moving the subject moves it directly into this position. A later rule then deletes the preposition in front of the deep structure object. The object noun phrase is not moved at all in the course of the derivation. There are however problems with this analysis.

If it is correct to derive adjectival forms from a complex sentence in deep structure, then the deep structure of (105) is (125).

(125)

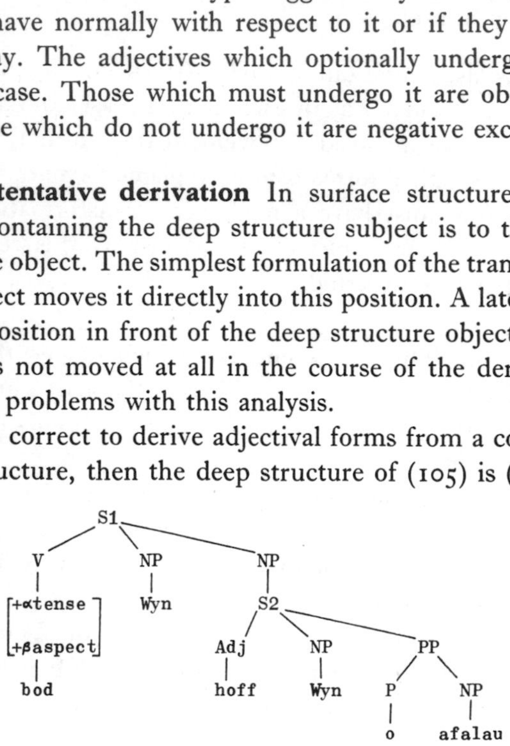

The subject of S2 is deleted by a modified version of T. Equi-Subject Deletion and the postposing rule applies, giving the output (126).

(126)

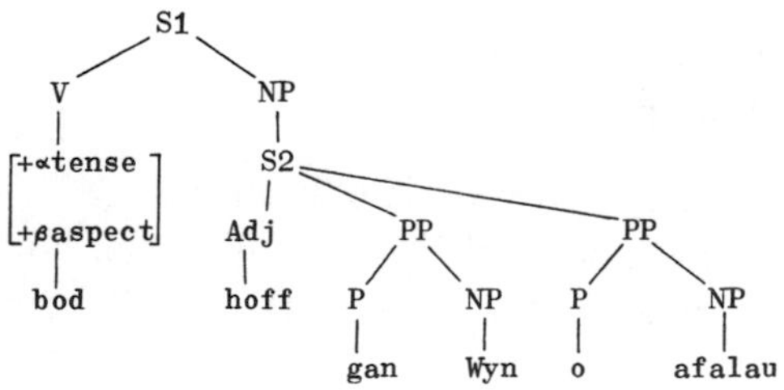

In order for the agent to be moved to a position to the left of the object noun phrase it must be inserted in S2 as shown. But this predicts that the agent prepositional phrase will not appear as the focus of a cleft sentence, since it was shown in section 2.2.2 that only prepositional phrases immediately dominated by the topmost sentence node can be clefted. It can be seen from (127) that the agent prepositional phrase is fully grammatical as the focus of a cleft sentence, so the predictions of the tree (126) are incorrect.

(127) Ai gan Wyn mae'n dda fod Ifor yno?
Question: by Wyn is good being Ifor there?
i.e. Is it Wyn who is glad that Ifor is there?

A further problem relates to the claim that the deep structure object noun phrase remains in the same place throughout the derivation. There is in fact some evidence that it must be the subject of the sentence at some point though not in surface structure. If this noun phrase is the focus of a cleft sentence as in (128) it takes a form of the verb *bod* (be) normally found only with a clefted subject.

(128) Afalau sydd yn hoff gan Wyn.
Apples that is fond by Wyn.

Compare this form *sydd* of *bod* with its appearance in (129) and (130) where it is the subject of the sentence that has been clefted.

(129) Ifor sydd yn darllen y llyfr.
Ifor that is reading the book.
(130) Ifor sydd yn wael.
Ifor that is ill.

In (131) and (132) however, where it is the object that is the focus, a different form of the verb *bod* is used.

(131) Ifor y mae Wyn yn ei wylio.
Ifor that is Wyn in his watching.
(132) Ifor y mae Ann yn hoff ohono.
Ifor that is Ann fond of him.

Another more problematical issue is the question of reflexives. It was suggested above in section 5.3.1 that the restrictions on reflexives in passive adjective forms may be accounted for in the same way as the similar restrictions on *cael* passives and impersonals, as a restriction on the movement rule. This movement rule in the *cael* and impersonal passives crucially involves moving one noun phrase over another identical noun phrase within the same simple sentence. The movement rule relating (125) to (126) in this analysis of the passive adjective does not move a noun phrase over another identical one and so the restrictions in the adjective forms cannot be related to those in the other passives.

It appears then that this analysis of the passive adjective is inadequate, and an alternative one must be developed which will allow clefting of the agent prepositional phrase, move the deep structure object into subject position and then to sentence-final, and help to explain the restrictions on reflexive pronouns.

5·3·4 A revised derivation In order to account for the possibility of clefting the agent prepositional phrase, it must be dominated by the topmost sentence node, S1. T. Adjectival Agent Postposing must convert the tree (133), to which T. Equi-Subject Deletion has already applied, into (134).

(133)

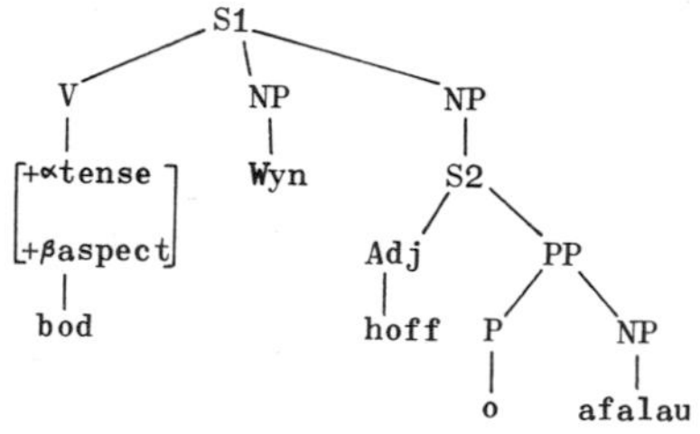

(134)

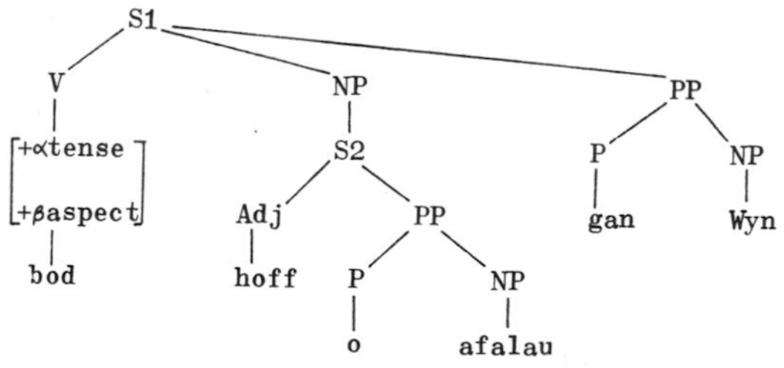

T. Adjectival Agent Postposing now does cross one noun phrase over another but they are not in the same simple sentence, so some other movement rule is needed to handle the restrictions on reflexives.

At this point in the derivation the object noun phrase is moved into subject position, thus accounting for the cleft form (127) where it appears to have been clefted from subject position. It does not however remain in subject position since such forms as (135) are ungrammatical.

(135) *Mae afalau yn hoff gan Wyn.
Is apples fond by Wyn.

It must be moved into sentence-final position to give the correct surface structure. On this account then the tree (134) is converted to (136), and this in turn is converted to (137).

(136)

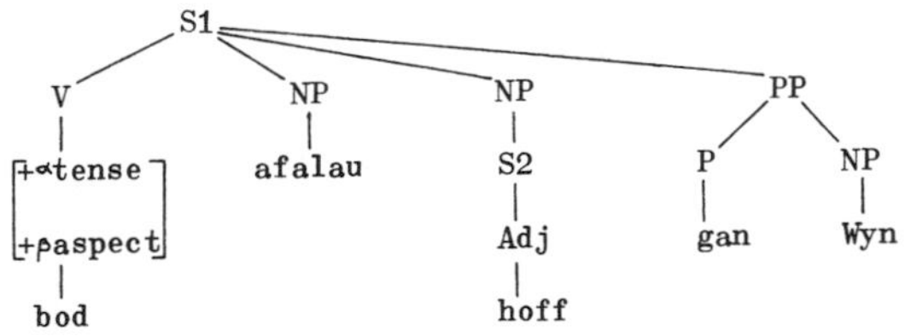

(137)

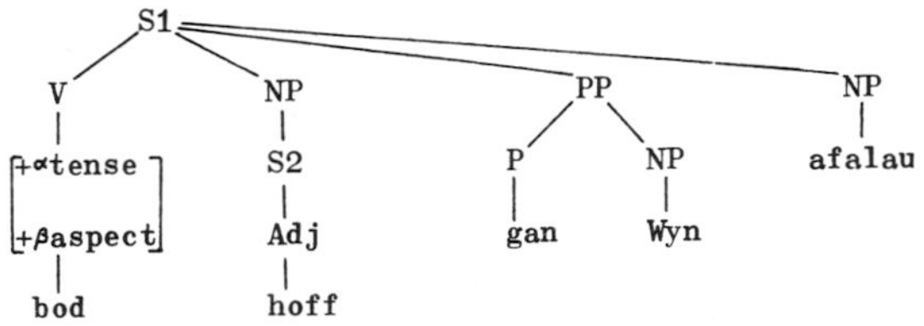

The final postposing rule which converts (136) into (137) does now move a noun phrase over another noun phrase within the same simple sentence, so that it may fit in with the restrictions on reflexives.

This apparently more complicated derivation does then succeed in accounting for data which was not explained on the first analysis. The operation of T. Adjectival Agent Postposing gives the correct structure for clefting the agent phrase. The object noun phrase does appear in subject position at one stage in the derivation. And the final rule which moves this noun phrase to the end of the sentence appears to fit the suggested restriction on reflexives. And the steps involved resemble similar through not identical processes elsewhere in the language.[5]

T. Adjectival Agent Postposing is already being discussed as similar to the other agent postposing rules. The rule which moves the object of the embedding into the matrix as subject also has parallels. For instance, in section 2.6.2 pairs of forms like (138) and (139) were discussed.

(138) Mae'n hawdd i Ifor weld Carys.
Is easy for Ifor seeing Carys.

(139) Mae Carys yn hawdd i Ifor ei gweld.
Is Carys easy for Ifor her seeing.

The rule which relates these two forms moves the object of the embedding, here *Carys*, into its derived position as subject of the matrix sentence. This rule may differ in detail from the rule involved in the passive adjective, but the general process is the same.

The last rule, which moves the derived subject into sentence-final position over a prepositional phrase, also has parallels. For instance, in the possessive forms (140) and (141) there are alternative forms with the subject either in normal subject position or in sentence-final position.

(140) Mae llyfr gennyf i.
Is (a) book with me.
i.e. I have a book.
(141) Mae gennyf i lyfr.
Is with me (a) book.

The rule required here is very similar to the one required in the passive adjective form. The main differences are the absence of the adjective and the fact that the postposing rule is optional rather than obligatory. In both cases the postposed subject appears in soft mutation form. In (141) *llyfr* (book) is mutated to *lyfr* and in (142) *llyfrau* is mutated in the same way to *lyfrau*.

(142) Mae'n hoff gan Wyn lyfrau.
Is fond by Wyn books.

5.3.5 The derived unspecified subject One problem in formulating T. Adjectival Agent Postposing is whether it leaves behind an unspecified noun phrase in subject position or whether it merely chops out the subject noun phrase, leaving nothing behind. There is in fact no evidence either way in these adjectival forms. The object noun phrase could be either attached to the noun phrase node which was left behind in subject position, or moved bodily into the space left by the removal of the original subject noun phrase. In either case all trace of the original transformation has been lost.

There are indeed traces of an unspecified noun phrase in subject position in surface structure, but these seem to relate to the late rule that moves the derived subject to the end of the sentence rather than to T. Adjectival Agent Postposing. This is partly because no further movement rules have operated on the output of this transformation to distort the results, and partly because there is quite a clear correlation between the presence or absence of this unspecified noun phrase in surface structure and the nature of the sentence-final noun phrase.

If the sentence-final noun phrase is a tensed embedding then the pronoun *hi* (she) may optionally appear in subject position, as in (143). It may be omitted as in (144).

(143) Mae hi'n dda gennyf y bydd Wyn yno.
Is it good by me that will be Wyn there.

(144) Mae'n dda gennyf y bydd Wyn yno.
Is good by me that will be Wyn there.

If the sentence-final noun phrase is a noun or a tenseless embedding then there is no overt *hi* in surface structure. Compare (142) and (145) with (146) and (147).

(145) Mae'n gas gennyf ysgrifennu llythyrau.
Is bad by me writing letters.
i.e. I dislike writing letters.

(146) *Mae hi'n hoff gan Wyn lyfrau.
Is it fond by Wyn books.

(147) *Mae hi'n gas gennyf ysgrifennu llythyrau.
Is it bad by me writing letters.

It may be that there is also at some stage in the derivation of (142) and (145) an instance of the pronoun *hi* in subject position which is then deleted before surface structure. In favour of this suggestion is the fact that *bod* appears in all these forms in its 3sg inflection. It does not agree with the postposed subject as might be thought, since if this postposed subject is a pronoun as in (148) the verb retains the 3sg inflection and does not agree with the pronoun.

(148) Mae'n hoff gan Wyn fi.
Is fond by Wyn me.

(149) *Yr wyf yn hoff gan Wyn fi.
Am fond by Wyn me.

(148) with a postposed pronoun is odd, but (149) where the verb agrees with it is utterly ungrammatical. The inflection of the verb can be explained if there is a pronoun *hi* in subject position at the point in the derivation when agreement rules apply.

This pronoun *hi* is found as an unspecified noun phrase subject in other adjectival forms such as (150) and (151).

(150) Mae hi'n hwyr.
Is it late.
(151) Mae hi'n oer.
Is it cold.

It may be deleted here too, giving (152) and (153).

(152) Mae'n hwyr.
Is late.
(153) Mae'n oer.
Is cold.

Here it represents an unspecified noun phrase in subject position in deep structure and takes the place of the impersonal form of the verb *bod*, which is ungrammatical with adjectives, as in (154).

(154) *Yr ydys yn oer.
Is cold.

Just as the impersonal form of the verb may represent an unspecified noun phrase already in subject position in deep structure or one which results from a movement transformation, so on this analysis the pronoun *hi* may do so too. In the case of the passive adjectives it represents an unspecified noun phrase subject which results from a transformation.

It might be suggested that this analysis is wrong, and that the pronoun *hi* in the case of postposed tensed embeddings results from the application of T. Sentence Postposing, as discussed in section 3.3.3. In this case there will not necessarily be any parallelism between the tensed embeddings and the other forms. Rather than give up the explanation put forward above which is able to explain the verbal inflection, it may be more fruitful to rethink T. Sentence Postposing. There appear to be transformations which postpose items and leave behind an unspecified noun phrase. Examples are T. Impersonal Agent Postposing and the rule which postposes the derived subject in passive adjectives. It may be that T. Sentence Postposing is a rule of this type, and that the *hi* which remains in subject position is this unspecified noun phrase rather than the head noun of a complex noun phrase as was suggested above in section 3.3.2. The deep structure representation of the tensed embedding will thus be (155) with no head noun.

(155)
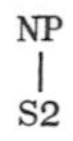

The pronoun *hi* here represents the unspecified subject of a verb as well as an adjective, as in (156) and (157).

(156) Mae hi wedi fy synnu fod Ifor wedi cyrraedd.
Is it after my surprising being Ifor after arriving.

(157) Mae hi'n amlwg fod Ifor wedi cyrraedd.
Is it clear being Ifor after arriving.

This is however paralleled elsewhere, since there are verbs which take the pronoun *hi* to represent a deep structure unspecified noun phrase subject, as in (158) and (159).

(158) Mae hi'n glawio.
Is it raining.

(159) Mae hi'n bwrw glaw.
Is it throwing rain.

Such forms cannot take an impersonal verbal form to represent this subject.

(160) *Yr ydys yn glawio.
Is in raining.

If this is correct there seems to be a general tendency for rules which postpose items to the right to leave behind an unspecified noun phrase in the original position. This suggests that T. Adjectival Agent Postposing may do so too, but there is no real evidence of this, as was stated at the beginning of this section.

5.3.6 The deep structure unspecified subject There is some evidence that T. Adjectival Agent Postposing does not apply if there is an unspecified noun phrase subject in deep structure. Forms such as (161) appear to be derived from deep structures of the type (162).

(161) Mae'r afalau yn dda.
Is the apples good.

(162)

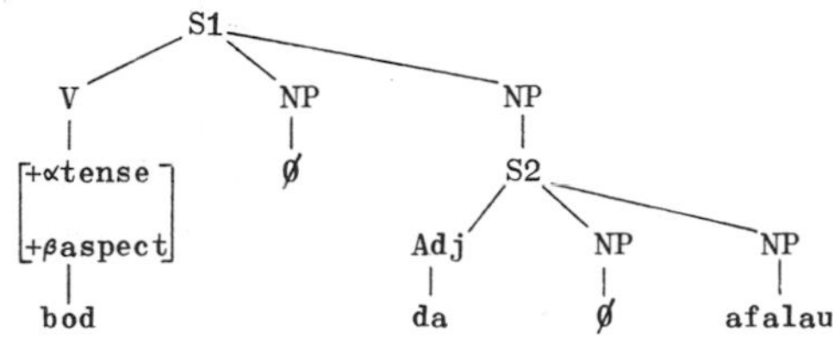

The source of the opinion expressed is not speified and there is no overt agent phrase. Compare (161) with (143) and (144) where the agent is overt with the adjective *da* (good). The object noun phrase has been moved into subject position, as in the other cases, but has not been postposed into sentence-final position. (163) where it has been postposed is ungrammatical.

(163) *Mae'n dda 'r afalau.
Is good the apples.

If the rule postposing subjects refers to the presence of a prepositional phrase in the sentence, as was suggested by the parallelism with possessive forms in section 5.3.4, then the failure of this rule to apply here implies that there is no prepositional phrase in the tree.

It might be suggested that the unspecified noun phrase subject has in fact been postposed into agent position but that the resulting prepositional phrase is deleted before the derived subject is moved to the end of the sentence. In this case some other explanation must be found for the failure of the derived subject to move in (161).

There is a possible argument from rule ordering that the prepositional phrase should still be present in the tree at the point when the derived subject is moved to the end of the sentence. It depends on the assumption that the same rule deletes instances of unspecified noun phrases in both subject position and other positions in the sentence, including the objects of prepositions. It has already been argued in section 5.1.3 that the rule deleting such noun phrases in subject position must follow the verbal agreement rules, and so it would also delete prepositional objects at the same point in the derivation, after verbal agreement. But the rule which postposes the derived subject must precede verbal agreement so that the verb can agree with the pronoun *hi* which is eventually left behind. This gives the ordering of rules shown in (164).

(164) T. Subject Postposing
↓
T. Subject-Verb Agreement
↓
T. Unspecified Noun Phrase Deletion

At the point when the derived subject is postposed then the prepositional phrase containing an unspecified agent is still in the tree.

On this analysis, only if the agent prepositional phrase is never generated in the first place is it missing from the tree at the crucial point in the derivation. This is possible if T. Adjectival Agent Postposing does not apply to such forms as (162) where the deep structure subject is an unspecified noun phrase.

5.3.7 Adjectival agent postposing The rule T. Adjectival Agent Postposing can be formulated as shown in (165).

(165) T. Adjectival Agent Postposing (optional)

```
SD. (S   V   NP  (NP (S  Adj  PP  ) ) )
         |
        bod

     1   2   3   4   5   6    7
```

Condition. 3 is a full lexical item.

SC. Adjoin 3 as right daughter of 1, in a prepositional phrase as object of the preposition gan.

Leave an unspecified noun phrase node in the position of 3.

5.4 The relationship with the passive

5.4.1 Formulation and restrictions T. Adjectival Agent Postposing resembles the other two agent postposing rules in several ways. All three rules move the subject noun phrase of a transitive sentence into a prepositional phrase as object of *gan*, and appear to leave an unspecified noun phrase in the original subject position. All three adjoin the prepositional phrase as right daughter to the highest available sentence node.

In some ways T. Adjectival Agent Postposing seems to resemble T. Impersonal Agent Postposing more strongly than the other. Both rules are optional, and both reorder the subject within a simple sentence. T. Agent Postposing on the other hand is obligatory and raises the noun phrase from an embedded sentence into the matrix sentence.

T. Adjectival Agent Postposing differs from the other rules in having an adjective rather than a verb in the sentence, and in moving the subject over the adjective rather than just over other noun phrases. This means that the subject is moved over an embedding whereas this is not possible for the other two rules.

Further, the deep structure object of the adjective may be a tenseless embedding, as in (145), though this is not possible for *cael* passives or impersonal passives. Compare (145), which is repeated here, with (166) and (167).

(145) Mae'n gas gennyf ysgrifennu llythyrau.
Is bad by me writing letters.
(166) *Cafodd ysgrifennu llythyrau ei orffen gan Wyn.
Got writing letters its finishing by Wyn.
(167) *Gorffenwyd ysgrifennu llythyrau gan Wyn.
Finished writing letters by Wyn.

Similarly, while the verb in a *cael* or impersonal passive must be agentive and nonstative, the adjectives in this construction are nonagentive and stative. Compare (168) and (169), where the adjective *caredig* (kind) is agentive and nonstative, with (170) and (171) where the nonagentive and stative adjective *hoff* (fond) cannot appear.

(168) Byddwch yn garedig iddo!
Be kind to him!
(169) Darfu iddi fod yn garedig iddo.
Happened for her being kind to him.

(170) *Byddwch yn hoff ohono!
Be fond of him.
(171) *Darfu iddi fod yn hoff ohono.
Happened for her being fond of him.

These environments were suggested in section 4.1.2 as tests for the features [± agentive] and [± stative]. While the adjective *hoff* (fond) can appear as a passive adjective, the related verb *hoffi* (like) which is also nonagentive and stative cannot appear in the *cael* passive or those impersonal passives where T. Impersonal Agent Postposing has applied. The restrictions on T. Adjectival Agent Postposing then are different from the restrictions on the other two rules.

5.4.2 An alternative formulation An alternative analysis of the passive adjective forms might be suggested which would bring them even closer to the *cael* passive. On this view the deep structure of (172) is as shown in (173).

(172) Mae'n gas gennyf law.
Is bad by me rain.
i.e. I dislike rain.

(173)

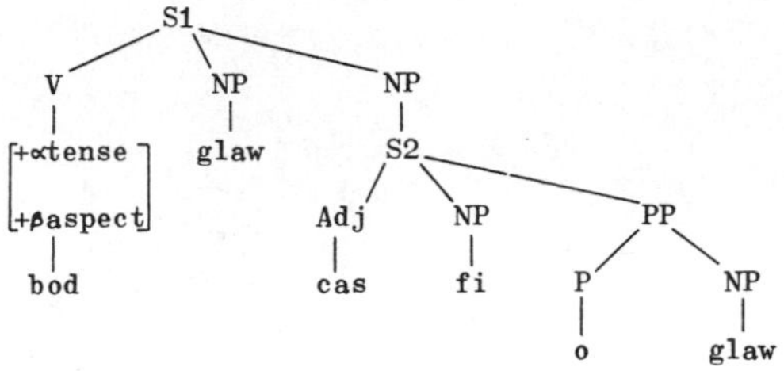

As in the *cael* passive, the subject of the matrix verb is identical to the object of the embedding. On the S1 cycle T. Adjectival Agent Postposing moves the subject of the embedding into a prepositional phrase in the matrix sentence, and another rule deletes the object of the embedding on identity with the subject of the matrix sentence. This derivation is very similar to that of the *cael* passive, and accounts for the object of the embedding appearing in subject position at some stage in the derivation. It was pointed out in section 5.3.3 that this is the case.

There are problems with this analysis however if the deep structure object of the adjective is a tenseless embedding, as in (145). The deep structure of this form will be (174).

(174)

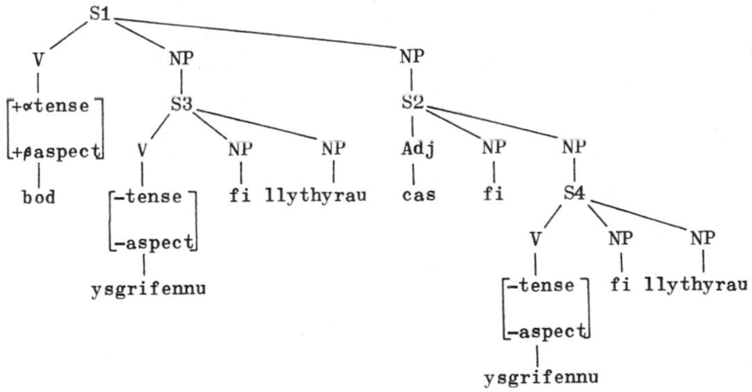

On the S2 cycle T. Equi-Subject Deletion applies, deleting the subject of S4, and giving the tree (175).

(175)

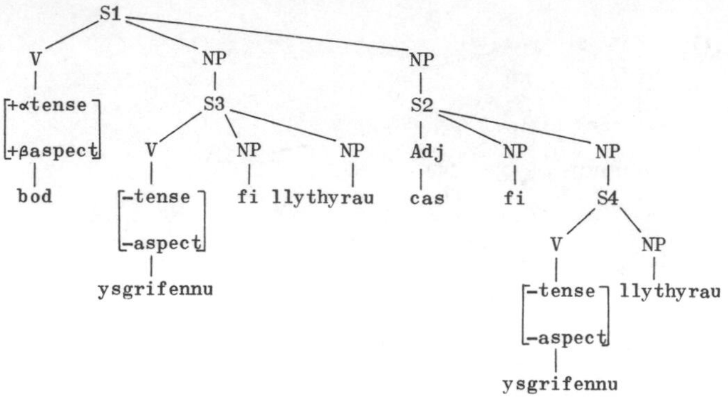

The subject of S1 and the object of S2 are no longer identical, and the rule which applies on the S1 cycle to delete the object of the embedding on identity with the subject of the matrix is blocked. If the version of T. Adjectival Agent Postposing needed here is specified as applying to a tree where the subject of the matrix and the object of the embedding are identical, like T. Agent Postposing, then it too is blocked.

This analysis predicts that such forms will be ungrammatical. In the case of *cael* passives this prediction is correct. (166) is ungrammatical and this blocking of the derivation was discussed in section 4.2.2. In the case of these adjectival forms however the prediction is incorrect as (145) is fully grammatical. This analysis must therefore be incorrect. The analysis developed above in section 5.3 will be retained.

5.4.3 Collapsing the rules It is not clear if it is possible to collapse all three agent postposing rules. The problems which arose in collapsing T. Agent Postposing and T. Impersonal Agent Postposing are multiplied when a additional rule is added. The structural descriptions of the three rules are given below for purposes of comparison.

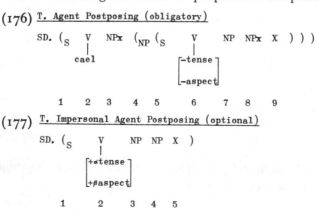

(176) T. Agent Postposing (obligatory)

```
SD. (S  V     NPx  (NP (S    V          NP  NPx  X  ) ) )
        |                    |
       cael               [-tense ]
                          [-aspect]

    1   2     3     4   5    6          7    8   9
```

(177) T. Impersonal Agent Postposing (optional)

```
SD. (S    V         NP  NP  X  )
          |
      [+αtense ]
      [+βaspect]

    1     2         3   4   5
```

(178) T. Adjectival Agent Postposing (optional)

```
SD. (S   V   NP   (NP (S  Adj  PP ) ) )
         |
        bod

    1    2   3    4   5   6    7
```

One way in which all three can be collapsed so that the structural change can be formulated in a unified way is shown in (179).

(179) T. Agent Postposing (combined)

```
SD. ⟨(S   V   NPx (NP ⟩ (S V  NP  ⎧NPx                     ⎫ ) ⟨ ) ) ⟩
          |                       ⎩(NP (S  Adj  PP ) )     ⎭
        cael

    1     2    3   4      5 6  7    8
```

The structural change will specify that the noun phrase numbered 7 is postposed into a prepositional phrase and that this is attached to the highest available sentence node as right daughter. Even this extremely complex formulation however is inadequate. It does not make clear that if the full reading with *cael* is chosen then only the NPx option from within the curly brackets is possible. The *cael* reading cannot include the adjectival option. Nor does it specify that the verb numbered 6 must be tenseless on the *cael* reading, tensed on the impersonal reading, and *bod* on the adjectival reading. All the other restrictions on embeddings, unspecified noun phrases and stative verbs must also be expressed, as must the optional-obligatory split between the different readings.

Thus while it is not out of the question that a formulation may be developed to allow all three rules to be collapsed into one, this seems very unlikely and the result is bound to be very complex indeed.

There are many problems involved in attempting to collapse only the two rules T. Agent Postposing and T. Adjectival Agent Postposing. One involves moving the subject of the embedding, the other the subject of the matrix. One is obligatory and the other optional. The restrictions on the rules differ. Similarly, trying to collapse T. Impersonal Agent Postposing and T. Adjectival Agent Postposing is fraught with problems, as the restrictions differ and one affects a simple sentence, the other a complex sentence. It does not seem worth following up either of these possibilities in detail. Not one of the three rules can be easily collapsed with any other one, and the difficulties become apparently unsurmountable when all three are brought together.

5.5 Picture nouns

5.5.1 Picture nouns Nouns of the type often referred to as 'picture nouns' (e.g. Postal 1971 p. 185) appear in two apparently synonymous forms. Examples are given in (180) to (183).

(180) llun Rembrandt o'r dyn
(the) picture (of) Rembrandt of the man
i.e. Rembrandt's picture of the man

(181) y llun o'r dyn gan Rembrandt
the picture of the man by Rembrandt

(182) disgrifiad y gyrrwr o'r ddamwain
(the) description (of) the driver of the accident

(183) y dysgrifiad o'r ddamwain gan y gyrrwr
the description of the accident by the driver

In each pair there is a regular formal relation. In the first of the two forms the picture noun is in the leftmost position. It is followed by a possessive noun phrase, as can be seen if a pronoun replaces the noun Rembrandt in (180).

(184) ei lun o'r dyn
his picture of the man

In (184) the noun has been replaced by the pronoun *ef* (he) which appears in normal possessive form as a preposed pronoun. Finally there is a prepositional phrase. In the second of the two forms the picture noun is preceded by a definite article, and followed by the same prepositional phrase as appeared in the first form. This in turn is followed by a prepositional phrase containing the preposition *gan* (by) and a noun phrase identical to the possessive noun phrase of the first form. This relation is summarised in (185) where corresponding items are identically numbered.

(185)

Form A		Picture $Noun_1$	NP_2	$Prep_3$	NP_4		
Form B	Def	Picture $Noun_1$	$Prep_3$	NP_4	gan	NP_2	

The noun phrases in the two forms are identically restricted. If they are acceptable in the A form then they are also acceptable in the B form, as in (180) to (183) above. On the other hand if they are not acceptable in the A form then they are not acceptable in the B form either.

(186) *llun y bwrdd o'r dyn
(the) picture (of) the table of the man
(187) *y llun o'r dyn gan y bwrdd
the picture of the man by the table

The noun phrase *y bwrdd* (the table) is unacceptable in both forms.

The formal parallelisms between the two forms and the identical selection restrictions they display can be accounted for if they are transformationally related. A single deep structure explains the selection restrictions, and a movement transformation gives the different ordering of items in surface structure. In this case it becomes necessary to decide which of the two forms reflects the underlying order of constituents and which results from the application of a movement rule.

The A form appears to be the more basic of the two. In the case of picture nouns such as *disgrifiad* (description) which are related to a verb of similar meaning, here *disgrifio* (describe), the ordering of the noun phrases in the A form is closer to that of the active sentence containing the corresponding verb. Compare (182) and (188).

(188) Disgrifiodd y gyrrwr y ddamwain.
Described the driver the accident.

In both the noun phrase *y gyrrwr* (the driver) is understood as the actor and in both the noun phrase *y ddamwain* (the accident) is the thing described, and in both they appear in the same order.

It is not possible to be so clear in the case of picture nouns which are not related to a verb, but it is still possible to set up a parallelism justifying the choice of the A form as basic. The picture noun *disgrifiad* (description) is in some way the result of the action of describing, so that (182) is the result of (188). The picture noun *hanes* (story) has no corresponding verb, but is similarly in some way the result of the action of speaking. The form (189) might be seen as the result of the action in (190).

(189) hanes Wyn am yr ymfudwyr
(the) story (of) Wyn about the emigrants
(190) Soniodd Wyn am yr ymfudwyr.
Spoke Wyn about the emigrants.

Again the noun phrase *Wyn* is understood as the actor in both cases, and the noun phrase *yr ymfudwyr* (the emigrants) is the topic of the story, and they appear in the same order in both forms. The parallelism with the active holds here too.

If the active form of the verb is taken as basic, as has been done so far in this study, then the parallelism shown here suggests that the A form of the picture nouns should be taken as basic too, with the B form derived by a movement transformation. The A form will be referred to as the active and the B form as the passive. The movement transformation linking them moves the 'subject' of the picture noun into a prepositional phrase as the object of *gan* (by) and will be referred to as T. Nominal Agent Postposing.

5.5.2 The deep structure The formulation of this transformation will vary with the deep structure adopted for these picture nouns. In a discussion of similar forms in English it has been suggested by Lakoff (1970a p. 56ff) that they should be derived from deep structure verbs. Those nouns which have no corresponding verb result from the obligatory application of the rules giving surface structure noun forms. He points out that this analysis can explain the similar grammatical relations in the verbal and nominal forms, such as those in (182) and (188) above. On the other hand, it has been suggested by Chomsky (1970) that such nouns should be derived from deep structure nouns. This will allow for the fact that not all verbs have a corresponding noun form and that the meaning of the verb and noun may differ. The similarities between the verb and noun forms will be accounted for by similar feature specifications for the two items in the dictionary.

If the picture nouns are to be derived from deep structure verbs, as suggested by Lakoff, the verb must be in a tenseless embedding dominated by a noun phrase node. This explains the lack of inflections for tense and aspect, and the distribution of these forms which always appear in the same positions as noun phrases. In (191) the picture noun is in subject position and in (192) it is the object of a preposition.

(191) Rhoddodd llun Rembrandt o'r dyn bleser mawr imi.
Gave (the) picture (of) Rembrandt of the man great pleasure to me.

(192) Clywais i am lun Rembrandt o'r dyn.
Heard I about (the) picture (of) Rembrandt of the man.

In this the picture nouns resemble the tenseless embeddings discussed in Chapter 1.

There are however differences between the picture nouns and the tenseless embeddings. The form of the picture noun *disgrifiad* (description) is different from the form of the uninflected verb *disgrifio* (describe) which appears in the tenseless embedding. And they also differ in meaning, with the picture noun referring to the result of the action and the uninflected verb, like the inflected verb, referring to the action itself.

There are also differences in syntax between the two forms. For instance, while the embedding containing the uninflected verb must undergo T. Equi-Subject Deletion if its subject is identical to the subject of the matrix sentence, this is not true of picture nouns which retain the subject. Compare (193) where the subject of the embedding has been deleted with (194) where the subject of the picture noun has not.

(193) Dymunai Ifor weld y tŷ.
Wanted Ifor seeing the house.

(194) Gwelodd Ifor ei lun o'r tŷ.
Saw Ifor his picture of the house.

Again if the subject of an uninflected verb differs from the subject of the matrix sentence, then it undergoes T. Subject Raising, to give (195). This is not so in the case of a picture noun which appears as (196).

(195) Dymunai Ifor i Huw weld y tŷ.
Wanted Ifor for Huw seeing the house.

(196) Gwelodd Ifor dy lun o'r tŷ.
Saw Ifor thy picture of the house.

A third difference is that picture nouns may undergo T. Nominal Agent Postposing but uninflected verbs may not.

(197) *Dymunai Ifor weld y tŷ gan Huw.
Wanted Ifor seeing the house by Huw.

(197) where this rule has applied to an uninflected verb is ungrammatical, but (181) where it has applied to a picture noun is fully grammatical.

These differences may merely reflect a different type of embedding from that discussed in Chapter 1, though the precise nature of the difference is not clear. It may however be an indication that the picture nouns are not to be derived from a deep structure verb in an embedding at all, but rather from a deep structure noun as suggested by Chomsky. This view is further supported by the fact that picture nouns display many more characteristics of nouns than do tenseless embeddings. For instance, the picture noun forms may appear in all noun phrase positions in the sentence, even as agent of the *cael* passive, as in (198).

(198) Cafodd Huw ei synnu gan lun Rembrandt o'r dyn.
Got Huw his surprising by (the) picture (of) Rembrandt of the man.

It was pointed out in section 4.2.3 that tenseless embeddings may not appear in this position. Where the tenseless embedding takes a manner adverb as in (199) the picture noun takes an adjective as in (200).

(199) Mae Wyn yn ysgrifennu yn fywiog.
Is Wyn in writing in a lively manner.
(200) hanes bywiog Wyn am yr ymfudwyr
(the) story lively (of) Wyn about the emigrants

Relative clauses and quantifiers are also possible with picture nouns but not with tenseless embeddings.

It appears that these forms may be more correctly derived from deep structure nouns, but it is not possible to be sure that a different form of embedding will not provide a satisfactory analysis. The transformation T. Nominal Agent Postposing will therefore be formulated in terms of both possibilities, and the choice is left to later study.

5.5.3 Nominal agent postposing T. Nominal Agent Postposing seems to be an optional rule, since both the active and passive forms are grammatical. No cases have emerged of picture nouns which may only appear in the active form or only in the passive.

It applies to transitive forms. In the picture noun there is a prepositional object corresponding to the direct object of the verb, as was seen in (182) and (188). In some cases, such as (201), there is no overt prepositional object, but in such cases one could optionally be present, as in (181).

(201) y llun gan Rembrandt
the picture by Rembrandt

There are no instances where the rule applies to a picture noun which can never take a prepositional object. The rule is most simply formulated if it is assumed that in cases like (201) there is a prepositional object present in deep structure with an unspecified noun phrase as its object. This is later deleted by the same rule as deletes the unspecified agent phrase in the *cael* passive. This was discussed above in section 2.5.3.

It is not clear to what position the subject is moved, since the test of clefting cannot be applied. It was shown in section 2.2.2 that a prepositional phrase inside a noun phrase cannot be the focus of a cleft sentence. Only the whole noun phrase can appear as focus. This is true of picture noun forms, as can be seen from (202) and (203).

(202) *Gan Rembrandt y gwelais i y llun o'r dyn.
By Rembrandt that saw I the picture of the man.

(203) Y llun o'r dyn gan Rembrandt a welais i.
The picture of the man by Rembrandt that saw I.

It is clear from this only that the prepositional phrase is inside the noun phrase. Since the rule resembles the other agent postposing rules in moving the subject to the rightmost position in the form it seems reasonable to assume that it also resembles them in attaching it to the highest node available as right daughter. This means attaching it to the noun phrase node.

It is also unclear if the rule applies to cases where the deep structure subject is an unspecified noun phrase. The surface structure of such forms has no overt subject or agent, as in (204).

(204) y llun o'r dyn
the picture of the man

There is some evidence however which suggests that T. Nominal Agent Postposing does not apply in these cases. This evidence is also relevant to the question of whether the rule leaves behind an empty noun phrase node in the original noun phrase position.

In the case of some picture nouns, such as *llun* (picture), the prepositional object may appear in surface structure as a possessive noun phrase as in (205).

(205) llun y dyn
(the) picture (of) the man

It can be seen that this noun phrase is a possessive from the fact that if it is replaced by a pronoun, as in (206), this pronoun appears in normal preposed possessive form.

(206) ei lun
his picture

The prepositional object may not appear in this possessive position if there is an overt agent phrase, as in (207) and (208).

(207) *llun y dyn gan Rembrandt
(the) picture (of) the man by Rembrandt

(208) *ei lun gan Rembrandt
his picture by Rembrandt

This ungrammaticality cannot be due to a general restriction on possessives co-occurring with a prepositional phrase, since this is the structure of the active picture nouns such as (180) and (182).

An alternative explanation must be found for the ungrammaticality of these forms. One possibility is that the prepositional object of (205) and (206) has been preposed onto the empty noun phrase node of the deep structure subject. In the case of (207) and (208) the deep structure subject has been postposed by T. Nominal Agent Postposing and has left no empty noun phrase, so that the prepositional object must remain in its original position and cannot become a possessive. The two sets of forms can only be distinguished if T. Nominal Agent Postposing has not applied in (205) and (206), as its application would remove the empty noun phrase node from these too. It appears then that this rule does not apply if the deep structure subject is an unspecified noun phrase, and that it does not leave behind an unspecified noun phrase in the original subject position.

5.5.4 Alternative formulations Two formulations are given here to allow for the two possible deep structure origins of the picture noun forms. The formulation given in (209) assumes a verbal deep structure. It is only a rough approximation since, as was pointed out in section 5.5.2, it is not clear what form the embedding would take.

(209) T. Nominal Agent Postposing (optional)

```
SD. (NP  (S    V       NP  PP ) )
               |
           [-tense ]
           [-aspect]

     1   2     3       4   5
```

Condition. 4 is a full lexical item.

SC. Adjoin 4 as right daughter of 1, in a prepositional phrase as object of the preposition gan.

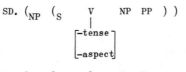

The formulation given in (210) assumes a deep structure noun origin for these forms.

(210) T. Nominal Agent Postposing (optional)[2]

SD. $(_{NP}$ N NP PP)

1 2 3 4

Condition. 3 is a full lexical item.

SC. Adjoin 3 as right daughter of 1, in a prepositional phrase as object of the preposition gan.

5.5.5 Determiners The transformation has been formulated without reference to the determiner of the noun phrase. This omission must now be justified.

There are constraints on the determiner of the active form. The determiner of the whole noun phrase depends on the determiner of the possessive. For instance, in (211) the determiner of the possessive is definite and so the determiner of the whole is definite too.

(211) disgrifiad y gyrrwr o'r ddamwain
(the) description (of) the driver of the accident

In (212) however the possessive is indefinite and so too is the whole noun phrase.

(212) disgrifiad gyrrwr o'r ddamwain
(a) description (of a) driver of the accident

There is no phrase-initial determiner in these forms but they parallel simple definite and indefinite noun phrases in distribution. In a certain type of copula sentence only an indefinite noun phrase can appear as complement, as in (213) and (214).

(213) Mae hwn yn lyfr.
Is this (a) book.

(214) *Mae hwn yn y llyfr.
Is this the book.

The indefinite picture noun phrase can appear as complement of this type of copula as in (215), but not the definite picture noun phrase as in (216).

(215) Mae hwn yn ddisgrifiad gyrrwr o'r ddamwain.
Is this (a) description (of a) driver of the accident.

(216) *Mae hwn yn ddisgrifiad y gyrrwr o'r ddamwain.
Is this (the) description (of) the driver of the accident.

This relation between the determiner of the possessive and the determiner of the whole noun phrase is normal throughout the language and not limited to picture nouns. In (217) and (218) the same relation holds though the possessive here is expressing ownership.

(217) llyfr bachgen
(a) book (of a) boy
(218) llyfr y bachgen
(the) book (of) the boy

Only the indefinite form can appear as complement of the copula.

(219) Mae hwn yn lyfr bachgen.
Is this (a) book (of a) boy.
(220) *Mae hwn yn lyfr y bachgen.
Is this (the) book (of) the boy.

There are no such constraints on the passive picture noun phrase, as there is no possessive. In (221) and (222) the determiners of the agent and prepositional object remain the same but the determiner of the whole varies.

(221) y disgrifiad o'r ddamwain gan y gyrrwr
the description of the accident by the driver
(222) disgrifiad o'r ddamwain gan y gyrrwr
(a) description of the accident by the driver

In (221) and (223) the determiner of the whole stays the same but the determiner of the agent varies.

(223) y disgrifiad o'r ddamwain gan yrrwr
the description of the accident by (a) driver

And in (221) and (224) the determiner of the prepositional object varies with no effect on the determiner of the whole.

(224) y disgrifiad o ddamwain gan y gyrrwr
the description of (an) accident by the driver

There is no correlation at all.

The position may be summarised. If the subject of the picture noun phrase is a possessive, then the determiner of the whole noun phrase is identical to that of the possessive. If the subject appears in an agent phrase then there are no constraints on the determiner of the whole.

If the determiners are specified in deep structure and the transformation formulated in a way that takes them into account, then it must be specified that the rule is optional if the determiners of the subject and the whole phrase are identical, but obligatory if they are different. This is a considerable complication in the rule, and appears to confuse two separate issues. The application of T. Nominal Agent Postposing is basically a stylistic issue, and determiners are a result of anaphoric relations within the text.

If the rule does not refer to determiners then this confusion is avoided, but some other way must be found to ensure that only the correct forms are generated. There are two possibilities. The rule may apply randomly, with the unacceptable forms rejected later in the derivation. Or the determiners may not be present in deep structure and may be specified in the course of the derivation. A general rule will specify the determiner of the possessive and this will be copied onto the higher noun phrase. If there is no possessive then the general rule will itself specify the determiner of the higher noun phrase.

5.6 The relationship with the passive

Like the other three agent postposing rules T. Nominal Agent Postposing moves the subject noun phrase to the right into a prepositional phrase as the object of the preposition *gan* (by). Like them it applies to transitive forms. It resembles the impersonal and adjectival forms more closely than the *cael* passive in being an optional rule and apparently not applying to an unspecified noun phrase subject. It resembles the *cael* passive and the impersonal in applying to a verb, at least on one formulation, and in applying to agentive, nonstative verbs at that. The verbs which correspond to picture nouns can appear in the test sentences for both these features. An example is *disgrifio* (describe) which corresponds to *disgrifiad* (description).

(225) Disgrifiwch y ddamwain!
Describe the accident!

(226) Darfu iddo ddisgrifio'r ddamwain.
Happened for him describing the accident.

On the formulation given in (210) this rule differs from the others in applying to a noun form. Other differences also appear in the formulation. It appears that this rule, unlike the others, does not leave an empty noun phrase in subject position. And the agent phrase may well be attached to the higher noun phrase node even on the verbal analysis.

Another difference appears in the reflexive forms. The *cael* passive, the impersonal passive and the passive adjective all reject reflexive pronouns. In the case of the passive picture nouns it is possible to have a reflexive prepositional object as in (227).

(227) llun ohono ef ei hun gan Rembrandt
(a) picture of himself by Rembrandt

A reflexive agent phrase is not possible however.

(228) *llun o Rembrandt ganddo ef ei hun
(a) picture of Rembrandt by himself

This may indicate a general difference between sentences and noun phrases or may be a sign that T. Nominal Agent Postposing is different from the other rules.

The difficulties of collapsing the rules increase with each additional rule introduced into the set. The collapsed structural description attempted above in (179) was extremely complicated and yet did not succeed in expressing all the differing restrictions on the subrules. It does not seem possible to collapse either version of T. Nominal Agent Postposing with it to give a joint structural description which will cover all the possibilities. And here the structural change is different too in not leaving behind an empty noun phrase. No attempt will therefore be made here to formulate a general agent postposing rule to cover all four constructions – the *cael* passive, the impersonal passive, the passive adjective and the passive picture noun.

5.7 Conclusions

The purpose of this chapter was to see if the rule T. Agent Postposing which appears in the derivation of the *cael* passive could be independently motivated. In order to do so it was necessary to establish that this rule also appeared in the derivation of other constructions. Three cases were examined where this might have been the case, but in none of them was the rule involved identical with T. Agent Postposing. Separate rules were required in each case. The rule T. Agent Postposing has therefore not been independently motivated in the strict sense since it is still a distinct rule appearing only in the derivation of the one construction. It does appear however to be one of a set of very similar rules, all of which move an underlying subject into a prepositional phrase as object of *gan* (by). To this extent then it has been given an indirect motivation.

6 *A deep structure agent phrase?*

It has been assumed throughout this study that the agent phrase of the passive should be derived by a postposing rule, which was formulated in Chapter 2 as T. Agent Postposing. Difficulties arose however in the last chapter in trying to give independent motivation to this rule, and there is in fact some evidence that the whole approach is mistaken. It is possible that the agent phrase is already present in sentence-final position in deep structure, not postposed into this position in the course of the derivation. This alternative analysis is now explored. In section 6.1 certain constructions containing the verb *cael* and the preposition *gan* will be examined and it will be argued that the prepositional phrase should be present in deep structure. In section 6.2 the *cael* passive will be compared with these forms and the possibility discussed that the prepositional phrase in this case too should be present in deep structure.

6.1 Constructions with *cael* and *gan*

6.1.1 Lexical object *Cael* may appear as the verb of a simple sentence with a lexical noun or a pronoun as direct object. Here it has the meaning 'receive'. The subject is the recipient, the object the thing received and the object of the preposition *gan* is the source.

(1) Cafodd Wyn anrheg gan ei frawd.
Got Wyn (a) present by his brother.[1]
i.e. Wyn got a present from his brother.

In (1) *Wyn* is the recipient, *anrheg* (a present) is the thing received, and *ei frawd* (his brother) is the source. The prepositional phrase may be omitted as in (2). In this case there is no mention of the source.

(2) Cafodd Wyn anrheg.
Got Wyn (a) present.

In the *cael* passive and the other forms discussed in Chapter 5 where the prepositional phrase with *gan* is derived by a postposing rule, an alternative synonymous form exists where the object of *gan* appears in subject position. For instance, in the case of the *cael* passive and the impersonal passive this alternative form is the active.

It is not so simple to find a similar alternative to (1) where the object of *gan* will appear as subject of the sentence. The most promising synonymous form is a sentence containing the verb *rhoi* (give), as in (3).

(3) Rhoddodd ei frawd anrheg i Wyn.
Gave his brother (a) present to Wyn.

The *cael* form (1) and the *rhoi* form (3) are synonymous. The object of *gan* in (1) appears as the subject of (3). And in addition the subject of (1) appears as the object of the preposition *i* (to) in (3). This relationship is summarised in (4), with corresponding items being identically numbered.

(4) cael NP_1 NP_2 gan NP_3
rhoi NP_3 NP_2 i NP_1

If the *gan* prepositional phrase is to be derived by a postposing rule of the type discussed in Chapter 5, then the two forms (1) and (3) must be derived from the same deep structure. The *rhoi* form retains the ordering of constituents in the deep structure form. In the derivation of the *cael* form a postposing rule applies.[2]

There are problems with this analysis however. In the *cael* passive and the other forms discussed in Chapter 5 the verb, adjective or nominal which appears in the basic form also appears in some shape in the derived form. For instance in the *cael* passive the inflected verb of the active appears in the passive as an uninflected verb.

(5) Darllenodd Ifor y llyfr.
Read Ifor the book.

(6) Cafodd y llyfr ei ddarllen gan Ifor.
Got the book its reading by Ifor.

In the case of the *cael/rhoi* forms however the verb of the one does not appear in the other. Each sentence has a completely different verb. The transformational relationship between (1) and (3) must therefore involve not only reordering the noun phrases but also changing the verb. The two verb forms furthermore differ in syntactic features as well as in phonological shape. *Rhoi* is agentive but *cael* is not as can be seen from (7) and (8).

(7) Rhoddwch y llyfr iddo!
Give the book to him!
(8) *Cewch y llyfr ganddo!
Get the book by him!

The transformational link will be very complex if it is to account for all these differences.

There are other pairs of sentences with the same kind of relationship as the *cael/rhoi* forms. In (9) and (10) for instance *prynu* (buy) corresponds to *cael* and *gwerthu* (sell) corresponds to *rhoi*.

(9) Prynodd Wyn lyfr gan ei frawd.
Bought Wyn (a) book by his brother.
(10) Gwerthodd ei frawd lyfr i Wyn.
Sold his brother (a) book to Wyn.

The relationship of these two forms is shown in (11). The similarity of this to (4) is clear.

(11) prynu NP_1 NP_2 gan NP_3
gwerthu NP_3 NP_2 i NP_1

It might be expected that the existence of such a similar pair provides extra motivation for the transformational linking of (1) and (3). In fact however it adds to the difficulties. The phonological shape of the verbs differs again, so that the transformational link is again not limited to reordering the noun phrases. In this case however the two verb forms do not differ in their syntactic features as both are agentive.

(12) Prynwch lyfr ganddo!
Buy (a) book by him!
(13) Gwerthwch lyfr iddo!
Sell (a) book to him!

The pattern is therefore not identical to the *cael/rhoi* pair and if a simple transformational link is to operate in both cases it must allow for idiosyncratic changes in the phonological form of the verb and equally idiosyncratic changes in its syntactic features. The attempt to generalise the rule merely complicates it.

Another problem arises from the fact that *cael* is not the only verb which might be considered to have this relationship with *rhoi*. A second verb *derbyn* (receive) also appears in sentences which are synonymous with sentences containing *rhoi*. For instance (14) is synonymous with (3).

(14) Derbyniodd Wyn anrheg gan ei frawd.
Received Wyn (a) present by his brother.

As in the case of *cael* the object of *gan* in (14) is identical to the subject of (3), and the subject of (14) is identical to the object of *i* in (3). Should either of these two verbs be able to replace *rhoi*, thus splitting off this set from other sets such as *prynu/gwerthu* where only one replacement is possible? Or should only one of the two be chosen, and if so which one?

Both have some claim to replacing *rhoi*. *Derbyn* is agentive like *rhoi*, as can be seen from (15), so the complicating changes of syntactic features needed with *cael* are avoided.

(15) Derbyniwch y llyfr ganddo!
Receive the book by him!

On the other hand *cael* is the more widespread verb of the two and can appear as an alternative to *rhoi* in constructions where *derbyn* is not possible. These forms, which have nominal direct objects, are discussed in detail in section 6.1.3 below. Here the ungrammaticality of the form with *derbyn* is shown in (16).

(16) *Derbyniodd y pregethwr wrandawiad da gan y gynulleidfa.
Received the preacher (a) hearing good by the congregation.
i.e. The preacher got a good hearing from the congregation.

If one of the two verbs is chosen as the transformed version of *rhoi* then there are two possibilities for the other. It may be considered as the obligatory transform of some verb which is never found in its basic form. Or it may be seen as a basic form in its own right, not resulting from any transformation. But if one of these forms is basic then the motivation for the transformational derivation of the other is undermined. Once it is admitted that one *gan* prepositional phrase is basic then it is not clear why another one should not be.

If all the forms discussed in this section are basic then the problems of the transformational link do not arise. It does not matter that the verbs differ in phonological shape and in syntactic features in an idiosyncratic way, nor that they do not always appear in symmetrical pairs.

The links that do exist between them can be expressed by similarities in their lexical specifications. On this view the *gan* prepositional phrase will be present in deep structure like the *i* prepositional phrase. *Cael*, like *rhoi*, takes a direct object and a prepositional phrase in deep structure.

6.1.2 Embedded object *Cael* may also take a tensed embedding as a direct object. In this construction it is used in the sense of receiving information, of finding out a fact. The object of *gan* is the source of this information,

(17) Cefais i gan Wyn fod pawb yno.
Got I by Wyn being everyone there.
i.e. I found out from Wyn that everyone was there.

The prepositional phrase may be omitted as in (18), where there is no mention of the source of the information.

(18) Cefais i fod pawb yno.
Got I being everyone there.
i.e. I found out that everyone was there.

In (19) the object of *cael* is a tenseless embedding whose subject has been deleted by T. Equi-Subject Deletion on identity with the subject of *cael*.

(19) Caiff Ifor fynd yno gennyf i.
Gets Ifor going there by me.
i.e. I allow Ifor to go there.

Here the subject of *cael* receives permission to do the action referred to in the embedding. The object of *gan* is the source of the permission. The prepositional phrase may be omitted here again as in (20), where there is no mention of the source of the permission.

(20) Caiff Ifor fynd yno.
Gets Ifor going there.
i.e. Ifor may go there.

These examples, with an embedding as object of *cael*, have no equivalent synonymous forms with *rhoi*. (21) and (22) are both ungrammatical.

(21) *Rhoddodd Wyn imi fod pawb yno.
Gave Wyn to me being everyone there.
i.e. Wyn told me that everyone was there.

(22) *Rhoddaf i fynd yno i Ifor.
Give I going there to Ifor.
i.e. I allow Ifor to go there.

If (17) and (19) are transformationally derived, then the postposing rule must be obligatory to prevent the generation of (21) and (22). This adds yet another complication to these already raised in section 6.1.1. The postposing rule will be obligatory if the object of *rhoi* is an embedding but optional if the object is a lexical noun or a pronoun. If both *rhoi* and *cael* are basic forms then the ungrammaticality of (21) and (22) can be accounted for by an idiosyncratic selectional feature of *rhoi*. Whereas *cael* can take an embedding as direct object, *rhoi* cannot.

It does not seem helpful then to derive the object of *gan* from the subject of a *rhoi* sentence in these cases. Another possibility exists here, that of deriving the object of *gan* from a noun phrase in the embedding as was done with the *cael* passive in Chapter 2. A noun phrase would be moved up into the matrix sentence into sentence-final position by a rule very similar to T. Agent Postposing. This analysis does not work here either however. The tensed embedding in (17) is a full sentence with no sign of any noun phrase having been moved out of it. And the tenseless embedding in (19) seems to parallel the embedding in such forms as (23) in having lost only its subject on identity with the subject of the matrix sentence.

(23) Hoffwn i fynd yno.
Should like I going there.

In the *cael* passive there were good semantic and syntactic reasons why the object of *gan* should appear in deep structure as subject of the embedding. There is no reason why the object of *gan* should appear in the embedding in either the tensed form (17) or the tenseless form (19). This alternative transformational derivation for the *gan* prepositional phrase does not hold either then, and it appears that the prepositional phrase must be present in deep structure.

6.1.3 Nominal object A nominal form related to a verb can also appear as object of *cael*. For instance, *gwrandawiad* (hearing) in (24) is related to the verb *gwrando* (listen).

(24) Cafodd y pregethwr wrandawiad da gan y gynulleidfa.
Got the preacher (a) hearing good by the congregation.

The subject of *cael* is identical to the object of the nominal, and the object of *gan* is identical to the subject of the nominal, as can be seen by comparing (24) with (25) which contains the corresponding verb *gwrando*.

(25) Gwrandawodd y gynulleidfa ar y pregethwr.
Listened the congregation to the preacher.

The two forms (24) and (25) are more or less synonymous and in both the noun phrases have the same function. *Y pregethwr* (the preacher) is the speaker and *y gynulleidfa* (the congregation) is the hearer. The subject and object of the nominal are not overt. The meaning of *cael* here it is not so clearly a case of 'receiving' as in the other cases discussed in sections 6.1.1 and 6.1.2, but structurally it is similar to them, having a direct object and a prepositional phrase with *gan*. As in the other cases, the prepositional phrase can be omitted to give (26).

(26) Cafodd y pregethwr wrandawiad da.
Got the preacher (a) hearing good.

Here there is no mention of the hearers and the meaning is similar to that of the impersonal form (27).

(27) Gwrandawyd ar y pregethwr.
Listened to the preacher.

There is an alternative form with the verb *rhoi* as in (28).

(28) Rhoddodd y gynulleidfa wrandawiad da i'r pregethwr.
Gave the congregation (a) hearing good to the preacher.

The subject of *rhoi* is identical to the subject of the nominal, and the object of *i* is identical to the object of the nominal, as can be seen by comparing (28) with the active verbal equivalent (25). These two noun phrases are not overt in the nominal.

The relationship of the *cael* form (24) and the *rhoi* form (28) is identical to that of the *cael/rhoi* forms discussed in section 6.1.1. The subject of *cael* in (24) is identical to the object of *i* in (28), and the object of *gan* in (24) is identical to the subject of *rhoi* in (28). In attempting to relate the two forms transformationally the same problems, with one exception, arise as did in section 6.1.1. The one exception to this is that *derbyn* (receive) cannot replace *cael* if the object is a nominal, as was shown by the ungrammaticality of (16), and so there is a straightforward relationship between *cael* and *rhoi*, rather than a three-cornered one involving *derbyn* too. All these problems are avoided if both the *cael* and *rhoi* forms are basic.

If this is the case, then the subject and object of the nominal must be deleted on identity with noun phrases in the matrix sentences. If the matrix verb is *cael* the subject of the nominal is deleted on identity with the object of *gan*, and the object of the nominal on identity with the subject of *cael*. If the matrix verb is *rhoi* then the subject of the nominal is deleted on identity with the subject of *rhoi*, and the object of the nominal on identity with the object of *i*.

An alternative transformational derivation of the prepositional phrase with *gan* is possible, on the lines of that suggested for the *cael* passive in Chapter 2. On this analysis the subject of the nominal is moved into the matrix sentence into a prepositional phrase with *gan* in sentence-final position, by a rule very similar to T. Agent Postposing. It might be suggested that this movement transformation is needed to account for the ungrammaticality of (29) where the agent is a reflexive pronoun.

(29) *Cafodd y pregethwr wrandawiad da ganddo ef ei hun.
Got the preacher (a) hearing good by himself.

In section 4.3.2 it was suggested that cyclic reflexivisation blocked T. Agent Postposing and prevented the derivation of reflexive agents, as in (30).

(30) *Cafodd y pregethwr ei rybuddio ganddo ef ei hun.
Got the preacher his warning by himself.

If the derivation of the two forms includes a similar postposing rule, then the similar restriction can be explained.

It appears however that this approach is mistaken. Reflexive pronouns are ungrammatical as object of *gan* not only in cases like (29) and (30) where the prepositional phrase may result from a postposing rule, but also where the *gan* phrase is already present in deep structure. For instance, the reflexive pronoun is ungrammatical in this position in the forms which were discussed above in sections 6.1.1 and 6.1.2, where the direct object of *cael* is a lexical noun, or an embedding.

(31) *Cafodd Wyn anrheg ganddo ef ei hun.
Got Wyn (a) present by himself.

(32) *Cafodd Wyn ganddo ef ei hun fod pawb yno.

Got Wyn by himself being everyone there.
i.e. Wyn found out by himself that everyone was there.

(33) *Caiff Wyn fynd yno ganddo ef ei hun.
Gets Wyn going there by himself.
i.e. Wyn allows himself to go there.

The restriction in these cases cannot involve movement transformations. And a generalisation is lost if the restriction which accounts for the ungrammaticality of (31) to (33) is different from that which accounts for the ungrammaticality of (29) since all four forms share other grammatical characteristics.

It is not clear what form this restriction should take, but it seems to be a requirement that the subject and prepositional object of *cael* should be distinct. There is some further evidence that this is a deep structure restriction rather than one related to a movement transformation in that it is found with *rhoi* forms too. The object of the preposition *i* may not be a reflexive pronoun.

(34) *Rhoddodd Wyn anrheg iddo ef ei hun.
Gave Wyn (a) present to himself.

In section 6.1.1 it was argued that even if the *cael* forms were transformationally derived, the *rhoi* forms were basic with the prepositional phrase already present in deep structure. This seems in fact to be quite a widespread restriction, appearing with other verbs besides *cael* and *rhoi*. For instance it appears with *gwerthu* (sell) and *prynu* (buy).

(35) *Gwerthodd Ifor lyfr iddo ef ei hun.
Sold Ifor (a) book to himself.

(36) *Prynodd Ifor lyfr ganddo ef ei hun.
Bought Ifor (a) book by himself.

It is possible that the restriction will appear with all verbs that form symmetrical pairs of the type formed by *cael/rhoi* and *gwerthu/prynu*.

There is therefore no clear evidence that the *cael* form with a nominal object as in (24) is transformationally derived. It is therefore assumed that it resembles the other forms discussed in sections 6.1.1 and 6.1.2 in being a basic form, generated directly in deep structure.

6.1.4 Another instance of *gan* The *cael* forms considered so far are not the only forms where a prepositional phrase with *gan* seems to be present in deep structure. Another such case will be presented in this section.

Parallel to forms containing *cael* and a lexical noun object, such as (37), are possessive forms such as (38).

(37) Cafodd Emyr lyfr.
Got Emyr (a) book.
(38) Mae llyfr gan Emyr.
Is (a) book by Emyr.

The *cael* form expresses the acquiring of the book, and the possessive form the state of having it. In both the noun *Emyr* is the owner, and the noun *llyfr* (book) the thing owned.

There are syntactic parallelisms between the two forms. The subject of (37) is identical to the object of *gan* in (38), and the object of (37) is the subject of (38). This relationship is summarised in (39).

(39) cael NP_1 NP_2
bod NP_2 gan NP_1

Again the question arises if the object of *gan* should be derived from some other form, such as the *cael* form, where it is the subject of the sentence.

Similar problems arise on the transformational derivation of the prepositional phrase here as arose in the previous sections over the transformational derivation of the *cael* forms. Here too it is necessary to change the verb in the course of the derivation, and to change not only the form of the verb but also syntactic features, since *cael* is transitive but *bod* is intransitive. And here again we do not find a symmetrical pair, since there is a third verb which might be analysed as an alternative to *cael*. This verb is *perthyn* (belong), which resembles *bod* in expressing continuing possession.

(40) Mae llyfr yn perthyn i Emyr.
Is (a) book in belonging to Emyr.
i.e. Emyr has a book.

The subject of *cael* here too is identical to the object of the preposition and the object of *cael* is identical to the subject of *perthyn*. As before this three-cornered situation raises problems for a transformational derivation and suggests that the analysis would be simpler if the three forms were all basic.

There are in fact more problems here than in the case of the *cael/rhoi* pair. The *cael* and *bod* forms differ in meaning, acquiring versus possessing, so this is yet another problem for the transformational link. And they differ in selectional restrictions, since *cael* may express the source of the thing possessed while *bod* may not.

The final problem in deriving the *bod* possessive form from the *cael* form relates to the question of whether the *cael* form is itself transformationally derived or basic. If it is transformationally derived then the derivation of *bod* will involve double the problems, both those in the derivation of *cael* from *rhoi* and those in the derivation of *bod* from *cael*. And if *cael* is not transformationally derived, but a deep structure form, then the effort to derive one *gan* prepositional phrase transformationally, the one in the *bod* form, means assuming that another such *gan* phrase is present in deep structure, the one in the *cael* form. The attempt to derive this *gan* prepositional phrase by a transformation leads either to great complication or to inconsistency. It seems better to assume that the *cael* and *bod* forms are both basic.

6.2 The *cael* passive

6.2.1 A deep structure agent The *cael* passive resembles the forms discussed above in section 6.1 in several ways. It contains the matrix verb *cael*, a direct object, and a prepositional phrase with *gan*. This prepositional phrase may be optionally omitted.

(41) Cafodd Wyn ei rybuddio gan Ifor.
Got Wyn his warning by Ifor.
(42) Cafodd Wyn ei rybuddio.
Got Wyn his warning.

The *cael* passive is closest to the permission forms (19) and (20) examined in section 6.1.2, in that both have a tenseless embedding as direct object. The two forms differ in the identity relations between the noun phrases in the matrix and the embedding. In the permission forms the only identity relation holds between the subject of the matrix and the subject of the embedding. In the passive the subject of the matrix is identical to the object of the embedding, and the object of *gan* is identical to the subject of the embedding. From the point of view of these identity relations the *cael* passive is closest to the forms with a nominal direct object discussed in section 6.1.3.

The same tree structure is needed to account for the various forms with *cael* and *gan*. In section 2.2.2 it was shown that the prepositional phrase in the *cael* passive could be moved into sentence-initial position as the focus of a cleft sentence, as in (43).

(43) Gan Ifor y cafodd Wyn ei rybuddio.
By Ifor that got Wyn his warning.
i.e. It was by Ifor that Wyn was warned.

It was argued that this meant that the prepositional phrase was directly dominated by the top S node in the tree. The same pattern of clefting holds for the other forms with *cael* and *gan*. In all of them the prepositional phrase can be the focus of a cleft sentence, as in (44) to (47).

(44) Gan ei frawd y cafodd Wyn anrheg.
By his brother that got Wyn (a) present.

(45) Gan Wyn y cefais i fod pawb yno.
By Wyn that found out I being everyone there.
i.e. It was from Wyn that I found out that everyone was there.

(46) Gan Wyn y cefais fynd yno.
By Wyn that got I going there.
i.e. It was from Wyn that I got permission to go there.

(47) Gan y gynulleidfa y cafodd y pregethwr wrandawiad da.
By the congregation that got the preacher (a) hearing good.
i.e. It was from the congregation that the preacher got a good hearing.

These similarities suggest that the possibility should be considered that perhaps the prepositional phrase in the *cael* passive should also be present in deep structure. A deep structure like (48) will be required for the *cael* passive (41).

(48)

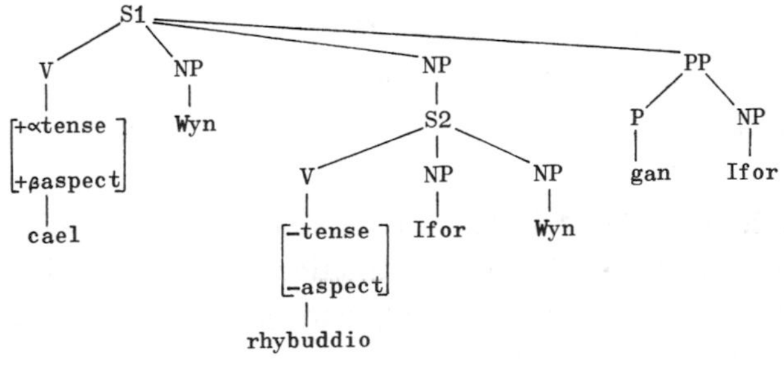

This resembles the deep structure suggested in Chapter 2 in most features. It differs only in the additional presence of a prepositional phrase with the preposition *gan* in the matrix sentence in sentence-final position. The object of *gan* is identical to the subject of the embedding. The original T. Agent Postposing is no longer required in the derivation since there is already a prepositional phrase present. Instead a deletion rule is needed to delete the subject of the embedding on identity with the object of *gan* in the matrix sentence. The output of this rule will be the tree structure (49).

(49)

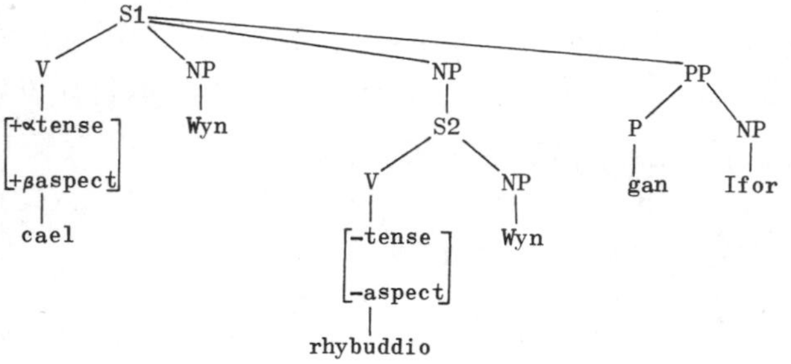

The deletion rule replaces T. Agent Postposing in the derivation, and the derivation procedes otherwise as before, to give the output (41). This is because the later rules presuppose that the subject of the embedding has been lost and it is irrelevant if this is through the application of a movement rule or a deletion rule. The new deletion rule can be formalised as in (50) below.

(50) T. Passive Subject Deletion (obligatory)

SD. ($_S$ V NPx ($_{NP}$ ($_S$ V NPy NPx ($_{PP}$ P NPy))))

V (2) = cael; V (6) = [–tense, –aspect]

1 2 3 4 5 6 7 8 9 10 11

SC. Delete 7.

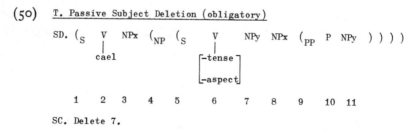

6.2.2 Which analysis? It is difficult to find evidence to choose between this analysis and the earlier transformational one. Several constraints on the passive can be handled equally easily on either view. For instance, only one prepositional phrase with *gan* may appear in the passive, as can be seen from the ungrammaticality of (51).

(51) *Cafodd Wyn ei rybuddio gan y dyn gan y ddynes.
Got Wyn his warning by the man by the woman.

On a transformational analysis this results from the fact that there is only one subject noun phrase in the embedding to be postposed by T. Agent Postposing. There is no way of generating the second prepositional phrase. On the deep structure analysis suggested above in section 6.2.1 this reflects a general restriction on *cael* forms, which seem unable to have more than one prepositional phrase of the same type in the same sentence. (52) is ungrammatical in the same way as (51).

(52) *Cafodd Wyn anrheg gan ei frawd gan ei chwaer.
Got Wyn (a) present by his brother by his sister.

The same type of restriction in fact appears with other verbs, with (53) again being ungrammatical in the same way. Here there is a doubled prepositional phrase with *i*.

(53) *Rhoddodd Ifor y llyfr i Wyn i Emyr.
Gave Ifor the book to Wyn to Emyr.

Other data is similarly ambiguous. The failure of the preposition *gan* to alternate with the preposition *oddiwrth* (from) in the passive may be explained on either analysis. (54) where *oddiwrth* appears in the passive is ungrammatical, but (55) where it appears with a lexical object is grammatical.

(54) *Cafodd Wyn ei rybuddio oddiwrth Ifor.
Got Wyn his warning from Ifor.
(55) Cafodd Wyn anrheg oddiwrth ei frawd.
Got Wyn (a) present from his brother.

On the transformational analysis this results from only the one preposition being inserted by the rule. On the deep structure analysis it results from the fact that the passive has an embedded sentence as the direct object of *cael.* (56) and (57) which also have an embedded sentence as direct object are also ungrammatical. The alternative only appears where the direct object is a lexical noun or a pronoun.

(56) *Cafodd Wyn oddiwrthi hi fod pawb yno.
Got Wyn from her being everyone there.
i.e. Wyn found out from her that everyone was there.

(57) *Caiff Wyn fynd yno oddiwrthyf i.
Gets Wyn going there from me.
i.e. I allow Wyn to go there.

There is no alternative form with *rhoi* (give) in the case of the passive, though there is in the case of *cael* forms which take a lexical object.

(58) *Rhoddodd Ifor ei rybuddio i Wyn.
Gave Ifor his warning to Wyn.

Compare the ungrammaticality of (58) with the grammaticality of (3). This discrepancy may be explained on either analysis. On the transformational analysis of the *cael* passive it is a separate form which does not participate in the *cael/rhoi* alternation. On the deep structure analysis the ungrammaticality of (58) resembles the ungrammaticality of (21) and (22). In all three cases the direct object is an embedding and *rhoi* is not possible. In the case of (21) and (22) *rhoi* must be restricted not to allow an embedding as object, and this restriction can be extended to passives too.

Restrictions which were discussed in Chapter 4 in terms of the transformational analysis can be equally well handled in terms of the deep structure analysis. For instance, in section 4.2 it was pointed out that embeddings may not appear as subject or agent of the passive, and it was pointed out how these restrictions might be explained. Blocked derivations and restrictions on T. Agent Postposing were invoked. It was however also pointed out that these restrictions could be handled in terms of selection restrictions on *cael*, and on the deep structure analysis this is the explanation that must be adopted. Embeddings are on this view ruled out as subject of *cael* or object of *gan*. In this the passive parallels the other constructions containing *cael* and *gan*. In no case can an embedding appear in these two positions.

Similarly, in Chapter 4 restrictions on reflexive pronouns were discussed and it was pointed out that the object of *gan* cannot be a reflexive pronoun. On the transformational analysis, this restriction was explained in section 4.3.2 as being due to a blocked derivation. On the deep structure analysis a different explanation must be found, and one is readily available. It was pointed out above in section 6.1.3 that reflexive pronouns are ungrammatical as object of *gan* in all constructions which include *cael* and *gan*, and that this type of restriction appears with other verbs too. The passive is on this view subject to the same restriction on its deep structure as the other *cael* forms. No additional mechanism is needed.

There do not seem to be any clear cases where it is possible to account for restrictions on one of the two analyses but not on the other. Apparent problems do not prove to be serious. For instance, it was shown in section 4.1.2 that the verb of the embedding must be agentive and non-stative. On the transformational analysis this can be explained either by a restriction on T. Agent Postposing or by selection restrictions on *cael*. On the deep structure analysis it must be explained by a selection restriction on *cael*. This might appear an odd restriction since in other *cael* constructions it is not found. It does not appear in the construction expressing permission, where the object of *cael* is a tenseless embedding as in the passive. (59) is fully grammatical although the verb of the embedding *gwybod* (know) is nonagentive and stative.

(59) Caiff Ifor wybod yr ateb cyn bo hir.
Gets Ifor knowing the answer before will be long.
i.e. Ifor may know the answer before long.

However this discrepancy is not really a problem. The passive and permission embeddings already differ in the identity relations holding between the noun phrases in the embedding and those of the matrix sentence. It is therefore not surprising that other differences should appear.

6.2.3 An impasse There appears then to be something of an impasse. We have two adequate means of generating the passive and no way of deciding between them. Both analyses can handle the data and both express parallelisms between the passive and other constructions. Unfortunately in opting for one of the two one loses the parallelisms expressed by the other. If the transformational analysis is adopted then the parallelisms with the other structures discussed in Chapter 5 can be shown, that is with the impersonal passive, the passive adjectives, and the passive nominals. If the deep structure analysis is adopted then the parallelisms with the structures discussed in this chapter can be shown. It does not seem possible to have both at once.

It is not possible to subsume both sets of parallelisms under either of the analyses. The transformational analysis will not work for the structures discussed in this chapter, as was shown in section 6.1. And on the other hand it is not possible to analyse the structures discussed in Chapter 5 in terms of a deep structure analysis. One example of the difficulties raised by this latter possibility will be discussed.

It appears that the impersonal passive must involve a postposing transformation, since the alternative deep structure analysis requires the impersonal forms to violate independently established selectional restrictions. For instance, it was pointed out in section 6.2.2 that *cael* may only take one prepositional phrase with *gan* in deep structure, and that (52) with two such deep structure prepositional phrases is ungrammatical. In the impersonal passive, however, two prepositional phrases with *gan* are fully grammatical, as in (60).

(60) Cafwyd anrheg gan ei frawd gan Wyn.
Got (a) present by his brother by Wyn.

If both prepositional phrases are already present in deep structure then the impersonal passive is exceptional in violating this selectional restriction. If on the other hand (60) is derived by a postposing transformation from the same deep structure as the equivalent active (61) this problem disappears.

(61) Cafodd Wyn anrheg gan ei frawd.
Got Wyn (a) present by his brother.

Here only one of the two prepositional phrases is present in deep structure and the other one is added by the postposing rule.

Furthermore verbs which do not normally co-occur with a prepositional phrase containing *gan* accept it in the impersonal passive. For instance, *rhybuddio* (warn) cannot normally appear with such a prepositional phrase, as can be seen from the ungrammaticality of (62).

(62) *Rhybuddiodd Ifor y dyn gan Wyn.
Warned Ifor the man by Wyn.

But in the impersonal passive form (63) the prepositional phrase is fully grammatical.

(63) Rhybuddiwyd y dyn gan Ifor.
Warned the man by Ifor.

Here again, if the deep structure analysis is adopted then the impersonal passive is exceptional in violating the normal selection restrictions. But on the transformational analysis the problem does not arise. The deep structure is restricted in the normal way and the prepositional phrase is added at a later stage in the derivation.

Similar arguments can be developed in the case of the passive adjectives and the passive nominals.

6.2.4 A common weakness In the discussion so far the favourable side of both analyses has been shown. Both are capable of handling restrictions on the passive and both highlight similarities between the passive and other structures. It should perhaps be pointed out that just as they have the same advantages they share at least one weakness. It was shown in Chapter 5 that there were difficulties in comparing the *cael* passive with the other passive constructions, and that the postposing rule of the *cael* passive T. Agent Postposing was not identical to any of the other postposing rules set up to account for the other constructions. T. Agent Postposing remains uneasily isolated, similar but not identical to other rules, and with no truly independent motivation.

The same problem arises on the deep structure analysis of the *cael* passive. T. Agent Postposing has been replaced by T. Passive Subject Deletion and this rule too has no real independent motivation. It is similar to the rule required in the deletion of forms like (64) where the object of the matrix verb *cael* is a nominal rather than a tenseless embedding. This type of form was discussed above in section 6.1.3.

(64) Cafodd y pregethwr wrandawiad da gan y gynulleidfa.
Got the preacher (a) hearing good by the congregation.

Here too the subject of the embedding is deleted on identity with the object of *gan* in the matrix sentence. The two deletion rules are not identical however. The one affects tenseless embeddings and the other embedded nominals, and other discrepancies appear suggesting they are restricted in different ways. For instance, verbs which are fully grammatical in the *cael* passive, like *rhybuddio* (warn), are not grammatical in the nominal form.

(65) Cafodd Wyn ei rybuddio gan yr heddlu.
Got Wyn his warning by the police.

(66) *Cafodd Wyn rybuddiad gan yr heddlu.
Got Wyn (a) warning by the police.

T. Passive Subject Deletion is also isolated then, similar to at least one other rule but not identical with it, and with no real independent motivation.

6.3 Conclusions

The transformational derivation of the agent phrase, which was assumed in Chapters 2 to 5, is not the only possibility. There exists a viable alternative analysis where the agent phrase is already present in deep structure. The movement transformation T. Agent Postposing must be replaced by a deletion transformation T. Passive Subject Deletion. The rest of the derivation remains identical. Both analyses can be equally well justified and there does not seem to be any motivated way of choosing between them. But the analyses each highlight the similarity of the *cael* passive to different sets of constructions, and the choice of either will mean losing the other set of parallelisms.

7 *Conclusions*

Two possible derivations of the *cael* passive have been suggested in the course of this study. The first view to be put forward was the transformational analysis. On this view the deep structure of the form (1) is that shown in (2).

(1) Cafodd Wyn ei rybuddio gan Ifor.
Got Wyn his warning by Ifor.

(2)

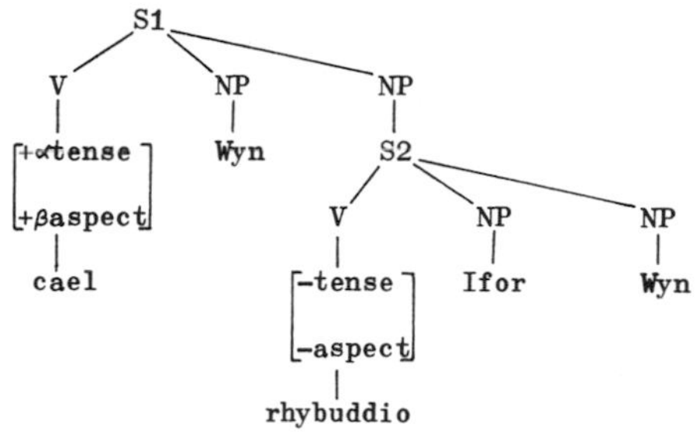

A tenseless active sentence is embedded as direct object of the verb *cael*. The subject of *cael* is identical to the object of the embedding. The subject of the embedding is moved by T. Agent Postposing into the matrix sentence as object of *gan* in a sentence-final prepositional phrase. The output of this transformation is the structure (3).

(3)

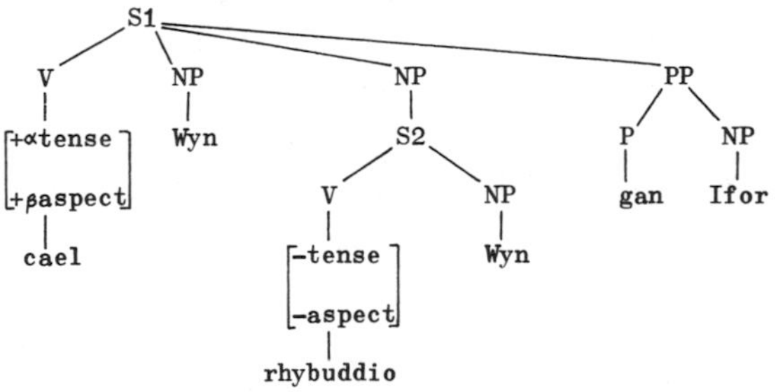

The object of the embedding is pronominalised on identity with the subject of the matrix, and this pronoun is copied into the determiner of the noun phrase dominating the embedded sentence. The verb of the embedded sentence is given the appropriate mutation form and the pronoun left behind in the original object position is deleted. The object of *gan* is given the appropriate soft mutation form. The verb *cael* is inflected to agree with its subject. The surface structure resulting from these rules is that shown in (4).

(4)

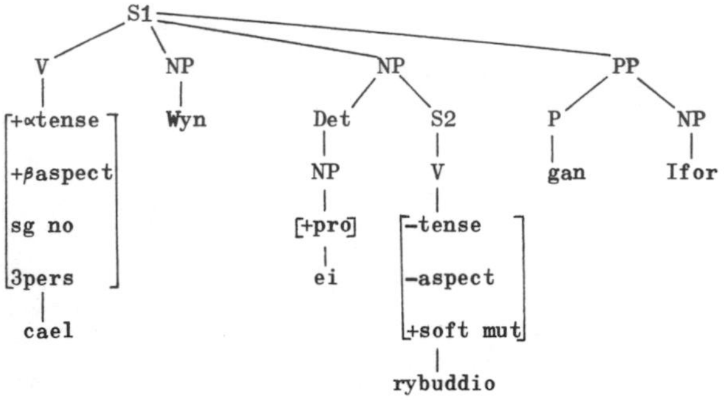

On the alternative analysis, the deep structure analysis, the deep structure representation of (1) is as shown in (5).

(5)

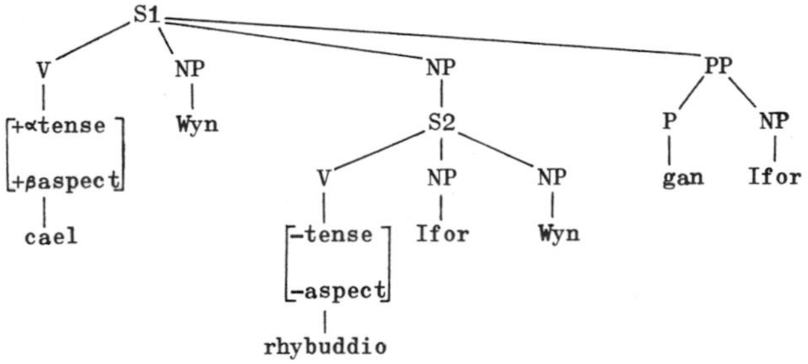

Here again there is a tenseless embedding embedded as object of *cael* and the object of the embedding is identical to the subject of *cael*. (5) differs from (2) however in the presence of a prepositional phrase in sentence-final position in the matrix sentence. The preposition is *gan* and the object of *gan* is identical to the subject of the embedding. The subject of the embedding is deleted on identity with the object of *gan* by T. Passive Subject Deletion, giving the output (6).

(6)

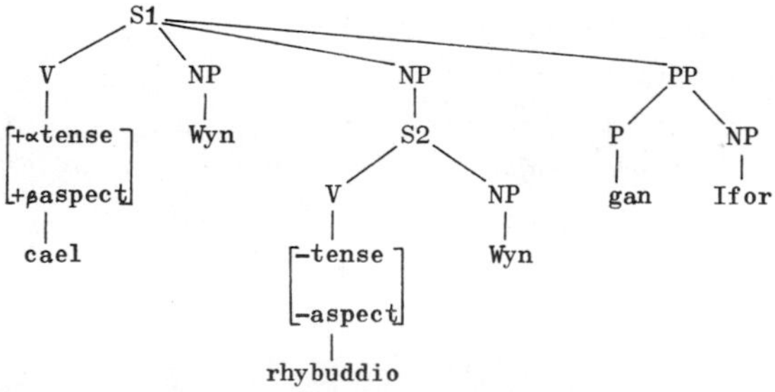

This tree is identical to (3), the output of T. Agent Postposing on the other analysis. And from this point on the two derivations are identical.

In (1) both noun phrases are full lexical nouns. If the subject of *cael* is a pronoun then it may optionally be deleted, as in (7).

(7) Cefais fy rhybuddio gan Ifor.
Got (I) my warning by Ifor.

If the object of *gan* is a pronoun then the preposition is inflected to agree with it, as in (8), and the pronoun may be optionally deleted to give (9).

(8) Cafodd Wyn ei rybuddio ganddi hi.
Got Wyn his warning by her.

(9) Cafodd Wyn ei rybuddio ganddi.
Got Wyn his warning by (her).

If the object of *gan* is an unspecified noun phrase then the whole prepositional phrase is deleted, as in (10).

(10) Cafodd Wyn ei rybuddio.
Got Wyn his warning.

Both derivations are identical with respect to these points.

This derivation of the passive, in either of the two variants suggested, reveals similarities between the passive and other constructions in Welsh. Like the periphrastic sentence forms, it is a complex sentence with a lexical verb embedded below an auxiliary verb. The auxiliary verb is tensed but not the embedded lexical verb. In turn this relates the passive to other embedded forms where the matrix verb is lexical rather than auxiliary. The passive appears to differ from these forms only in the identity relations required between the noun phrases in the matrix and the embedding. No other form appears to require identity of the subject of the matrix and the object of the embedding. This difference in identity relations explains the need for a different rule to remove the subject of the embedding in the case of the passive.

The rules which appear in the derivation of the passive, with the exception of the rule removing the subject of the embedding, are also required in the derivation of other forms. Those rules which affect the agent phrase are required for all prepositional phrases, and the agreement and subject deletion rules which affect the matrix sentence are required for any simple sentence with a tensed verb. The rules which affect the pronoun object, itself pronominalised by a very general rule, are the same as those needed for the derivation of a pronoun object in other tenseless embeddings and the subject of certain tensed embeddings, and can also be applied to possessive noun phrases where there is no embedding.

If the first analysis suggested above is adopted, then the rule T. Agent Postposing which is required to move the subject of the embedding into agent position is similar to postposing transformations which appear in other forms, and parallels can be shown between the *cael* passive, the impersonal passive, the passive adjective and the passive nominal. If on the other hand the second deep structure is adopted, then it is possible to relate the passive to the set of constructions containing *cael*, a direct object, and a prepositional phrase with *gan*.

It has been possible then to integrate the description of the passive into the syntactic patterning of Welsh, and only a minimal amount of new apparatus has been needed to account for it. As a tenseless embedding it resembles a series of other constructions, requiring in addition only an identity relation between the subject of the matrix and the object of the embedding. This is a new type of restriction since the other constructions operate purely in terms of identity relations between the subject of the matrix and the subject of the embedding. It is only a minor extension of identity relations between subjects however, falling into the same general class of identity relations between noun phrases in the matrix and embedded sentences.

The rule removing the subject of the embedding is also a new piece of apparatus purely to account for the passive, but it also is only a development of a rule type already required to account for other constructions. This holds on both of the derivations suggested. If it is a postposing rule it is of the same type as T. Impersonal Agent Postposing and the other rules discussed in Chapter 5. If it is a deletion rule then it resembles the rule required to derive the embedded nominal forms in Chapter 6, section 6.1.3. No drastically new rule type, with no similarity to those needed elsewhere in the grammar, is required purely to account for the correct forms of the passive.

The possibility of serious cross-linguistic comparative work is also raised by this analysis, since an embedding analysis has been suggested for English by two writers. K. Hasegawa (1968) has suggested that the *be* passive as in (11) and the *get* passive as in (12) should both be derived in this way, and R. Lakoff (1971) has suggested this for the *get* passive alone.

(11) John was run over.

(12) John got run over.

When independent work on different languages, using arguments based on evidence internal to the languages concerned, leads to very similar analyses for the 'same' construction in each of them, then the existence of language universals becomes a serious possibility.

Certain theoretical implications follow from the analysis developed in this study. Throughout the study syntactic similarities between different constructions have been stressed and the deep structures and transformations formulated have been designed to highlight these relationships. Some of the constructions which are syntactically similar in deep structure and derivation are very different in semantic interpretation, one example being periphrastic verb forms and tenseless embeddings below lexical verbs which were discussed in Chapter 1. Conversely constructions which are semantically very similar to each other are given a very different syntactic analysis, differing in deep structure and in transformational derivation. If the syntactic derivation is to reflect syntactic parallelisms then it must obscure semantic ones.

If the reverse position were adopted and constructions which are semantically related were derived from the same deep structures then it would not be possible to reflect the syntactic relationships. For instance it would be necessary to derive periphrastic and simple sentences from the same deep structure and to derive active and passive sentences from the same deep structure. The difficulties in showing the syntactic similarities of the periphrastic forms and the passives to the semantically unrelated lexical embeddings would be immense.

The position which emerges from this analysis then is of the clear separation of syntactic and semantic analysis. Constructions which are related on the one level are not necessarily related on the other level. And the type of description which can reveal one set of relationships is not able to handle the other set. In this study it has been assumed that deep structures and transformational rules are appropriate to express syntactic relationships and that some other mechanism will be needed to express semantic relationships elsewhere in the grammar. This position is compatible with that adopted by Chomsky (1965) in that he allows for a separate set of semantic interpretation rules to operate on the deep structure representations to give the semantic analysis. They are quite separate from the transformational rules. This position is however opposed to that of generative semantics[1] where a distinction between two such sets of rules is rejected and it is assumed that syntactic patterning is directly related to semantic patterning.

In spite of the encouraging results achieved in this study it would be wrong to give the impression that the outcome is completely satisfactory. Two equally plausible derivations were put forward for the passive and it was necessary to choose between them. In choosing one it was necessary to reject the other and so to lose the parallelisms it revealed. The next step must be to find some way of integrating both accounts so that neither set of parallelisms is lost. This will mean developing a more comprehensive model which can supersede the one used here, but any such model must be able to account for all the data and relationships which this account has revealed.

Appendix

1 THE THEORETICAL FRAMEWORK

The theoretical assumptions on which this study is based are those of Chomsky (1965). Those assumptions which relate specifically to syntax will be briefly summarised here, using simplified examples.

The syntactic structure of sentences can be represented by a phrase structure tree. For instance, the structure of (1) can be represented by (2).

(1) Mae Ifor wedi gweld Emyr.
Is Ifor after seeing Emyr.

(2)

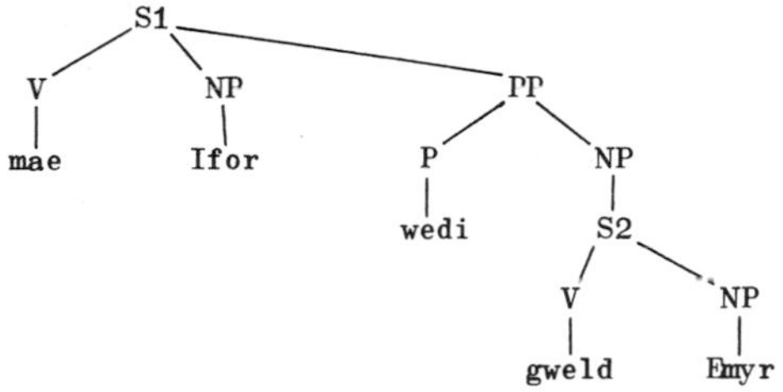

Each item in the sentence is given a label to show its syntactic category. The items are grouped together into progressively larger constituents of the sentence, with each constituent being also labelled to show its category. The lines in the diagram represent these groupings.

This tree diagram shows only the immediately observable structure of the sentence. It is hypothesised that it is necessary to have a more abstract representation of a sentence too, in order to show aspects of it which are obscured in the observable form. For instance, in (2) it is not clear that the noun phrase *Ifor* is to be understood as the subject of the verb *gweld* (see) as well as the subject of the verb *mae* (is). A more abstract representation would make this clear, as in (3).

(3)

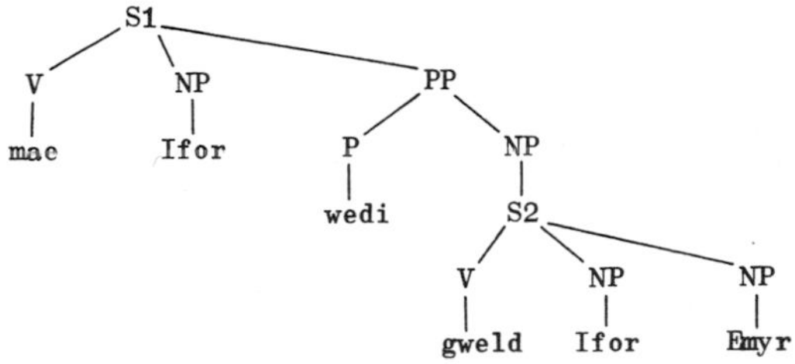

The tree structure (2) is termed the surface structure representation and the tree structure (3) is termed the deep structure representation.

The grammar is organised so that the deep structure is generated by a set of rules, and it is then altered by another set of rules to give the less explicit surface structure representation. The rules relating these two representations are termed transformational rules, and an example of such a rule is the one which deletes the subject of the verb *gweld* (see) in (3) to give the form (2). Several transformations may apply in order to change one deep structure into the corresponding surface structure representation. In some cases they need to apply in a particular order relative to each other, and in other cases it may not matter in which order they apply. One important form of ordering is that it is assumed that rules may apply cyclically. By this it is meant that in a tree such as (4) where there are several sentences, the rules will apply first to the lowest one in the tree, that is to S3, then to S2, and finally to S1.

(4)

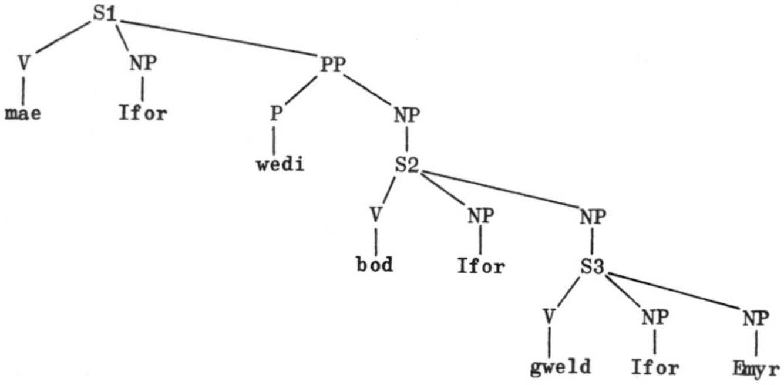

In this way the subject of S3 will be deleted first, then the subject of S2. Other rules will have to apply to the whole tree after these cyclic rules have applied. These are known as postcyclic rules.

Transformations not only delete items as in the example discussed above, but also move items from one point to another. For instance, the deep structure of (5) is (6) and its surface structure is (7). In order to convert (6) into (7), one of the transformations must move the noun phrase *Emyr* to the right to a new position in the tree.

(5) Rhybuddiwyd Ifor gan Emyr.
Warned Ifor by Emyr.

(6)

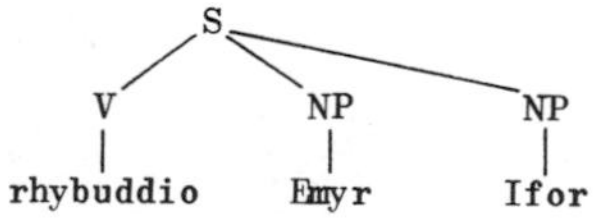

(7)

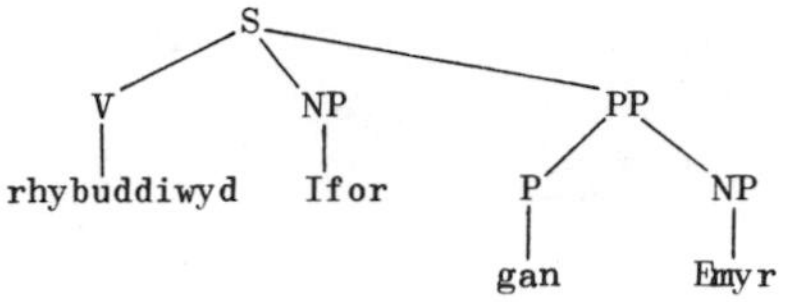

Not only are items moved bodily as in this case, but they can also be copied in a new position in the tree. For instance, the deep structure of (8) is (9), and its surface structure is (10).

(8) Ifor y soniais i amdano ef.
Ifor that spoke I about him.
i.e. It was Ifor that I spoke about.

(9)

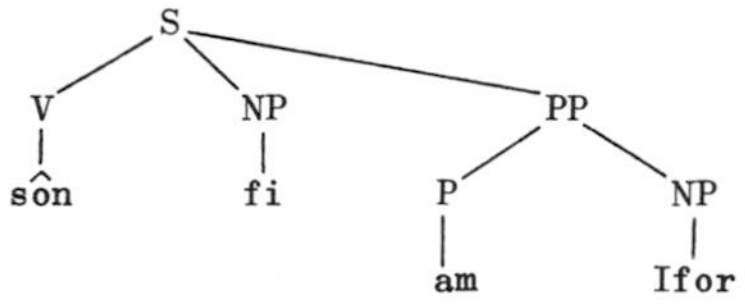

(10)

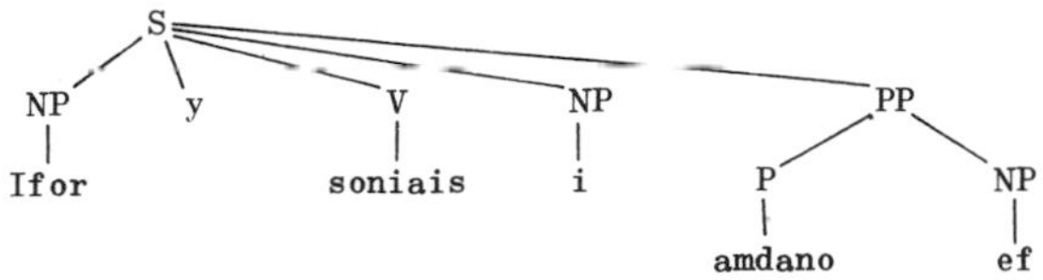

One of the transformations involved in converting (9) into (10) will copy the noun phrase *Ifor* in a new position in the tree, leaving the original one in its original position, to be pronominalised by a later rule.

Transformations may also add items. For instance, in converting (6) into (7) the preposition *gan* has been added. And in converting (9) into (10), the item *y* has been added to the left of the verb.

The items in sentences are not units which cannot be broken down further. They have not only a form, like *Ifor*, but are also specified by syntactic features. These features specify such things as tense and aspect in verbs, and number, person and gender in nouns. For instance, the deep structure of (11) would include the feature specifications shown. And of course there should be feature specifications in the trees already discussed in a simplified way.

(11) Gwelodd ef y tŷ.
Saw he the house.

(12)

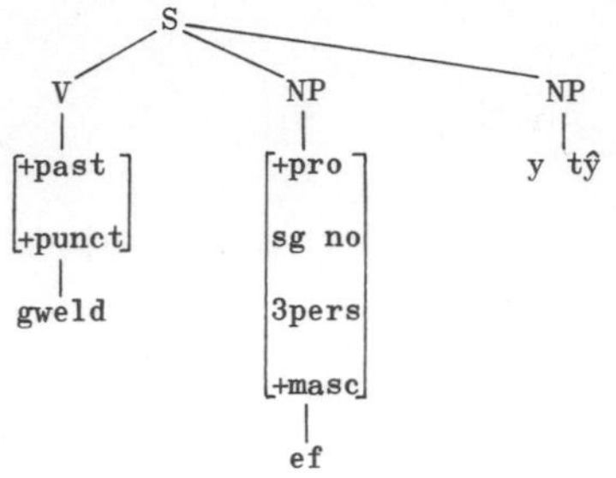

Transformations may affect features just as they may affect whole items. For instance, they may copy features from one item onto another. In order to convert (12) into (13), it is necessary to copy the features for number and person from *ef* onto the verb. This is to ensure that the verbal inflection will agree with *ef*.

(13)

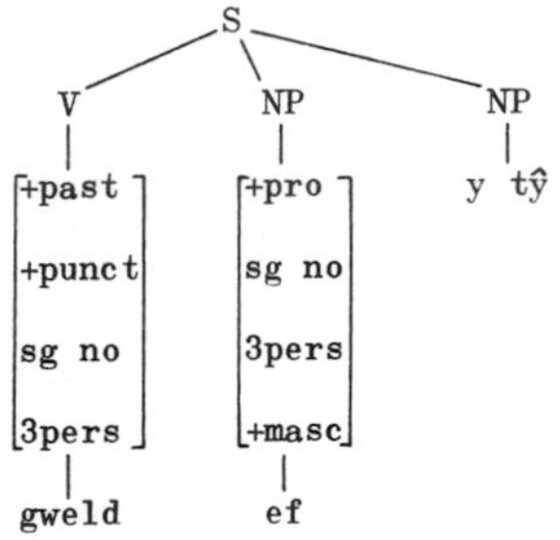

Transformations may add features. In the derivation of (10) from (9), it is necessary to add the feature [+pro] to the noun phrase *Ifor* to convert it into the pronoun form *ef*. Transformations may also alter the value of a feature from + to −, or from − to +.

The syntactic rules are only part of the grammar, which also deals with semantics and phonology. The deep structure representation is interpreted by semantic rules to give the meaning of the sentence. And the surface structure is interpreted by phonological rules to give the complete specification of the spoken sentence.

2 FORMALISING TRANSFORMATIONS

The formalism used here for expressing transformations is that developed by the UCLA team (Stockwell, Schachter and Partee 1973 pp. 14ff).

The structural description of the rule is shown by a labelled bracketing, a notation equivalent to the tree structures shown in section 1 above. Each item is numbered. Then the structural change indicates the change that must be carried out on the sentence. An example is given in (14). The structural description represents the tree (3).

(14) T. Deletion

SD. ($_{S}$ V NP ($_{PP}$ Prep ($_{NP}$ ($_{S}$ V NP NP))))

1 2 3 4 5 6 7 8 9 10

SC. Delete 9.

In this way it is possible to be explicit about the item referred to and the change carried out.

The structural change may delete an item, move one, or copy one. In the case of movement or copying transformations it is necessary to specify where in the tree the item is to be adjoined. In order to be explicit about this a set of terms has been developed to describe the position of items in the tree. Two items which are both immediately dominated by a single node, as in (15), are sister constituents. A is the left sister of B, and B is the right sister of A.

(15)

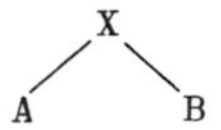

Another relation used is the daughter relation. A and B are daughter constituents of X, A being the left daughter of X and B the right daughter. A movement transformation or a copying transformation will specify in these terms where the item is to be attached. For instance, to convert (16) to (17), the rule will be formulated as in (18).

(16)

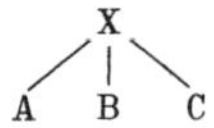

(17)

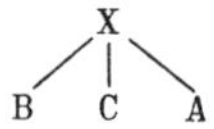

(18) T. Movement

SD. ($_{X}$ A B C)

1 2 3 4

SC. Adjoin 2 as right daughter of 1.

Similarly, in order to convert (16) into (19), the rule will be formulated as in (20).

(19)

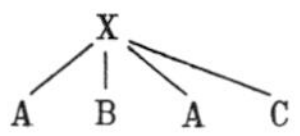

(20) T. Copying

SD. ($_{X}$ A B C)

1 2 3 4

SC. Copy 2 as left sister of 4.

Rules affecting features may also be formulated in this system. For instance, the rule copying the features of the subject onto the verb, in deriving (13) from (12), may be expressed as in (21).

(21) T. Feature Copying

```
SD. (S     V           NP        NP )
           |           |
       [+past  ]   [sg no ]
       [+punct ]   [3pers ]

    1      2           3         4

SC. Copy the features [sg no] and [3pers] from 3 onto 2.
```

3 ABBREVIATORY VARIABLES

Certain notational devices have been adopted in order to collapse several very similar transformational rules into one, and so express the generalisation that they are all dealing with the same type of relationship. For instance, the rule (21) might be rewritten with a variable instead of the noun phrase numbered 4. This will allow the rule to apply not only to transitive sentences like (11) but also sentences like (22) to (24) where the agreement of verb and subject also appears but there is not simply a direct object following the subject.

(22) Rhedodd ef.
Ran he.

(23) Soniodd ef am y dyn.
Spoke he about the man.

(24) Rhoddodd ef y llyfr ar y bwrdd.
Put he the book on the table.

Such variables are shown by capital letters from the end of the alphabet, such as X, Y, and Z. The revised structural description of the rule is shown in (25). Here X represents anything following the subject, be it an object, a prepositional phrase, both or zero.

(25)

```
SD. (S     V           NP        X )
           |           |
       [+past  ]   [sg no ]
       [+punct ]   [3pers ]

    1      2           3         4
```

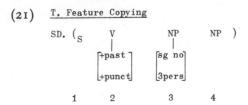

Similarly, in order to allow the rule to apply to a wider variety of sentences, where the subject pronoun is of a different person and number to *ef*, but where it is necessary to copy these features from the subject onto the verb in the same way, variables are used to express the features. In this case the variables are Greek letters. If the rule (21) is rewritten to take account of this, its structural description will appear as in (26).

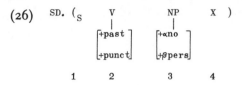

(26)
$$\text{SD. } \big(_{\text{S}} \quad \begin{array}{c} \text{V} \\ | \\ \begin{bmatrix} +\text{past} \\ +\text{punct} \end{bmatrix} \end{array} \quad \begin{array}{c} \text{NP} \\ | \\ \begin{bmatrix} +\alpha\text{no} \\ +\beta\text{pers} \end{bmatrix} \end{array} \quad \text{X} \big)$$
$$1 \qquad 2 \qquad 3 \qquad 4$$

This now merely specifies that whatever the number and person features of the subject pronoun they are to be copied onto the verb. It can now account for (27) to (29) as well as (11).

(27) Gwelais i y tŷ.
Saw I the house.

(28) Gwelaist ti y tŷ.
Sawest thou the house.

(29) Gwelsom ni y tŷ.
Saw we the house.

Such variables may be used for the tense and aspect features too to show that the rule applies on other tense and aspect specifications.

If either of two or more different items may appear in a particular structural description in a certain position, then they are collapsed by the use of curly brackets. For instance, if the same structural change affects the two structural descriptions (30) and (31), then they may be collapsed as in (32).

(30)
$$\text{SD. } \big(_{\text{X}} \ \text{A} \ \text{B} \ \text{C} \ \big)$$
$$1 \quad 2 \quad 3 \quad 4$$

(31)
$$\text{SD. } \big(_{\text{X}} \ \text{A} \ \text{D} \ \text{C} \ \big)$$
$$1 \quad 2 \quad 3 \quad 4$$

(32)
$$\text{SD. } \big(_{\text{X}} \ \text{A} \begin{Bmatrix} \text{B} \\ \text{D} \end{Bmatrix} \text{C} \ \big)$$
$$1 \quad 2 \quad 3 \quad 4$$

In this way it can be shown that either of the two forms B and D may appear in position 3. One of them, but not both, must be present for the rule to apply.

Another bracketing convention has been adopted here, though it is not used by the UCLA team. This is the device of angled brackets, which is taken from phonological formalism (Harms 1968 p. 66). If the same change affects two structural descriptions like (33) and (34), they are to be collapsed as in (35).

(33) SD. (X A B C)
1 2 3 4

(34) SD. (X D A B C E)
1 2 3 4 5 6

(35) SD. (X ⟨D⟩ A B C ⟨E⟩)
1 2 3 4 5 6

This indicates that either the whole structural description is met or only that part of it not contained in the angled brackets. And if the item contained within one of the pair of angled brackets is present, then so too must be the item within the other pair. In such a case as this it is the larger structural description which must be tested first. If it is not met then the lesser one may be tested. If the larger one is met however then the lesser one is ignored. The rule may apply only once, not twice, one on each of its structural descriptions. This is ensured by the disjunctive ordering convention developed by Chomsky and Halle (1968 pp. 30ff), again in the context of phonology.

Notes

INTRODUCTION

1 Examples are R. M. Jones (1963), A. R. Thomas (1967b), M.-L. Kean (1974), M. R. Allen (1975), G. M. Awbery (1973a).

2 Traditional approaches to some of the data considered in this study can be found in J. Morris Jones (1913), M. Richards (1938), S. J. Williams (1959), J. J. Evans (1959), J. T. Bowen and T. J. Rhys Jones (1960), and M. D. Jones (1965). A more structuralist orientation is found in T. A. Watkins (1961), A. R. Thomas (1967a), and M. Jones (1970). For a detailed discussion of their standpoints see G. M. Awbery (1973b).

3 A literal English translation of each example will be given. In some cases, as here, an idiomatic English translation will also be given. This will be done whenever a new construction is introduced in order to make clear what its normal English equivalent would be, and when a particularly complicated example is under discussion.

CHAPTER I. ACTIVE SENTENCES

1 My translation.

2 For a discussion of how mutations may be handled in a transformational framework, see G. M. Awbery (1973a). A very detailed discussion of Welsh mutations from a traditional standpoint can be found in T. J. Morgan (1951).

3 The details of which tense and aspect combinations are realised by each of the inflected and periphrastic forms of the verb are not relevant here. These issues are discussed in R. M. Jones (1966a and b), A. R. Thomas (1967a), and M. Jones (1970).

4 E.g. M. Richards (1938 p. 17).

5 Possible historical reasons for the lack of mutation of the uninflected verb following *yn* are mentioned in T. A. Watkins (1960), where it is also considered that *yn* is a preposition.

6 This analysis resembles the account of English auxiliaries given in J. R. Ross (1967). The arguments used differ in detail, but the same main points are stressed, the verb-like syntax of the auxiliary verb, and the resemblance of the embedding both to a noun phrase and a sentence.

7 A similar, but more general, rule is formulated for English in P. S. Rosenbaum (1967 p. 6). The rule given here for Welsh will be generalised as the discussion progresses.

8 It will however be shown in Chapter 3 that some of these rules cannot in fact be cyclic.

9 Alternatively, the rule T. Pronoun Prepositional Object Deletion can be formulated with the preposition marked for person, number and gender. In this case it cannot be triggered until after T. Preposition Agreement has applied and extrinsic ordering of the two rules will not be needed.

10 This type of approach is discussed in N. A. Chomsky (1970).

11 The terms present and imperfect are the traditional labels for these morphological forms. They are used purely for convenience here and have no implications for the tense and aspect features involved.

12 These forms are discussed further in Chapter 3.

CHAPTER 2. PASSIVE SENTENCES

1 This tree, like many subsequent ones, has been simplified to the extent that the features of person and number which should have appeared on the verb as a result of agreement rules have been omitted. This has been done to avoid cluttering up the diagrams. The tense and aspect features are retained as they figure importantly in the discussion.

2 A few informants accept (34) as grammatical, providing more backing for my analysis.

3 It is shown in A. Berman (1974) that similar problems arise on a VSO analysis of English.

4 Note that the mutated form *ferch* in (50) is not a violation of this rule. The mutation in (50) is due to a different rule, mutation of a feminine noun following a definite article.

5 It will be shown in Chapter 3 that some of these forms cannot be cyclic.

6 It appears that the rule deleting *cael* was more general at an earlier stage in the language, as it could also be deleted below *yn* and *ar* (M. Richards 1938 p. 55).

7 ∅ is used as a symbol here and later for the unspecified noun phrase whether present already in deep structure or resulting from a transformation.

8 For a discussion of the possibility of a simple sentence analysis of adjectives see n. 5 of Chapter 5.

9 For these terms see S. J. Williams (1959 p. 55).

CHAPTER 3. MORE PASSIVES

1 See L. R. Gleitman (1969).

2 Further, even if the two forms could be collapsed the result would be *ei* (his) not *eu* (their).

3 T. Pronominalisation must be able to derive a plural pronoun from a conjunction of nouns in order to account for such forms as (i).

(i) Dywedodd Wyn ac Ifor eu bod yn aros.
Said Wyn and Ifor their being in waiting.

The underlying subject of the embedding must be the conjoined form *Wyn ac Ifor*.

4 The two prepositional phrases can be reversed to give (ii). This is a very common optional transformation.

(ii) Cafodd y blawd ei gymysgu â halen gan Catrin.
Got the flour its mixing with salt by Catrin.

5 If T. Conjunct Splitting were last-cyclic it might precede T. Agent Postposing. This analysis would then require an additional rule to delete the lower prepositional phrase, so there is no benefit to be gained from it.

6 This resembles the deep structure adopted for such embeddings in English by P. S. Rosenbaum (1967).

7 It is however argued in Chapter 5, section 5.3.5 that this analysis of embeddings may be incorrect. On this second view there is no head noun and only the NP node immediately dominating S. The pronoun *hi* results from the application of T. Sentence Postposing. On this view T. Pronominalisation may not precede T. Sentence Postposing and the additional deletion rule is necessary.

8 The ungrammaticality of (106) is discussed below in Chapter 4, section 4.3.2.

CHAPTER 4. RESTRICTIONS ON THE PASSIVE

1 The traditional terms present, imperfect and pluperfect are used here for convenience only and have no implications for the tense and aspect features involved.

2 Attempts have been made to account for similar restrictions on embeddings as subject of the passive in English in P. S. Rosenbaum (1967), J. E. Emonds (1970) and G. Lakoff (1970b). The explanations offered by Rosenbaum and Emonds rely on drawing a distinction between those embeddings which count as noun phrases and those which do not. Those embeddings which do not count as noun phrases may not appear as subject of the passive. It has however been pointed out in Chapter 1 of this study that these embeddings must be analysed as noun phrases. This type of explanation for their ungrammaticality in the passive cannot then be invoked. Lakoff's explanation involves global constraints on derivations, but appears to rely on a simple sentence analysis of the passive and breaks down when faced with the present complex sentence analysis. A detailed discussion of these positions can be found in G. M. Awbery (1973b).

3 The ungrammaticality of embeddings as agent of the passive in English is discussed in J. E. Emonds (1970). Here again he relies on an analysis of embeddings where they do not count as noun phrases. In the context of this analysis of Welsh embeddings such an explanation is unhelpful. His suggestions are discussed in detail in G. M. Awbery (1973b).

4 An alternative explanation for the ungrammaticality of reflexives as agent of the passive is presented in P. M. Postal (1971) for English. He suggests that movement transformations may not move a noun phrase over another identical noun phrase within the same simple sentence. The rule postposing the agent is of this type as it moves the agent over the object in the same simple sentence. T. Agent Postposing in Welsh appears to be a rule of this type too, so that it may be possible to adapt his explanation to the Welsh data. One problem which does arise however, is that Postal claims that the constraint only holds if neither noun phrase has yet been pronominalised. This is not possible in the case of the Welsh passive. It has been argued above that T. Reflexivisation is a cyclic rule. It will therefore apply on the S2 cycle, while T. Agent Postposing does not apply till the S1 cycle.

5 Difficulties arise if reciprocal forms are derived from conjoined sentences as suggested by L. R. Gleitman (1969). On this analysis the deep structure of (81) consists of a conjunction of (i) and (ii).

(i) Cael Wyn (rhybuddio Ifor Wyn).
Get Wyn (warn Ifor Wyn).
(ii) Cael Ifor (rhybuddio Wyn Ifor).
Get Ifor (warn Wyn Ifor).

As T. Agent Postposing is a cyclic rule it will apply to these forms separately before they are collapsed on the S1 cycle. It will not be possible to generate the tree (82) where the sentences have been collapsed but T. Agent Postposing has not yet applied. Either a different deep structure source for these forms must be formulated or a different explanation for the ungrammaticality of the passives must be found. The first choice seems the most desirable as it does not mean losing the clear parallelisms between the reflexive and reciprocal forms, which was exploited in the explanation offered in the text.

CHAPTER 5. OTHER AGENT TRANSFORMATIONS

1 E.g. M. Richards (1938 p. 52) and M. D. Jones (1965 p. 52). The preference for the impersonal is based on its brevity and compactness.

2 This is only true on a VSO analysis. On a NP–VP analysis it is possible to distinguish the subject and object in terms of tree structure alone. The subject is dominated by the S node and the object by the VP node.

3 Note that this confusion of subject and object would not be possible on a NP–VP analysis since the object would still be dominated by the VP node.

4 For the loss of a preposition preceding a tensed embedding, see the discussion in section 3.4.2.

5 In this study adjectives have been derived from deep structure complex sentences, similar to those underlying periphrastic verbal forms. It is possible however that this is incorrect and that they should be derived from deep structure simple sentences, of the type shown in (i).

(i)

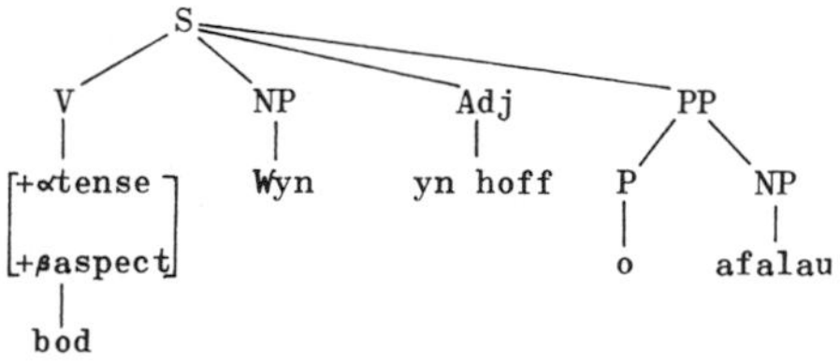

In this case the prepositional phrase is dominated by the top S node throughout the derivation so that there is no problem in deriving the cleft form (127). T. Adjectival Agent Postposing moves the subject across a noun phrase in the same simple sentence, thus possibly accounting for the restriction on reflexives. It is still necessary to move the object into subject position and then into sentence final position. The broad lines of the derivation remain the same on this account as on the deep structure account.

CHAPTER 6. A DEEP STRUCTURE AGENT PHRASE?

1 *Gan* will still be translated in this chapter as *by* in order to highlight the similarity between these forms and those discussed so far, although *from* would be a more natural English translation. To use *by* for the passives and *from* for these would suggest a much bigger split than is in fact found.

2 A transformational link between such forms as (1) and (3) in English was suggested in G. Lakoff (1970a p. 126), but was not formalised. It was termed the Flip Rule.

CHAPTER 7. CONCLUSIONS

1 For a discussion of generative semantics see G. Lakoff (1971).

Bibliography

Allen, M. R. (1975) 'Vowel mutation and word stress in Welsh', *Linguistic Inquiry*, Vol. VI, No. 2

Awbery, G. M. (1973a) 'Initial mutation in a generative grammar of Welsh'. *University of Leeds Phonetics Department Report*, No. 4

(1973b) 'The Passive in Welsh', dissertation submitted for the degree of Ph.D. of Cambridge University.

Berman, A. (1974) 'On the VSO hypothesis', *Linguistic Inquiry*, Vol. v, No. 1

Bowen, J. T. and T. J. Rhys Jones (1960) *Teach Yourself Welsh*, The English Universities Press Ltd

Chomsky, N. A. (1965) *Aspects of the Theory of Syntax*, M.I.T. Press

(1970) 'Remarks on nominalisation', in *Readings in English Transformational Grammar*, ed. R. A. Jacobs and P. S. Rosenbaum, Ginn and Co.

Chomsky, N. A. and M. Halle (1968) *The Sound Pattern of English*, Harper and Row

Emonds, J. E. (1970) 'Root and structure-preserving transformations', dissertation submitted for the degree of Ph.D., Massachusetts Institute of Technology

Evans, J. J. (1960) *Gramadeg Cymraeg*, Gwasg Aberystwyth.

Gleitman, L. R. (1969) 'Co-ordinating conjunctions in English', in *Modern Studies in English*, ed. D. A. Reibel and S. A. Schane, Prentice-Hall Inc.

Harms, R. T. (1968) *Introduction to Phonological Theory*, Prentice-Hall Inc.

Hasegawa, K. (1968) 'The passive construction in English', *Language*, Vol. 44, Pt 2

Hughes, J. (1822) *An Essay on the Ancient and Present State of the Welsh Language*, London

Jones, M. (1970) 'Preliminary outline of the finite verbal phrase in Welsh', *Studia Celtica*, Vol. 5

Jones, M. D. (1965) *Cywiriadur Cymraeg*, Gwasg Gomer

Jones, R. M. (1963) 'Gramadeg cenhedlol a graddio'r iaith', *Bulletin of the Board of Celtic Studies*, Vol. 20, Pt 3

(1966a) 'Tympau'r modd mynegol', *Bulletin of the Board of Celtic Studies*, Vol. 22, Pt 1

(1966b) 'Ffurfiau cwmpasog y ferf', *Bulletin of the Board of Celtic Studies*, Vol. 22, Pt 1

Kean, M.-L. (1974) 'The strict cycle in phonology', *Linguistic Inquiry*, Vol. v, No. 2

Lakoff, G. (1966) 'Stative adjectives and verbs in English', *Report* No. NSF-17 to the National Science Foundation

(1971) 'On generative semantics', in *Semantics – An Interdisciplinary Reader in Philosophy, Linguistics and Psychology*, ed. D. D. Steinberg and L. A. Jakobovits, Cambridge University Press

(1970a) *Irregularity in Syntax*, Holt Rinehart and Winston Inc.

(1970b) 'Global rules', *Language*, Vol. 46, Pt 3

Lakoff, G. and S. Peters (1969) 'Phrasal conjunction and symmetric predicates' in *Modern Studies in English*, ed. D. A. Reibel and S. A. Schane, Prentice-Hall Inc.

Lakoff, R. (1971) 'Passive resistance' in *Papers From the Seventh Regional Meeting of the Chicago Linguistic Society*, Chicago Linguistic Society, Chicago, Illinois

Morgan, T. J. (1952) *Y Treigladau a'u Cystrawen*, University of Wales Press

Morris Jones, J. (1913) *A Welsh Grammar*, Oxford University Press

Postal, P. M. (1971) *Cross-Over Phenomena*, Holt Rinehart and Winston Inc.

Richards, M. (1938) *Cystrawen y Frawddeg Gymraeg*, University of Wales Press

Rosenbaum, P. S. (1967) *The Grammar of English Predicate Complement Constructions*, M.I.T. Press

Ross, J. R. (1967) 'Auxiliaries as main verbs', in *Studies in Philosophical Linguistics*, series 1, ed. William Todd, Evanston, Illinois

Stockwell, R. P., P. Schachter and B. H. Partee (1973) *The Major Syntactic Structures of English*, Holt Rinehart and Winston Inc.

Thomas, A. R. (1967a) 'Constituents of the periphrastic verbal phrase in Welsh', *Studia Celtica*, Vol. 2

(1967b) 'Generative phonology in dialectology', *Transactions of the Philological Society*, Basil Blackwell, Oxford

Watkins, T. A. (1960) 'CC y/yn berfenwol', *Bulletin of the Board of Celtic Studies*, Vol. 18, pt. 4

(1961) *Ieithyddiaeth*, University of Wales Press

Williams, S. J. (1959) *Elfennau Gramadeg Cymraeg*, University of Wales Press

Index